Fred The Needle

THE AUTHORISED BIOGRAPHY

Fred The Needle

THE UNTOLD STORY OF SIR FRED ALLEN

By Alan Sayers and Les Watkins

Hodder Moa

Front endpaper: Lieutenant Fred Allen (fifth from left) with members of his platoon, Guadalcanal, 1942.

Back endpaper: Fred Allen addresses the All Blacks class of 2002 . . . more than 30 years after his legendary stint with the men in black came to an end.

Pages 6–7: Fred Allen with, from left, three of his most famous pupils: Brian Lochore, Kel Tremain and Colin Meads.

National Library of New Zealand Cataloguing-in-Publication Data
Allen, Fred, 1920–
Fred the needle : the untold story of Sir Fred Allen / Fred Allen ;
co-writers Alan Sayers, Les Watkins.
Includes bibliographical references and index.
ISBN 978-1-86971-225-9
1. Rugby Union football players—New Zealand—Biography.
I. Sayers, Alan. II. Watkins, Les. III. Title.
796.333092—dc 22

A Hodder Moa Book
Published in 2011 by Hachette New Zealand Ltd
4 Whetu Place, Mairangi Bay
Auckland, New Zealand
www.hachette.co.nz

Designed and produced by Hachette New Zealand Ltd
Printed by Everbest Printing Co. Ltd., China

This book is dedicated to Norma Edith Allen, a very special lady without whose love and support her husband's legendary achievements would not have been possible.

Contents

Acknowledgements

Co-authors Alan Sayers and Les Watkins wish to thank the following people and organisations for their valued assistance in the writing of this book: Marianne Allen and daughters Katia and Inés, Ken Baguley, former Auckland Mayor John Banks and his team at Auckland City Council, the British Barbarians, Gareth Edwards, Lindsay Knight, Keith and Vera Lawson, the Hon Murray McCully, Sir Colin and Lady Meads, Barry McCrystal, Matija and Nola McGowan, Ron Palenski, Greg Sayers, Kevin and Loretta Skinner, Shaun Usher and Christina Sayers Wickstead.

We are also grateful to the remarkable team at Hachette New Zealand, especially editorial director Warren Adler and managing director Kevin Chapman for their professionalism and infectious enthusiasm.

Finally, we express loving thanks to our wives, June Sayers and Kathleen Watkins, for their endless patience and invaluable input.

Foreword

I am honoured to write an introduction to the life story of Sir Fred Allen, the most dynamic and inspiring individual I have known in 60 years' involvement in sport.

The first time I saw Fred I was only 11 years old. It was the year I went to Auckland as a member of the King Country primary schoolboys' team to play in the final of the Roller Mills Shield competition at Eden Park. After the game we had special seats in the stand to watch Auckland play Wellington.

I saw some great players in action that day, but none impressed me more than an Auckland five-eighths named Fred Allen. As I watched him in action, little did I know I was admiring the man who would one day play an important role in my life, a man whose philosophy would reach out and encompass me.

I first encountered Fred during training for the 1956 North Island–South Island game. I had been selected for the North XV and he was the coach. During one of his team talks he gave me a scathing dressing down and I was not impressed. For some time my feelings towards Mr Allen were not exactly friendly.

Things worsened before a test match in Auckland when I yawned during one of Fred's team talks. He nearly jumped over the table in front of him. 'Am I boring you Pinetree?' he said. 'Because if I am, there's a bus leaves on the hour, every hour, for Hamilton and you'll be on the next one.'

In 1967, however, during the All Blacks' unbeaten tour of Canada, England, Scotland, Wales and France, my feelings changed. Other hardened veterans had also felt the lash of Fred's tongue, but once we came to recognise his ability, his integrity and his intense loyalty to his players, our differences dissolved and we soon became a close-knit unit.

By the end of the tour, the bond between Fred and me had reached full strength and I found myself his number one disciple. I believed in him implicitly and there was nothing I would not do to help him. At one team meeting I appealed to the players to carry his message of 15-man rugby back to their clubs and provinces when they returned home.

We went through our 17 games undefeated and because of our fast, open style of play we won the praise and affection of rugby supporters wherever we played. The 1967 All Blacks were, they said, the greatest team ever to tour their countries — all because of the speedy, accurate, intelligent rugby taught by Fred Allen.

One of his great skills was the motivation of his players. He recognised that each man was an individual who, if the right psychology was applied, could be moved into producing something extra. I've seen him achieve this many times.

He also had the remarkable ability to bond men from all walks of life into one closely knit unit and once that was achieved his teams kept on winning and winning.

Fred Allen was not a man to be trifled with. But although he could be fearsome at times he was always fair, and I never once found him to be otherwise. It was because of this quality, along with his loyalty and integrity, that he acquired such enormous respect from his players.

He is, without doubt, the strongest disciplinarian ever to coach the All Blacks. To don the black jersey was, for him, a privilege for which you were expected to meet certain standards — to train hard, to give of your best, to respect your opposition and uphold the traditions of the game both on and off the field.

I recently read that Fred Allen's coaching would not be successful today. I refute that statement for the reason that position, possession and pace, as taught by Fred, are still, and always will be, the fundamentals of winning rugby.

I also believe that were he coaching today, Fred's vast knowledge of rugby, along with his lengthy experience, would enable him to make all the changes necessary for success in the modern game.

And there's another thing I'm sure of — because of their off-field behaviour one or two of today's players would soon be on their way home.

This great man's mana increases with the years, a fact clearly demonstrated on his 90th birthday when the City of Auckland honoured him with a civic luncheon in the Town Hall to which 100 distinguished guests were invited.

We came from near and far to pay homage to a man we had all grown to admire, respect and even revere.

I say with absolute confidence that Fred Allen's enormous contribution to our national game as All Blacks captain, selector, coach, administrator and ambassador around the world will never be equalled.

Sir Colin Meads
Te Kuiti

Preface

The inspirational life of Frederick Richard Allen has earned the admiration and respect of thousands, not only in his own country but also in every other rugby-playing nation in the world.

For many years this great New Zealander has declined to have a book written about his life. 'There are things I would not say for fear of hurting people,' he told the writers who approached him.

But the all-clear was given in 2010 and for the first time all who know and admire him will be able to read what he has to say about the game he loves, his personal life and the triumphs and disasters along the way.

Fred was a child of the Great Depression whose home life was one of poverty and family feud — and it was during those bitter years that he first displayed a character of such strength and proportion it would stay with him for the rest of his life.

From the moment he picked up an oval ball at the age of seven, rugby became young Fred's burning passion, a passion that has burned brightly for more than 80 years and will undoubtedly continue for the rest of his life.

Leadership and discipline, even as a boy, came naturally to him. In his teenage years he captained every team in which he played, even though he was often the smallest player in the side.

On the outbreak of the Second World War, he fibbed about his age in order to fight for his country. He was in many a bloody battle, was promoted in the field, was twice wounded and was lucky to survive. When he returned from active service, such were his strength of character, qualities of leadership and razor-sharp intelligence it was obvious he was destined for greatness.

Today he remains the only true unbeaten coach in All Blacks history, having guided our national side through 37 games against major rugby-playing countries without a single defeat. No other national coach has possessed his aura of authority or magnetic charisma. Wherever he goes today, be it the shopping plaza, his local RSA or his beloved Eden Park, people still gravitate towards him to pat him on the back or shake his hand. Scarcely a day goes by that he doesn't receive requests to attend functions of various kinds. It is impossible to cope with them all, but Fred Allen does the best he can for the game he loves — and for the things in which he believes.

Today Sir Fred is the patriarch of New Zealand rugby, a leader extraordinaire and an individual with the rare capacity to bring out the best in others. His record of service to his country as sportsman, soldier, administrator and ambassador, as well as community worker, is unsurpassed.

It is a mark of the man that throughout his adult life he has carried in his wallet a neatly folded piece of paper on which are written the following words:

The duration of an athletic contest is only a few minutes while the training for it may take many weeks of arduous work and continuous exercise of self-effort.

The real value of sport lies not in the actual game played in the limelight of applause, but in the hours of dogged determination and self-discipline carried out alone, imposed and supervised by an exacting conscience.

The applause soon dies away, the prize is left behind, but the character you build is yours forever.

The lines on this sheet of paper reveal the underlying philosophy of an exceptional motivator who has not only inspired countless young New Zealanders to give of their best on the field of play but has also prepared them for the much more difficult game of Life.

We need people who inspire us, people we can respect, people who set the highest standards and then set out to painstakingly achieve their goals. They are important people in today's world — and Fred Allen is one of them.

A Loving Son

A little boy cherishes his first pair of rugby boots, even though a number of sprigs are missing.

Mrs Florence Allen, affectionately known by friends and neighbours as Flossie, gave birth to her fifth child on 9 February 1920 in the historical South Island town of Oamaru. When she and her husband Fred named the baby Frederick Richard, they were, of course, completely unaware that their child was destined for great things.

Flossie already had three daughters, Audrey, Merle and Mabel, as well as a son named Alec, and before long baby Fred was joined by another brother, Frank, to bring the tally of children to six. At this stage the family moved from Oamaru for a brief spell in Invercargill before finally settling in Christchurch.

Feeding and clothing a family of eight on the meagre housekeeping provided by her husband, an underpaid railway employee who was very fond of his beer, was always a struggle for Flossie, whom Fred speaks of with great affection.

'She was a wonderful woman, my mother,' Fred says. 'She had a fine upbringing in Southland and she was the strength and driving force behind our family. She was the one who encouraged all her children into sport, and when I was seven she scraped together enough money to buy me my first rugby boots, even though they were second-hand with some of the sprigs missing.

'Damned if I know how Mum managed it, but manage it she did. Then she took me by the hand to the local football ground where she introduced me to the club's officials who just happened to be looking for an eight-year-old to complete a "nippers" team.

'The following Saturday morning, although I was only seven, I found myself running on to the field with a bunch of kids a year older than me. I didn't know any of them and I had no idea of what I was supposed to do. I just chased after that ball as hard as I could and when I got my hands on it and had my first run, I was hooked.

'That night, when Mum came to tuck me into bed, she found me wearing my new rugby jersey over my pyjamas. It was a couple of sizes too big, but I wouldn't let her take it off because I wanted to wear it forever. Mum just smiled that wonderful smile of hers and kissed me goodnight.'

Another of Fred's boyhood memories is the 'one and only time' he ever tried to steal something.

'We had neighbours with a big apple tree in the back of their section and that was a real temptation for me as an 11-year-old. I thought they were out one day so I climbed over our back fence and started to help myself. But the neighbours weren't out at all and they spotted me through a window.

'Instead of coming out and boxing my ears as most people would have done in those days, they called the police and in next to no time a policeman arrived on his bike and was under the tree ordering me down.

'But I was much too scared to obey. I just clung there in the middle of all those beautiful apples, scared out of my wits as that big constable stood on tiptoes and whacked away at my arse.

'I got one helluva fright — as well as a sore arse — but it didn't do me any harm. It just gave me more respect for people in authority and that's why I think today's anti-smacking brigade have got it all wrong.'

Fred's mother reckoned that every boy should have a dog, so one day she got him a Labrador from the pound.

'I think she got him for nothing. He was just a puppy when she brought him home, but he grew into quite a big dog. My three sisters and I had an argument about what to call him, but we finally settled on Rover because he liked to roam around a lot.

'There were fields and ponds not far from where we lived and I used to take him looking for rabbits. I was about 10 or 11 at the time and Rover became a very good rabbit hunter. He could sniff them out a mile away and we had great fun chasing them.

'Rover and I became such good mates that Labradors have been my favourite

Fred (front row, third from left) was 'just a skinny little guy in those days'. Canterbury Primary School reps, 1933.

breed ever since. One night he was run over by a car and the next day I refused to go to school. I didn't want the other kids to see how upset I was. But Mum understood. She knew how I was feeling.'

In his last year at Phillipstown School, Fred was selected to play for the Canterbury Primary School Reps, something which greatly pleased his mother.

'I was a skinny little guy in those days, but I always felt confident when I saw Mum on the sideline, silently egging me on. I used to try my hardest because I wanted to make her proud of me.

'As I came up through the grades at the Linwood Club I had this burning ambition to play for Canterbury when I was bigger. I didn't dare think about the All Blacks because to me the All Blacks weren't just superstars; they were black-shirted gods.'

It was at Lancaster Park on 5 July 1930 that young Fred first witnessed his gods in action. It was the height of the Great Depression but somehow Flossie had saved enough money to take him to the All Blacks' test match against the touring British Lions. When the final whistle went young Fred was jumping up and down with sheer delight because the All Blacks had won by 13 points to 10.

The player who mesmerised Fred that day was legendary fullback George Nepia, who'd been the most spectacular player in the 1924–25 All Blacks, the squad hailed as The Invincibles.

Legendary All Blacks fullback George Nepia in action during the 1930 series against the British and Irish Lions.

'That was a day I shall never forget. I came home with Mum in the tram and all the way I never stopped talking about the marvellous things I'd seen,' says Fred. 'I couldn't believe just how far Nepia could kick that ball or how fast some of those All Blacks could run. And when an All Black scored and the huge crowd cheered and cheered, Mum included, it was the most exciting thing I'd ever seen.'

The bond between Flossie and Fred was strong and there is no doubt that she saw in him something special, not only as a sportsman but also as a young man. She was such a proud mother that when he was chosen for the primary school reps she scarcely missed a game in which he played.

'I always felt good when Mum was there,' says Fred. 'She wasn't one of those parents who ran up and down the sideline yelling. But any time I scored a try I would look over at her as I ran back into position and she would give me a smile and a little clap.

'When Mum died and my sisters were attending to everything, they found my primary schools representative cap in a box among her most precious belongings. She had kept it there all her life so I could have it when she was gone.'

Relations were not as good between Fred and his father, however. Fred remembers: 'He and I didn't get on at all. He used to hit my mother and I'd have a go at him to pull him away from her. I was about 13 at the time and he was far too strong for me so I always copped a few bruises as well.

'When he lost his job on the railways, Mum and he separated. As far as

Fred's beloved mother Florence 'Flossie' Allen pictured with Mabel, one of his three sisters.

I know he went to work somewhere near Timaru. I don't think he ever got another permanent job.

'I never saw him again until I came back after the war with the Kiwis Army team about 14 years later. He showed up and tried to attach himself to me, but I could never forgive him for the way he had treated my mother.'

During those formative years of Fred's life, Flossie and her family struggled through the worst depression in New Zealand's history. In December 1930 just over 11,000 New Zealanders were out of work and by 1933 the roll of unemployed had reached 80,000 in a population of one and a half million. More than 1000 Wellington school children were reported to be suffering from malnutrition. Canterbury was hit just as severely. Hundreds of fathers with children at school were out of work and many of these children were short of food. Among these victims were Flossie and her family. They desperately needed more money.

It was almost impossible to find work, but Fred had a bright idea. When he was 13 he often stopped to look at the delicious cakes and pies in the window of McLaughlin's bakery in Manchester Street. People living a mile or so away, he felt, would be just as tempted as he was if only they could see those goodies. So he plucked up courage, went into the shop, and put a business proposal to Mr McLaughlin.

He suggested that if he had a basket on the front of his old bike he could hawk Mr McLaughlin's wares from house to house. Impressed by the youngster's enterprise, the baker agreed to provide the basket and soon Fred was off on his first run as a freelance salesman.

'I sold quite a lot of cakes and pies but, with the small amount I could carry, there wasn't much profit in it,' recalls Fred, 'although when Mr McLaughlin paid me he always gave me a bonus of a big pink lamington.'

What gave Fred the greatest pleasure, however, was being able to give a small handful of coins to his mother each week. Flossie knew full well just how hard Fred was trying and she was overwhelmed with admiration by her son's concern for her and the family.

Another of Fred's great joys at that stage was being occasionally allowed to borrow his elder brother's car for joyrides. The car's engine, however, had seen better days and even the most modest hills presented a problem. Fred soon discovered, though, that reverse was the most powerful gear and passers-by were often surprised to see this youth driving backwards up the foothills on the edge of Christchurch.

Fred would have dearly loved to have gone to high school, but with the situation as serious as it was, a secondary education was out of the question. It was something he has regretted all his life.

When he turned 16 Flossie took him for a job interview at Ballantynes in Christchurch, the store regarded as the Harrods of the southern hemisphere. He was accepted as an errand boy with prospects of promotion. His salary was 17 shillings and sixpence a week, most of which he gave to his mother. 'The rest of it I spent on the things kids enjoy, like comics and Eskimo Pies, which in those days cost about threepence,' says Fred.

Ballantynes was a dignified and disciplined establishment in which the staff conformed to a strict dress code. Women were required to wear black dresses with white collars and flat-heeled shoes. Their stocking seams had to be perfectly straight and they were banned from painting their fingernails or wearing jewellery of any kind. All male staff had dark suits and white collars and were instructed to wear hats when entering or leaving the store. That applied even to the lowliest of juniors like Fred.

'One of my main jobs when I began in furnishings was lugging rolls of material across Lichfield Street to the factory. If I'd been caught without my hat, even if I was only going across the road, I'd have been in deep trouble.'

Ballantynes' training system involved its youngest employees moving from department to department to gain an insight into the entire business. This rotation policy meant that Fred spent some time learning the art of window-dressing and it was during this period he discovered just how strong Ballantynes was on modesty.

Linwood Club's all-conquering under-18 side of 1936. Proud skipper Fred Allen is holding the ball in the front row.

When displaying female underwear, great care was taken to show it in the most discreet way. The life-like plaster models of shapely women were decorously hidden under dressing-gowns with only the tiniest hint, a peep-show glimpse, of the garment beneath. Male plaster models received similar treatment. The idea of them being on public show in woollen long-johns was far too vulgar for Ballantynes and they, too, were half hidden under dressing-gowns.

It is hard to imagine Fred Allen doing such 'delicate' work behind a shop window in the main street of Christchurch. But the type of work didn't worry him one bit because each week he was taking home enough money to lessen the burden on his beloved Flossie. And to him that's what mattered most.

When Fred turned 17 his natural athletic talent started to really show and there was rejoicing in the Allen household when his Linwood Club's under-18 grade side won both the Evans and Redpath Shield championships in 1936. What made the occasion all the more special was the fact that young Fred Allen had captained the side, even though he was the smallest player in the team.

By this time the Canterbury selectors had him in their sights and selected him to represent his province at the age of 19. And if that wasn't enough, he was appointed captain of Canterbury the following year.

Flossie's joy knew no bounds.

True Patriot

Fred Allen once dropped an easy pass — a simple error that saved his life.

Fred prefers to keep his war record to himself. 'That was a long time ago,' he says — let's just get on with life.' But, in spite of his reticence, there are things the public should know. Although he was a New Zealand infantry lieutenant who several times escaped death by the barest of margins, he was also a member of an American unit sent on an extremely dangerous mission, a trainee fighter pilot who topped his class and a platoon leader who broke ranks to rescue 11 comrades from a deadly Japanese ambush.

When the Second World War broke out, young Fred desperately wanted to fight for his country. But the minimum age for enlisting was 21, and Fred had just turned 20. So he 'raised' his age a year, bluffed his way through, and entered Burnham Camp near Christchurch.

After several weeks' training, his 30th Infantry Battalion was ordered to Fiji where more extensive exercises were carried out. Then it was back to New Zealand for a short period before embarking for Guadalcanal in the Solomon Islands to help repel the Japanese war machine which was moving south at an alarming rate. In the previous few months most of the Western Pacific theatre had been overrun and millions of people had been enslaved and forced into hard labour under the cruellest of masters. Among the many territories overthrown were Malaya and the 'impregnable' British fortress of Singapore, as well as Hong Kong, the Philippines and half of New Guinea, less than 200 miles from the northern tip of Australia.

With the enemy now on its very doorstep, the future of Australia hung perilously in the balance — and with it the fate of New Zealand, whose population, because of wartime censorship, was completely unaware of the gravity of the situation.

After serving in Guadalcanal, where some of the war's bloodiest fighting took place, Fred's unit was transferred to the island of Vella Lavella, also the scene of terrible slaughter before it was recaptured by Allied forces.

During one daylight attack, a fragment from a Japanese shell punched a small hole clean through the back of Fred's neck, missing his spinal column by little more than a centimetre. It came close to leaving him permanently paralysed.

Fred's platoon, of which he was the leader, had been selected to join an elite American commando unit on a particularly hazardous raid, one he was determined not to miss because of the wound which, except for the discomfort, did not physically inconvenience him in any way. He asked the Army doctor, a close friend, not to report the injury and the doctor reluctantly agreed. He inserted a plug of sterilised gauze through the hole in Fred's neck and gave

Private Frederick Richard Allen, Burnham Camp, Christchurch, 1940. Fred, right, had 'raised' his age a year and bluffed his way into the army.

him the okay to proceed, provided Fred report to him the moment he returned.

The mission to New Guinea's Green Island, formerly called Nissan Island, just south of the equator, began at midnight on 30 January 1944 as the commandos, their faces darkened with special green paint, climbed down rope ladders on the side of an American destroyer. Waiting below were American landing craft assigned to take the raiders to secluded beaches inside the island's lagoon a mile away.

There was a huge swell running and, without warning, one of the landing craft bumped into the side of the destroyer. One of Fred's mates, who was first man down, was trapped between the two vessels. The hapless soldier screamed in pain as both his legs were crushed. He was lifted aboard the destroyer by members of the crew and carried below to the vessel's surgery where his legs were later amputated.

It was not a good start to such a stealthy operation and every man was very much on his toes as the landing craft proceeded towards the island. But the Japanese had neither heard nor seen them and the commandos waded ashore without incident.

The purpose of the mission is described in official war records, a section of which reads:

> . . . to report on the suitability of sites for airfields, landing beaches and approaches, naval and torpedo boat bases, and radar stations as well as the rise and fall of the tides and the depth of the lagoon — all of which are to be gathered in the 24 hours allowed ashore.

> Major A.B. Bullen will command the party to investigate airfield sites, while Lieutenant F.R. Allen's unit will reconnoitre the beaches on Barahun Island located in the lagoon.

Additional orders were to destroy any enemy patrols that discovered their presence and be offshore in their landing craft to be picked up by the American destroyers at midnight.

As the raiding party reconnoitred the island there were several engagements, one of which is recorded:

> Commander J.M. Smith, searching the coastline through binoculars, picked up the outline of a camouflaged barge hidden under overhanging branches and decided to investigate. As his landing craft touched the sand, Japanese waiting in the undergrowth only a few feet away poured machine-gun fire into the craft. In seconds 50 per cent of the occupants were either killed or wounded. Commander

Lieutenant F.R. Allen, 1943.

Smith, although wounded, took the dead coxswain's place and, after two agonising attempts had failed, retracted the boat from the beach.

Because of the shallow water near the shore and the huge surf, the American sailors guarding the landing craft had the utmost difficulty keeping them off the sharp coral reefs. But in spite of this hazard they were undamaged when the raiding parties returned to the beach in time to proceed to the pick-up point.

On the stroke of midnight the destroyers emerged from the darkness and the tired commandos scrambled aboard, their mission accomplished. The reconnoitring of Green Island had achieved its goals. It supplied the Allied chiefs-of-staff with the information needed to launch an all-out attack on the eight-mile-long atoll.

This task was assigned to infantry troops from New Zealand who carried out the assault on 15 February 1944. When all Japanese defences had been eliminated, Green Island became home for 17,000 Allied troops, the majority of them New Zealanders. Most of the others were American 'Seabees' (of the Construction Battalions — CBs) who worked around the clock to construct two airstrips from which to strike the enemy, along with roads, hospitals, docks and accommodation areas.

Green Island never caught the public imagination like Midway or Iwo Jima, but its capture was of great importance to the United States' effort to win the war. The Americans showed their appreciation in a short despatch: 'We hail our New Zealand comrades. Their collaboration, along with their strategic and fighting skills, has earned our lasting respect.'

The authors have recently learned that Lieutenant Allen was involved in another dangerous mission while on Vella Lavella — the rescue of a fellow platoon commander who had been ambushed in dense jungle with 10 of his men. A radio message had been received that Lieutenant 'Baldy' Howitson and his men were hiding in thick undergrowth, having succeeded in beating off the enemy, several of whom had been killed. Desperately short of ammunition, the trapped soldiers had little chance of surviving a second Japanese attack, which would certainly come after nightfall.

While his superior officers were deciding what action to take, Lieutenant Allen realised immediate action was essential if they were to reach the trapped soldiers before darkness fell. He led a squad of his own men through a mile of jungle, so dense that little daylight could penetrate the canopy above their heads, to reach their 11 comrades. An hour into their difficult journey, the increasing number of Japanese corpses showed them they were nearing their objective.

Having made contact with their comrades, some of whom had been

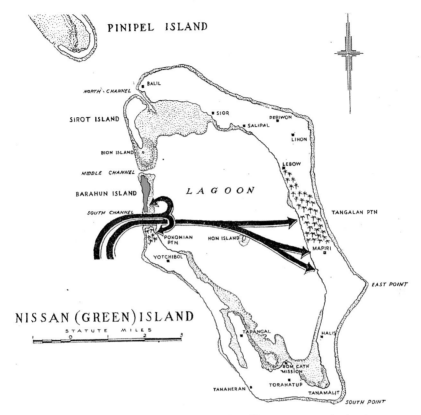

Barahun Island (highlighted in orange) where Fred and his unit were tasked with reconnoitring the beaches.

wounded, they handed over the boxes of ammunition they had brought with them before setting out on their return journey. To evade the enemy, they used a different route. It made the going a lot slower, but they still hoped to reach their company base before dark. They were aware of Japanese patrols nearby and expected an attack at any moment. But luck was with them and they arrived without incident.

When questioned by the authors about his motivation for this rescue, all Fred Allen would say was: 'Well, Baldy Howitson was a friend of mine.'

The first task assigned to Fred's unit when it arrived in the Solomons was a dangerous one, involving the unloading and storing of large drums of high-octane fuel for the Allied fighters and bombers. This huge stockpile was initially defended by a single Bofors anti-aircraft gun — until an enemy bomb scored a direct hit and both the gun and its entire New Zealand crew were blown to smithereens.

Japanese planes bombed the site at regular intervals and it was only by the greatest of good fortune that the highly inflammable pile never caught fire.

The most persistent raider became known to the camp as 'Washing Machine Charlie'. Night after night, just before midnight, the sleeping soldiers were woken by the drone of his plane, followed by the explosions of his bombs. These regular raids had such a psychological effect that something had to be done. So the American air base was contacted and arrangements made for Charlie's demise.

The following night, shortly before Washing Machine Charlie was due to make his run, a twin-engined Lockheed Lightning fighter was circling high above Charlie's flight path. When the sound of the Japanese plane was heard in the distance, the entire personnel on the ground below watched with great anticipation.

'We didn't have to wait long,' says Fred. 'Before Charlie released his bombs, the Lightning pounced with all guns firing and the ambush was over in seconds.'

As Charlie and his plane plummeted from the darkness in a ball of flame and hit the ground in an ear-splitting explosion, the New Zealanders cheered themselves hoarse. Then they went back to their beds and, for the first time in weeks, enjoyed a good night's sleep.

When their tour of duty in the Solomons was over, the division returned to New Zealand and it was then that Fred, who had always had passion for flying, was given the opportunity of joining the RNZAF with the aim of becoming a fighter pilot.

Fred (second from right) with members of his platoon in the Solomon Islands.

He gladly accepted and was posted to Woodbourne flying school at Blenheim.

Because of his lack of a secondary education, he realised he would be at a considerable disadvantage but, being the type of man he is, he studied night and day and was elated when he topped the written and oral examinations with a mark of 92 per cent. All his hard work was in vain, however, when Britain reduced the top age for fighter pilots to 21 and Fred, who was 24, missed out. Bitterly disappointed because of his desire to fight in the skies, Fred was released from the Air Force and given the opportunity of rejoining the infantry.

He still has the letter of congratulations sent to him by his station commander after his examinations:

RNZAF station 'Fareham'
Delta Blenheim 15.11.44

Lieutenant F.R. Allen was a pupil of mine for pre-entry examination which he passed with a credit mark of 92 per cent. This placed him at the top of his class. Lieutenant Allen showed great determination to learn to fly and has worked very hard and consistently during the course. Unfortunately new age regulations now prevent him becoming a fighter pilot.

He has also taken a very active part in camp sports, especially rugby football, and during his period of training he was selected as a Marlborough representative.

Lieutenant Allen also showed very fine qualities of leadership and was most popular among his men.

R.A. Evans, Flight Commander

Anxious to serve his country further, Fred now joined the famous New Zealand 27th Battalion, which had already performed meritorious service in Crete, Greece, the Western Desert and Tunisia. He served some time in the Middle East before the battalion was deployed to Italy, and it was during this campaign that Fred had his second close brush with death, one even more miraculous than the first.

His unit had just captured the Italian town of Villa Fontana as it fought its way north. During a pause in the fighting, Fred asked a tank commander to throw him his haversack, which was on top of the tank. The commander threw the bag, but Fred missed it, and had he not done so he would have been cut in half. It was the one pass in his entire life he was thankful he dropped. As he stooped to pick up the bag a German 88 mm shell burst close by. The tank commander, killed instantly, fell on top of Fred as he was bending down. The side of the tank inches above Fred's stooping body was sprayed with deadly

Fred (front row, third from left) was disappointed to miss the chance to become a fighter pilot, but satisfied to top his pre-entry class at Woodbourne flying school in Blenheim, 1944.

shrapnel, some of which ripped into Fred's shoulder and down one side, knocking him unconscious.

Stretcher bearers rushed to the two men, believing them to be dead. But Fred was still alive. He was taken to a field hospital to recover from his wounds before being sent to Rome to recuperate. By the time he was fit enough to rejoin his unit the war was almost over.

How fortunate it was for New Zealand that Lieutenant Fred Allen fumbled that easy pass, for in the years ahead that gallant soldier would coach the All Blacks to unprecedented glory and elevate New Zealand rugby to the top of the world.

Memories of war still linger in Fred's mind. 'There are unspeakable things a soldier can never forget,' he says, 'things like seeing your mates blown to bits beside you — it's impossible to wipe them out of your memory.

'What I saw was bad enough, but a nuclear war would be a million times worse. If we don't find the right leaders to take us into the future, civilisation is in peril.'

When Fred returned to civilian life, his self-discipline, his respect for authority and his keen intellect were clearly evident.

Because of the strict conditions under which he had worked at Ballantynes store, followed by his harrowing war experiences, he had developed into an exceptional leader and motivator of men. These were the qualities that would ensure his success in business and eventually place him firmly on the stairway to worldwide fame.

Kiwis in Khaki

One of the most influential teams in rugby history uplifts the people of Britain from the horrors of war.

A team of war-weary New Zealand soldiers is still remembered as one of the finest ever to grace the playing fields of England. Playing with a skill and panache never before seen in any of the four Home countries, the Kiwis Army team brought an entirely new dimension to the game of rugby.

The brainchild of General Sir Bernard Freyberg, officer commanding the New Zealand forces in the Middle East, the team was assembled for two purposes. The first was to resurrect the morale of Freyberg's battle veterans by playing the game they loved, and the second was as a goodwill gesture for the redevelopment of post-war Britain and France. The 33-match tour lasted six months and succeeded on both counts.

It also brought a new freedom to the men of the 2nd Expeditionary Force, and it succeeded beyond all expectation in uplifting the spirits of millions of British people who had suffered untold pain and hardship during the bombings of their cities and the deaths of their loved ones.

The Kiwis' open, free-flowing style of rugby drew enormous crowds and regenerated the joy and excitement of sport wherever they appeared.

The process of selecting the team was conducted with military precision.

The Kiwis pose for a photo before heading for another destination on the famous 1945–46 NZEF Army tour. Fred is seventh from left.

Hundreds of hopefuls were first interviewed in order to select 120 for field trials in Austria, and when these had been played the best 62 prospects were flown to England for a series of final trials at Margate.

One of these was an elated Fred Allen who was over the moon about playing his beloved game once again. He has vivid memories of flying from Italy to England in a Lancaster bomber for the final trials.

'The inside of the plane had no seating for passengers, but that didn't worry our party of 30 one little bit. We just stretched out on the floor, hardly believing our luck that all this was happening.

'Soon after we arrived in London our party was joined by the second contingent of 32, as well as three newly released British prisoners-of-war, included because of their rugby credentials.

'When the trials had been concluded at Margate in Kent, the team selections were read to a packed assembly.'

Fred remembers it well: 'There was terrific tension in the room as the names were announced. They were read in alphabetical order and mine was the first. I was absolutely thrilled — at last I was going to play some real rugby again. I could scarcely believe it.

'I was the happiest I had been for years. The names in the team included Bob Scott and Johnny Simpson who became among my closest friends.'

Every man selected was a warrior who had served his country on the battlefields of North Africa or Europe. After years of fighting, with their mates dying by their sides, they were more than eager to blot out the past — and playing rugby again was an excellent way to do it.

Although the idea came from General Freyberg himself, the man who made the team such a huge success was its manager Brigadier Allan Andrews, a young officer who narrowly escaped death on several occasions and was mentioned in despatches four times.

But the appointment of Major Charles Saxton, a former All Black from Otago, as coach and captain of the team, was the master stroke. Here was a man who thought outside the square, an innovator with new ideas on how the game should be played. The philosophy of Saxton's coaching is summed up in three words — 'position, possession and pace' — and under his guidance the newly formed team concentrated on putting these fundamentals into practice.

Rugby teams had previously operated more or less as two sections, with the heavier forwards pounding the opposition into submission before feeding the ball to the fleeter backs to score the tries. There was a saying in New Zealand that our teams played nothing but 'ten-man rugby'!

Saxton's philosophy introduced a different pattern. He wanted his team of 15 to gel together, with each man running, passing and backing up at maximum speed. He also called for more accurate handling and precise kicking to open spaces. So successful were his methods that before long the Kiwis were being hailed as one of the greatest and most spectacular teams ever to grace the playing fields of England. By the end of the tour they had played 33 matches and lost only two.

All this time Fred, who was proving to be one of the stars of the side, was absorbing Saxton's teachings with increasing enthusiasm. Not only was Saxton's fast, open style of play bringing excellent results — the final tally was 98 tries scored and just 22 conceded — it was also responsible for the games being the most enjoyable in which Fred had ever taken part.

He loved every minute of it. For him, this was the way rugby should be played and it didn't take him long to make a decision that would remain with him for the rest of his life. Should he ever be asked to prepare a team he would have no hesitation in using Saxton's revolutionary methods as the basis of his coaching.

When he made that decision little did he know that he would one day coach the mighty All Blacks through 37 games, including 14 tests in five countries, without a single defeat.

Fred's mother Flossie kept a scrapbook of the Kiwis tour packed with cuttings and photographs. She must have been very proud of her son's achievements for, in almost every game, his play was described in glowing terms by the overseas journalists.

Fred Allen was impressive in all his appearances and, in fact, it might be said that, but for his genius, the Kiwis would have been in serious difficulties in several of their games.

Fred Allen has played in every match and has always been the mainstay of the backline. Heady, neat and elusive he is the sure and constructive link between Saxton and the other backs.

The most thrilling game of the tour was against Wales at Cardiff Arms Park on 5 January 1946. It was in this nail-biting contest that the flying Kiwis winger, Jim Sherratt, scored one of the greatest match-winning tries of all time.

Halftime came with no points on the board and not long into the second spell the Welsh fullback Lloyd Davies landed a magnificent penalty goal from beyond halfway to give Wales a 3–0 lead.

The second half was played at a frenzied pace and there was only 11 minutes left on the clock when the Kiwis won a scrum 10 yards inside their own half. The Kiwis second-five, Ike Proctor, punted high downfield, hoping the Welsh fullback would make a mistake. But Davies took the ball cleanly and steadied himself for a long kick to touch — and that was when the mistake was made.

As he made contact with the ball, the fullback was slightly off balance and the kick failed by inches to reach the touchline. Seizing the opportunity, the Kiwis wing Sherratt raced in, scooped it up at top speed, and set off for the try-line 70 yards away. With the Welsh defence racing to cut him off, the big winger tore down field and it was apparent that only one defender, his Welsh opposite, Graham Hale, had any chance of stopping him. But Sherratt had a two-yard start and try as he may for the honour of his country, the Welshman was unable to close the gap as the flying New Zealander turned infield to dot down between the uprights. It is still remembered as one of the most brilliant tries ever scored at Cardiff Arms Park.

Bob Scott converted to give the Kiwis the lead 5–3. Then, with just a few minutes left, Scott landed two penalty goals, both from near halfway, and the final whistle blew with the Kiwis in front 11–3.

When the tour was over, the party, many now homesick, returned to New Zealand by sea. During the six-week voyage from London they had no rugby training and put on a great deal of weight. A fortnight with their families, during which they relaxed even more, did nothing to improve their condition.

By popular demand, a short tour of five matches against New Zealand provincial sides had been arranged. In their first game for three months the Kiwis put 12 points on the board in 15 minutes against Auckland and it looked as though they were about to annihilate the local side. But in the second half their condition began to wilt and in the end it was a thrilling draw at 20 points all with the Eden Park crowd of 50,000 screaming themselves hoarse.

In the second match the visitors defeated a combined Wairarapa-Bush XV 21–10 and then it was down to the South Island where they beat Canterbury 36–11 and Otago 19–8. By this time the pressure was beginning to tell and they lost to Wellington 11–18.

The tour was now over and the New Zealand Army team had achieved what they had set out to do. For countless spectators at both ends of the world their magnificent play had helped exorcise the bleak memories of war.

The Kiwis had also rejuvenated the game of rugby by incorporating a style that set new standards of innovation and entertainment, and by doing so, had become one of the most influential teams in rugby history. And not only that, the team had played with a skill and panache that had greatly impressed one of its own, five-eighths Fred Allen, who, in the years ahead, would become an international icon of the game.

From the moment the team disbanded Fred never faltered in his belief that rugby was a simple but highly effective game if played according to Charlie Saxton's beliefs. The forwards, especially the tight five, were of primary importance in gaining possession of the ball and from there on it was a matter of the ball beating the man if moved with precision and speed.

Despite the attentions of a Monmouthshire tackler, Fred manages to get his kick away.

Fullback Bob Scott was one of the stars of the Kiwis tour. Here he clears his line with Fred in support.

Another significant outcome of the tour was that the team produced no fewer than 16 future All Blacks, including Bob Scott and Johnny Smith, two of the greatest players of all time.

The team was fortunate to have renowned broadcaster Winston McCarthy, himself a soldier, accompanying the side throughout the tour. It was Winston who brought the tour alive for listeners at home in New Zealand as they sat glued to their short-wave radios in the early hours of the morning. Winston also saved every report of the tour and every photograph he could lay his hands on, as well as other memorabilia such as programmes, autographs, hotel menus, badges and the like. At the conclusion of the tour he meticulously pasted this entire collection into a large scrapbook.

On Winston's death in 1984 the book was bequeathed to commentator and radio host Keith Quinn, who later handed it to the New Zealand Army where, he believed, it rightfully belonged. This valuable record of the tour is now on permanent display in the Waiouru Army Museum.

In 1997 this immortal team was inducted into the New Zealand Sports Hall of Fame. The players assembled in Dunedin for the ceremony where its members then spent several happy days and evenings together. The player with the finest voice was Jim Kearney, who sang some beautiful songs, while Ike Proctor proved to be an excellent story teller.

'Iron Man' Johnny Simpson, a born humorist, who turned 75 on the day of the reunion, had this to say: 'I want to mention my mother who lived to 75.

She gave me two pieces of advice — respect your elders and don't get into cars with strange ladies.'

Fred was deeply saddened when he received a phone call from Johnny's wife Iris in November 2010 to tell him that his long-time friend had passed away. Johnny was 88 years old and had been blind for many years but he and Fred had never lost touch. Fred bitterly regretted being unable to attend the Iron Man's funeral but his heart-felt eulogy, read by Johnny's son Peter, described their wonderful friendship of 65 years.

'When Johnny played against the British Lions in 1950 he suffered a terrible injury to his knee which put an end to his international career,' Fred said. 'It was an injury which undoubtedly cost him the captaincy of the All Blacks the following year because of the forthcoming retirement of the current captain, another mighty player, Dr Ron Elvidge.'

Fred's eulogy ended with the words: 'Johnny has been a tremendous friend throughout most of my life and I shall miss him greatly. Farewell, Johnny, my old mate — one day we shall meet again on those beautiful rugby fields in the sky.'

Fred Allen and Johnny Simpson became friends in 1945 during the final selection trials for the Kiwis team in England. When that famous tour was over they both returned to Auckland to play club rugby, Fred for Grammar Old Boys and Johnny for Ponsonby. So outstanding was their form that both were selected to play in the representative side and then the All Blacks.

On the 1949 tour of South Africa, Johnny combined with Kevin Skinner, Otago, and Has Catley, Waikato, to become one of the finest front-row combinations of all time. Although the All Blacks, under the captaincy of Fred Allen, lost all four tests, history has since shown they were sent on a mission which had scant chance of success.

When Fred Allen was appointed coach of the Auckland rep side in 1957, he co-opted Simpson to look after the forwards. It was an excellent move as shown by the fact that Auckland not only won the Ranfurly Shield in 1959, they successfully defended it a record 25 times.

In the latter part of his life Simpson managed a hotel in Paraparaumu where he was also heavily involved in bowls. No mean player, he was president of the Kapiti Bowling Club in 1968 before serving a term as president of Bowls New Zealand. He also served on the national executive of the New Zealand Hotel Association.

(There is a plaster cast of Johnny Simpson's huge hands in the Rugby Museum in Palmerston North, and entry to the building is free to anyone who can match them in size. Many have tried but only two have succeeded.)

The Fashion Factory

Fred rejects a tempting offer to play league and rents a 'dungeon' below street level to start his first business.

In 1946 those wonderful days of touring with the famous Kiwis team were over. Fred had collected a lump sum of £250 for his years of military service which, he says, with a rueful smile, was hardly generous. Now he needed to find himself a job, but running rings around others on a rugby field didn't pull in the cash.

Well, that's not strictly true because a player with Fred's talent could pick up huge rewards in the league game. In fact, he could collect the sort of money most of his mates could hardly believe possible. But the snag was that to do so Fred would have to totally change his way of life. He'd have to say farewell to New Zealand and live in the industrial north of England.

He and two other stars of the Kiwis side had been head-hunted by the highly esteemed Wigan Warriors Rugby League Club. The others were centre three-quarter Johnny Smith who, because of his sublime skills, had been nicknamed 'The Master', and dashing winger Jim Sherratt — called 'Le Beau Cheval' by the French after scoring two exceptional tries against them in Paris.

'Wigan offered me a signing-on fee of £4500, which, quite honestly, struck me as mind-blowing,' says Fred. His reaction was hardly surprising because that advance payment roughly equated to what a highly regarded business executive could expect to earn in five years in London. And that amount was just the preliminary bait.

'The deal was for me to get £8 for each win and four for each draw — with nothing if we lost,' he says. 'Yes, it was bloody tempting — particularly for a young fella wondering how he's going to earn a living — because it was such a helluva lot of money.

'Making up my mind was a real struggle, but in the end I really didn't want to leave New Zealand. I knew I'd miss rugby very much, let alone the many friendships I'd made.'

Like Johnny Smith, who'd been offered an even bigger bait of £5000, he thanked Wigan and turned down the offer. So did Jim Sherratt. Not surprisingly, Fred and Johnny, together with 13 other members of the Kiwis, went on to play for the All Blacks.

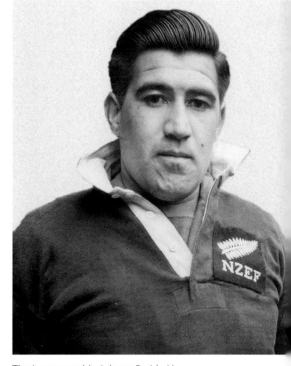

The incomparable Johnny Smith. He turned down a massive offer to go to rugby league after the Kiwis tour.

But what next for Fred? 'Well, I thought I ought to make use of what I'd learned at Ballantynes and do something in the fashion line. Maybe I should even have a crack at starting my own little business.'

One of Fred's friends had already established himself in the rag trade and needed someone to supply fabric belts for the garments he was making. That someone, Fred decided, was Fred! So he hunted around Auckland for cheap premises and found an unused storeroom below street level in Courthouse Lane for 15 shillings a week. 'It was a bit of a dungeon, about the size of a one-car garage, but it was good enough for me to make a start.'

At first there was just him making the belts, but soon he took on an assistant machinist to meet the growing demand.

'Then I realised I had a great opportunity to expand. At that time, just after the war, there were restrictions on what people could import but, as a returned serviceman, I could obtain a licence to import materials. And if I did that I could start making frocks as well as belts.'

That was the thinking behind the Fred R. Allen women's outer-garment manufacturing enterprise, launched with a borrowed £1000. It was to be

Man amongst mannequins . . . straight after the Kiwis tour Fred devoted much of his energy to building up his fashion business, Fred R. Allen Limited.

the centre of his life for just over 40 years. Except, of course, when he was concentrating on rugby — first as a player and then as a coach of international fame.

'But money was tight in those early days and I did sometimes wonder if I hadn't been stupid not to go to Wigan. I mean, you got no real pay from the stingy rugby union. I think I might have got five or perhaps six shillings a day, something like that. And that was only when you were on tour. Real mean they were.'

Because of the design and quality of Fred's garments it wasn't long before leading department stores such as Milne and Choyce and Smith and Caughey's in Auckland were stocking dresses bearing the Fred R. Allen label.

By then the business had expanded from the little dungeon to a larger office and showroom in Lorne Street where Fred, although the boss, helped the staff with all the daily tasks such as packing dresses, sweeping floors and tidying the workroom. Even in those days he knew instinctively that success was built on teamwork.

It was also important not to waste money. Fred's white-painted desk looked as though it had been bought for about $20 from some second-hand shop and his 'executive chair' wouldn't have cost half that much.

'Unlike other businesses in the area, there was no grog cupboard at Lorne Street,' says Fred. 'I didn't like the idea of breathing liquor over customers.'

Then came another shift to even bigger premises in Airedale Street where the firm was fortunate to have the services of one of New Zealand's top designer-cutters. Under Betty Kendall's supervision 20 machinists produced immaculately cut, high-class clothing for women.

'Our garments were non-dating without any gimmicks,' says Fred. 'They were not thrown out at sales because they'd still be fashionable the following year.'

Fred worked hard to build up the business. Each year, when he wasn't tied up with rugby, he travelled a least twice through the North and South Islands to show new lines and solicit orders at stores as far south as Bluff.

'It often meant driving through the night to keep appointments and that could be pretty arduous. If there were any hold-ups with ferries not sailing because of weather, or a strike or something, I could be properly stuffed. Looking back, I sometimes wonder how the hell I did it!'

His proudest moments as a salesman came when orders for his garments were regularly received from his former bosses at Ballantynes. 'Naturally, when I kept an appointment with their buyers I was extra certain that there wasn't a speck on my polished shoes and, of course, I carefully brushed my hat before getting out of the car.'

He was lucky on his last sales trip before leaving to coach the All Blacks on their victorious 1967 tour. He arrived back in Auckland in time to spend 10 days at home, and at the factory, before joining the team for the long voyage to Europe.

One of the most formidable players Fred encountered in Britain was the legendary Irish loose forward Bill McKay. Soon there was mutual respect between him and Fred, and that respect deepened into friendship in 1950 when McKay, the most experienced of the British Lions' forwards, featured in all their tests in Australasia.

The Lions thrashed the Wallabies but lost all three tests against Fred's All Blacks. During the second of those New Zealand encounters McKay was out of the game after 25 minutes with severe concussion and a broken nose.

'You can get a hint of how highly we all regarded him by where he spent his recovery,' says Fred. 'He was looked after by the legendary Maurice Brownlie, one of our greatest internationals, who'd invited him to his home in Gisborne.'

McKay's stay with Brownlie clinched his conviction that New Zealand was the country in which he'd really like to settle. So after qualifying as a doctor in Ireland — at Queen's University in Belfast — he returned in 1959 to start a practice in Gisborne.

It was then that Fred Allen received a surprising call. 'It was Bill McKay on the line saying that he and another of our mates, a farmer called Henry Harrison, had found a 350-acre farm that'd be a wonderful buy. It was a hill country place about 20 miles out of Gisborne and, as it was seriously run-down, could be snapped up at a bargain price.

'Would I join them as the third partner? I'd need about £10,000 but it would be a fantastic investment.

'I had to tell Bill right off there was no chance. I didn't have any money and was only just managing to keep my business going on an overdraft.

'So, sorry buddy, but no way can I manage it.'

A couple of days later McKay called again and urged Fred to try raising money. He got the same response.

'Then,' says Fred, 'something like a miracle happened. I'd hardly put the phone down when there was a knock at the door and there was a chap from an insurance company saying he had good news. Years earlier I'd bought a few of their shares — very few because I couldn't afford more — and I'd done so only because the agent pushing them was a mate.

'It seemed my few shares had gone into a draw, something I'd known nothing about, and I'd won a prize of £8000!'

The first thing Fred did was ring Bill McKay. 'Looks like we could be in business after all — if the bank will only lend me another £2000.'

The bank agreed and Fred Allen, frock-maker, farmer and All Black, drove to Gisborne to meet his partners and explore their property on horseback.

'Bill hadn't been kidding when he said the farm had been neglected. The fencing, the buildings and everything else were in a shocking state. Putting them right was going to cost big bucks and take a helluva lot of time. But we could all see the potential. So we agreed on a 10-year venture with Henry, a tough and experienced old farmer, running it for us.'

The trio chipped in regular sums to cover improvements and boost stock numbers and when the 10 years was up they sold.

'Each of us received an amount that today would be worth well in excess of $500,000 and that really set me up,' says Fred, 'so well in fact that I knocked down our holiday bach on the Whangaparaoa Peninsula and replaced it with a really fine house. I also bought a Corsair launch with room for seven to sleep in comfort.'

The windfall also enabled Fred to join wartime colleague, Alec McKenzie, as a racehorse owner. 'Gallopers, pacers, trotters, you name it, we were into it. Some of them were really good. I particularly remember one called Melodic which won 17 races and picked up about £18,000 in prize-money. Nowadays that would be worth a fortune.

'But no matter how well they were running I never bet on them. I'm just not a betting man.'

Fred was nearly 70 before he closed the clothing factory. 'Nearly all businesses were having a bit of a struggle in the late 1980s but I had two good reasons for not retiring earlier. First I had to consider my loyal staff who badly needed their jobs and then I had to consider myself.

'So many mates about my age had suddenly stopped work and the next thing they'd put their cues in the rack.

'I was determined that wouldn't happen to me.'

Triumph and Tragedy

Fred is selected to captain the All Blacks but elation turns to misery when his beloved Flossie is injured.

When Fred was at primary school his teachers could not help but notice how skilful he was at kicking and handling a ball, and it came as no surprise to them that he spent most of his time playing cricket or rugby. They told Flossie that her son was highly intelligent but his passion was more for sport than for study. They also told her he was 'an extremely well-behaved pupil, popular with his classmates and a pleasure to have in the classroom'.

Flossie was pleased with the teachers' summation of her second son. All she wanted was for her six children to be healthy and happy, and if young Fred wanted to play sport she would encourage him in every way she could. Because of the family's financial situation, she knew there was no chance of Fred pursuing a secondary and university education in order to enter a higher profession. He would always have to work hard and if he was healthy and strong through participation in sport it would be all the better.

So Fred's passion for bat and ball was given free rein throughout his teenage years and by the time he was 19 he had developed into a sportsman of outstanding ability.

The Canterbury selectors had been observing him for some time and before

Fred touches down for Auckland, against King Country at Eden Park, 1946. Auckland won 54–9.

long he found himself representing his province in two sports — as first-five in the rugby squad and as captain of the Brabin Cup cricket team.

So intelligently did the 19-year-old play in his first rugby appearances that the following year he was appointed captain of Canterbury. He had just turned 20. And the most astonishing fact about Fred's appointment was the fact that he was the smallest player in the side.

For some time Fred had been in a quandary, unable to decide which sport to pursue further, and it was when his captaincy was announced that he decided to forego cricket and concentrate on rugby. Little did he know of the honours and accolades that lay ahead.

He had been a slow grower during his formative years, but as the years went by he muscled up to 5 ft 10 in tall and 12 st 6 lb in weight. He had reliable hands, was fast off the mark and could sidestep off either foot. Add to these attributes his rugby intelligence and his boundless enthusiasm and it was obvious he was destined for greater things.

In the next few years Fred showed his class by representing a further three provinces — Marlborough in 1944 when he was in the Royal New Zealand Air Force, Waikato in 1944 when he was in military camp at Te Rapa and Auckland from 1946 to 1948 when the Second World War was over.

But in spite of these achievements it was his brilliant performances in the Kiwis immediately after the war that elevated him to the highest echelon of New Zealand rugby. During the Kiwis' tour of the British Isles and France he played in 28 of the 33 games, and when the side toured New Zealand he appeared in all five contests.

It was Fred's displays of intelligence, decision making and coolness under pressure, along with his ability to lead by example that caught the eye of the New Zealand selection panel. These were the qualities they were looking for, and in 1946 Fred was not only selected for the All Blacks home series against Australia, he was also appointed captain — and in his very first game!

For a rather surprised Fred it was a moment of supreme joy. The first thing he did was telephone his number one supporter, Flossie, and thank her for all she had done for him throughout the years.

A few weeks later Fred's family moved to Auckland where Flossie and his two brothers, Alec and Frank, rented a flat in Greenlane. Fred meanwhile had now earned sufficient money to rent his own unit in Atkin Avenue, Mission Bay, and purchase an old Chevrolet car.

One day in 1946 brother Frank was driving the Chev along Patteson Avenue, with Fred and Flossie as passengers, when a speeding car failed to give way at crossroads and smashed into their vehicle at speed, flipping it onto its side. Fred and Frank escaped with bruises but Flossie, seriously injured, was rushed to Middlemore Hospital.

Throughout the following weeks a distraught Fred did his best to concentrate on his duties as All Blacks captain, but his mind and thoughts were with his mother. He visited Flossie every day, looking forward to the time he would take her home. But sadly his mother never left hospital, where she passed away peacefully.

Fred had lost not only his mother but also his best friend. It was difficult for him to take, and he has always regretted that his mother died just at a stage where he was in a position to buy her things and make her life a great deal better than it had ever been. He also felt a deep sense of sadness that Flossie did not live long enough to see him lead the All Blacks on to the field for the first time against Australia in Dunedin, a test which New Zealand won. That would have meant so much to her.

Because of the war the All Blacks had not played a test match for almost nine years. There was a lot of rebuilding to do, but the inclusion of several members of the Kiwis Army team went a long way to solving the problem.

Fred believed that his first duty as captain was to get to know his players, and that is what he was determined to do from the moment the team was selected. His past record bore testimony to the fact that he had the instincts of a leader. Now, as captain of the mighty All Blacks, the question uppermost in his mind was 'How can I get the best out of this fine collection of players in order to win against the world's best?' But he was patient, observant and an excellent reader of men — qualities which would be of the utmost value in the years ahead.

His players came from all walks of life. There were heavyweights, middleweights and lightweights. There were men who were afraid of physical contact and there were men who enjoyed it. There were men who threw up with nervousness before a game and there were veterans who ran onto the field as though they had done it a thousand times before.

New Zealand's first test team since the outbreak of World War II. Fred (front row, third from left) was given the honour of leading the side against Australia at Dunedin on 14 September, 1946. It had been eight years, one month and one day since the All Blacks' last match.

But bonding these men together was a task that came relatively easy to him for the reason he had always been blessed with the instincts and understanding of a psychologist — as many of his players were about to find out. At the same time, to foster respect, he found it necessary to keep a perceptible gap between his team and himself. It was sometimes difficult, but always necessary. There were dozens of times when Fred wanted to join in with his players, especially on tour, and this he did on many occasions. He loved a handle of beer, he was sociable and an excellent singer, but he was aware from the beginning that it was of the utmost importance that he retain the respect of his men, without which he could never hope to succeed.

Although it wasn't his primary intention, he admits it was during these times of relaxation that he could not help but observe the true characteristics of his players. And it was because of these observations of their strengths and weaknesses that he was able to assist and direct them so ably, both on and off the field.

It was Fred's firm belief that a captain, as much as a coach, was the instigator of team pride. He insisted on a well turned out appearance at all times — a clean uniform, polished boots, washed laces and socks worn at the right height.

Fiercely protective of the All Blacks' good name, he felt it a captain's duty to put an instant stop to foul play — not to let it carry on until the referee stepped in. He also took great pride in winning. And he took particular pride when his team rallied back to winning form after losing a game.

He believed that a good team was a thinking team and he encouraged this in every way he could. 'I used to drum it into them,' he says. 'Use your head, look to the left, look to the right, take the best option and things like that.'

Fred's first test as captain was against Australia at Dunedin on 14 September 1946. Under his guidance, a fired-up All Blacks side romped home by 31 points to 8. In the second test in Auckland the Wallabies came back strongly, but again New Zealand prevailed, this time by 14 points to 10.

In 1947 a return series was played in Australia. Again too strong, the All Blacks won both contests, the first in Brisbane by 13 points to 5 and the second in Sydney by 27–14.

Fred had now been successful in his first four test matches and his reappointment as captain for the tour of South Africa in 1949 was a foregone conclusion.

Little did he know it, but the young All Blacks captain was about to embark on a mission well-nigh impossible to achieve. By the time the South African tour was over, everything he loved about the game of rugby would be destroyed, and life for Fred Allen would not be the same for a very long time.

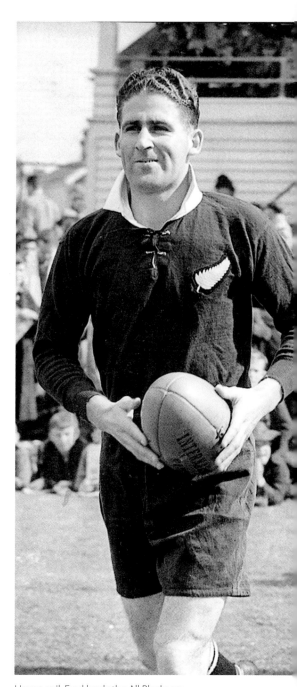

Home soil. Fred leads the All Blacks on to Eden Park for the second test against Australia in 1946. The All Blacks won the match 14–10 to clinch the two-test series.

The Tilted Playing Field

Disillusioned by the unfairness of the Springbok tour, Fred wants no further part of the game he loves.

'The whole thing was a disgrace to rugby!'

After six decades, Fred Allen breaks his silence to give his version of the All Blacks ill-fated tour of South Africa in 1949. So disgusted was he with what happened both on and off the field — and the 'gutlessness of the New Zealand Rugby Union' — that when the tour was over he vented his feelings in a most unorthodox way.

In front of the entire team he place-kicked his football boots from the deck of the liner *Dominion Monarch* into the Indian Ocean and vowed never to play rugby again. It was his way of showing his contempt for the manner in which a New Zealand team had been treated.

'If that's how the game is going to be manipulated, I want no further part of it,' he said. 'After what we've put up with in South Africa, I've had a gutsful!'

The All Blacks' problems started the day they left Auckland on the SS *Tamaroa*. She was little more than a cargo ship and the only exercise the team could manage on their 27-day journey was to use their specially issued skipping ropes or jog around the deck, which was difficult to do as the ship rolled through the Indian Ocean. There were a few twisted ankles and, with all the salt air, the players developed hearty appetites.

After the first couple of weeks at sea, they were bored out of their skins and one day they took out some of their frustration on broadcaster Winston McCarthy.

'He had been seconded to our team as official commentator by the New Zealand Government,' says Fred. 'He was a brilliant broadcaster but his incessant yapping had got on the nerves of some of the players. So one day they decided to do something about it.

'We were lolling around on deck when all of a sudden Johnny Simpson and Kevin Skinner picked McCarthy up like a sack of potatoes and hung him over the side by his ankles. We were right in the middle of the Indian Ocean and I thought, "Christ, I hope they've got a good hold on him."

'I found out afterwards that for a second or two each man was relying on the other. In fact, they nearly dropped him into the sea — they got almost as big a fright as McCarthy did. We'd have been in decent trouble if they'd lost their hold.

'I was more than relieved when they brought him back over the rail and stood him upright on the deck. Poor Winston just stood there in a state of shock, white as a sheet with his eyes glazed. It certainly cured him of his chattering for a while.'

The All Blacks arrived in less than ideal condition.

'During the voyage everyone put on weight, some over two stone, which meant

Top: A large Easter weekend crowd gathered at Queen's Wharf, Auckland, to farewell the 1949 All Blacks. Above: Homeward bound and Fred, after vowing never to play again, kicks his boots into the Indian Ocean.

that when we disembarked we were a long way from being in condition for a hard game of rugby, let alone against the Springboks.

'Immediately after our arrival, the Springbok coach Danie Craven took us by bus to Hermanus, in those days the Riviera of South Africa, where they plied us with food and drink at balls and cocktail parties — and all the time there wasn't a decent ground to train on.

'It was unbelievable hospitality but it wasn't doing us any good at all. It was going to take us a lot of hard work to trim down to our best form. There was a bit of skulduggery in all this. They certainly turned on the hospitality, but all the time it was tilting the field in their favour.'

During the 24-match tour, the All Blacks captain had been concerned about blatant offside play, illegal tackles, debilitating train travel for days on end over thousands of miles and locally selected referees. The four tests were controlled by two referees only: Eddie Hofmeyr, of Johannesburg (first and third tests), and Ralph Burmeister, of Cape Town (second and fourth tests). The All Blacks were given no other choices. Today this situation would be considered untenable.

As a captain of considerable experience Fred had always insisted on fair play and respect for the opposition, but what he and his team had endured fell well outside those guidelines. He was fully aware some of his players intended to expose the shortcomings of the tour the moment they arrived home. So before the ship berthed he called them together and urged them not to complain to the press, or anyone else, about the things that had gone on.

'I told them that although we had lost the tests four–nil it would still be the same in a thousand years. All the talk in the world wouldn't do any good and it certainly wasn't going to change the score.

'I didn't want them blaming Jim Parker, the manager, or his assistant Alex McDonald who was also the coach. If they were going to blame anyone, they should blame me.

'After a fair amount of discussion we made a pact not to complain or make excuses. As far as I know, none of them broke our agreement and I admired them for that.'

He concluded by telling them: 'Every one of you played the game according to the rules of good sportsmanship, but I can't say the same about the South Africans. No captain has ever been as proud of his team as I am of you.'

Fred had a great deal of sympathy for Parker and McDonald. 'They were nice guys,' he says, 'but Alex, at the age of 65, was past it. The heat in Africa affected him greatly and because he was sick most of the time I had no option but to take over the coaching, which distracted me from my other duties.'

Noted journalist T.P. McLean stated the position very clearly:

Fred gives an interview shortly after the All Blacks' arrival in South Africa in 1949. At left is assistant manager and coach Alex McDonald.

Fred Allen returned from the misery of the tour in a disturbed state of mind. He had been forced to carry the can for two elderly men, one as team manager the other as coach, and when each was proved incompetent, he bore much of the severe public criticism of the team.

Another critic of McDonald's selection as coach was prop forward Kevin Skinner: 'Alex played for the All Blacks in the early 1900s and captained them 12 times, but he was unqualified for the South African role — he was thinking 1905 and it was 1949.'

'The man the All Blacks desperately needed,' Fred says, 'was the Otago coach Vic Cavanagh. We'd have certainly drawn the series, and maybe won it, if we'd had him with us.

'Vic was far and away the outstanding coach of his generation — the finest coach never to be in charge of an All Blacks squad — but those stupid buggers in Wellington rejected his nomination and gave us Alex McDonald instead.

'The irony of this blunder was that while we were in South Africa, and in spite of 11 of his best players being with us, Cavanagh again showed his ability by guiding Otago through an unbeaten Ranfurly Shield season.'

Since that disastrous tour, thousands of words have been written about why New Zealand lost seven games out of 24, including all four tests.

'All that mattered to a rugby-mad New Zealand public was the final result,' Fred says. 'For the All Blacks to lose all the tests wasn't just a shock, it was a bloody disaster. But what riled me most was that some of the press articles said we'd been "thrashed", which was far from the truth.

'The All Blacks hadn't been thrashed. In each of the four tests we'd matched the Springboks every inch of the way and even scored more tries during the series. And I was very proud of the fact that in the entire 24 games played on tour, the South Africans crossed our line only eight times.

'So much of the media criticism was incorrect that for a long time after we arrived home I worried whether we'd done the right thing by agreeing to keep quiet. Perhaps we should have spoken up there and then.'

One minute before the Springboks ran onto the field for the first test their captain Felix du Plessis had told his players: 'Today South Africa plays New Zealand so consider your country at war!'

'That sums up the Springboks' attitude to win at all costs,' says Fred. 'In the first half their huge pack set out to grind down our forwards, but because of our strength up front they were unable to do so and we led at halftime by 11 points to 3.

It's a double for Fred against Natal at Durban. His two tries helped the All Blacks to an 8–0 win.

'In the second half it wasn't the Springbok team that won the game, it was one of their forwards, Okey Geffin, who was spot on with five penalty goals, one in the first half and four in the second. They couldn't penetrate our defence and those 15 points were the only points they scored.

'In the third test Geffin did it again — scoring all the Springboks' points with three penalties in their 9–3 victory. In the four tests he scored a total of 32 points.

'One of South Africa's leading rugby writers, H.B. Keartland, headed his account of the first test: "Springboks Climb From Shadow of Defeat to Hollow Victory". A follow-up story by Keartland was headed: "South Africa Won but Better Team was Beaten". His opinion was endorsed by prominent commentator R.K. Stent: "South Africa Lucky to Win First Test".

'Now I don't call that a thrashing,' says Fred.

'And, what's more, in the first test the All Blacks played more versatile football than the Boks. We scored a try by Peter Henderson, a dropped goal by Kearney and a conversion and penalty goal by our fullback Bob Scott, but those 11 points weren't enough.

'Had Scottie been in anything like his usual goal-kicking form we would have won. But a sudden lapse, which can happen to any kicker, caused him to miss five penalty attempts in succession. We just couldn't believe it — and neither could Bob, who otherwise played a magnificent game.

'I comforted him in the dressing room where he put his head between his hands and sobbed. He thought he had let New Zealand down, but he certainly didn't do that — all great kickers have their off days.

'For years he worried about his failure to put even a couple of those kicks over. But there was no need to punish himself because, unlike Geffin's kicks, most of Bob's attempts were long range and only missed by inches. And the number of times the ball hit the uprights, and failed to go through, was enough to make anyone sick.'

Another of Fred's concerns was the manner in which the referees let the Springbok No.8, Hennie Muller, roam offside and crash-tackle the inside backs, Jim Kearney and himself, often before they had the ball.

'Muller was a tremendous tackler and there were no replacements in those days,' says Fred. 'If a player went off injured that was it — from then on you were one man short. When a scrum went down Muller was offside most of the time and no matter how deep we stood, he came straight at us, often before the ball was out. He was so far offside it was a joke. And the referees let him get away with it!'

New Zealand's great front-row forward, Kevin Skinner, agrees: 'Both those refs allowed Muller to get away with murder,' he says. 'The number of times he hit our inside backs before they had the ball was a disgrace. Today he would have been off the field after the first infringement.

'Fred was in hospital — a couple of times if I remember right. He was badly bruised and had a lot of skin off him. We went to see him to cheer him up. They laid for him, alright. He wasn't very happy, I can tell you.'

Before the first test, the South African coach Danie Craven told Fred they were going to do something about All Blacks hooker Has Catley who, in the provincial games, had been getting the better of the Springbok front row in the scrums. He warned Fred they had a big, tough rooster who was going to sort Catley out.

Not one to take kindly to threats, Fred replied: 'I don't think that's a good idea, Danie. We've got three heavyweight boxers in our scrum, including the current holder of the New Zealand title.'

But Fred's words went unheeded and when the first scrum went down the South African loosehead prop, Hoppy van Jaarsveld, threw a vicious punch at Catley's head. Fortunately, the hooker turned just in time and the blow just grazed the side of his face.

'Had it hit him fair and square it would have split his head open,' Fred recalls. 'I realised what was happening so I rushed across to calm things down — but all I could hear was this voice saying, "I didn't do it, I didn't do it." It sounded like their tighthead prop, Okey Geffin.

'Then I heard Johnny Simpson say, "You're the one who did it, you bastard," followed by a loud whack. 'At that stage the ref broke up the scrum and here was this big Jaarsveld guy bent over double holding his hand over one eye, not looking very happy at all. Johnny, who wasn't nicknamed Iron Man for nothing, had given Jaarsveld the message loud and clear and that was the end of trouble from him.

'When the game finished, I went over to the Springbok captain du Plessis and congratulated him. It was the sporting thing to do. In the second test at Ellis Park I did the same thing and this time as we walked off the field he put his arm around me, and naturally I did the same to him. Just at that moment a photographer took a photo of us which was published around the world.

'What a roasting I got from the New Zealand press and the public! They resented the fact that I had a smile on my face when I should have looked downcast and miserable. I could scarcely believe it. What about sportsmanship? I'm glad I've got a different temperament from some of those buggers. Christ, if they only knew how I was hurting inside.'

It wasn't only on the field that things were stacked against the All Blacks. One

The photo that shocked a nation. Fred and Springbok captain Felix du Plessis walk off Ellis Park arm-in-arm after the Boks had beaten the All Blacks 12–6.

of their most serious concerns was the complex itinerary arranged by the South African Rugby Board. This involved long and debilitating train journeys — not in the luxurious express trains of today but in the old-type carriages with their uncomfortable seating. At one stage they were on a train for 10 successive days and nights and by that time they were thoroughly drained and mentally fed up.

After losing the first test, the All Blacks headed back to Johannesburg by rail, a trip of 35 hours. On the Saturday they played Transvaal and the same night they were back on the train to Bulawayo where they arrived two days later. Then they changed trains for a trip to Victoria Falls, which they reached on Tuesday morning. That same night they went back to Bulawayo, arriving on the Wednesday morning, and that same afternoon they played Rhodesia. They lost by 8 points to 10, which was hardly surprising.

Broadcaster Winston McCarthy wrote in his diary:

The All Blacks never looked the same combination after the Rhodesian trip, a journey that should never have been undertaken by rail with so many games left to play.

Travelling in South Africa is really tough. It would have been far better if the journey to and from Rhodesia had never been undertaken. Ten nights out of 12 in the train plus two matches in excessive heat was not in the best interests of a team that had three more test matches to play.

The All Blacks' misfortunes continued. Shortly after midnight on their way to Pretoria, their train ploughed headlong into an oncoming locomotive that had somehow got on to the wrong track. Many of the All Blacks were flung from their bunks against the walls of their cramped compartments.

Although most were shocked and bruised, the only serious casualty was forward Charlie Willcocks who was down to play in the next test but was unable to do so because of a badly wrenched shoulder. One of the engine crew was critically injured. He was attended throughout the night by All Black Ron Elvidge, a doctor, but died before an ambulance arrived.

After two more nights on the train, the All Blacks eventually arrived in Pretoria. 'It was pretty upsetting,' Fred says. 'Apart from losing one of our best forwards, the others were stiff and sore and we were all very short on sleep. What didn't go over well with the team was the fact that the New Zealand Rugby Union had accepted this exhausting itinerary on the grounds that it would "enable the players to become acclimatised"!

'What a lot of bullshit. All they were doing was continuing to bow and scrape to the South African Rugby Board, just as they did for 32 years from the first tour in 1928.'

When he returned home Bob Scott had this to say: 'Playing the Springboks was tough enough, but having to face them after those long and tiring journeys, which often left us little time for training, made it even more of an ordeal.'

Bob Howitt, editor of *Rugby News*: 'The setbacks in South Africa had been beyond Fred Allen's influence. He effectively took over the coaching to try and remedy the side's sagging fortunes, but the problems were insurmountable.'

On top of the coaching pressures, Fred suffered a number of niggling injuries throughout the first half of the tour. In a selfless move he took the unprecedented decision to drop himself from the final two matches of the test series.

Another factor which undermined the team was South Africa's apartheid policy, which again forced New Zealand to leave some of its finest players at home because of their Maori blood.

'What we would have given to have had stars like Johnny Smith, Vince Bevan and Ben Couch in our party,' says Fred. 'They'd have made all the difference. But because our weak-kneed administrators in Wellington had again kowtowed to the South African demands, we were robbed of some of our most talented players.

'What bloody hypocrisy! During the war we were all so proud of the 28th Maori Battalion. Those tough, brave men fought in Greece, Crete, North Africa and Italy where I was also fighting. They were one of the most decorated units in the New Zealand Army. Second-lieutenant Ngarimu won the Victoria Cross.

Top: The aftermath of the train accident which derailed the All Blacks on their way to Pretoria. Above: Des Christian and Fred survey the damage.

'And after the war,' Fred says, 'those who survived returned on the *Dominion Monarch*, the very same ship that brought the All Blacks back home.

'Just to think of it makes me sick! We should have told the South Africans where to shove their tour!'

When the defeated All Blacks disembarked in Auckland, Fred knew that both he and the manager, Jim Parker, would be subjected to searching questions. The reporters interrogated them at length, especially Fred, but he remained true to his agreement and said nothing that was likely to harm the relationship between New Zealand and South Africa.

'I was disillusioned and angry and there were many things I wanted to tell the New Zealand public,' he says, 'but before we landed I had made that bond with the players and that was good enough for me. I was aching inside, believe me. All I wanted to do was get home as quickly as possible and try to forget what had happened.

'But even when I tried to relax I couldn't help wondering whether or not I'd done the right thing for the future of rugby.'

For years Fred hoped for the day when apartheid would be abolished and South Africa, along with the New Zealand union, would apologise for the wrong they had done to black and Coloured people — and to sport.

It took more than 60 years for South Africa to make the first move when the president of the South African Rugby Union, Oregan Hoskins, said: 'Apartheid is an evil that shattered millions of lives over the years.'

He made a full apology to the Maori players excluded from the tours of 1928, 1949 and 1960, describing them as 'innocent victims of the racist ideology of our former government'.

'But even more importantly,' he added, 'this is also the opportunity to apologise on behalf of rugby to black South Africans who were denied the opportunity to represent not only their country but also their provinces during those long dark years.'

The New Zealand Rugby Union also issued a statement: 'On behalf of the union, we wish to say sorry first and foremost to those Maori players who were not considered for selection for teams to tour South Africa or to play South Africa.

'We also wish to take the opportunity to apologise to New Zealand as a whole for the division that rugby's contact with South Africa caused across the country over many years.

'It was a period in which the respect of New Zealand Maori rugby was not upheld and that is deeply regretted.'

One man who was particularly elated when the apologies were made was 76-year-old Oma Nepia, of Palmerston North, son of the legendary fullback George Nepia.

'My father was bitterly disappointed when he was not selected to play against South Africa,' Oma said. 'It was a very sad thing to happen to such a fine man. But thankfully all is well since apartheid disappeared and the family was delighted when the South African Rugby Union elected Dad as its first non-white honorary member.'

Thank goodness there was a lighter side to the 1949 tour — the attitude of local women to Fred's All Blacks. Everywhere the New Zealanders went they were besieged by pretty girls. One admirer in Port Elizabeth sent them a photograph and a letter saying: 'Take me back to New Zealand with you and I will serve you like a slave.'

'Hardly surprising that the offer wasn't taken up,' says Fred. 'I mean how could a fella have explained that to his wife back home?

Fred, as captain, attracted a great deal of attention. The local newspapers reported he had been given the nickname 'Doodgool' which means 'Knock 'em Cold' in Afrikaans.

The team's hooker, Has Catley, impressed so much with his scrummaging he was called 'Katnael' — or 'Cat Claw'.

Ron Elvidge's speed also impressed the girls and he became 'Weerlig' which means 'Lightning'.

Bob Scott was a little surprised to read in the local press that he was famous as 'Komkommer' — the 'Cucumber' — because he was so cool.

This type of attention in the papers was causing a certain amount of embarrassment for the All Blacks, except for one, the heftiest man in the team, who had been nicknamed 'Doodval' — a word indicating that anyone he fell on could be crushed to death. He was lock forward Harry Frazer, who had met a young lady in Johannesburg called Ethel Blythe and was keeping a deep secret from his teammates. Although they were all at the same hotel in Cape Town, the All Blacks had absolutely no inkling that Harry had become a married man.

Until they read the news in the local paper!

The 'Log O' Wood'

When a close friend suggests he turn his hand to coaching, Fred's interest in rugby begins to return.

To get his mind off the many problems troubling him, Fred busied himself in his work at F.R. Allen Ltd and found further relaxation in travelling throughout New Zealand twice a year to obtain orders for his firm's garments. But wherever he went there was no escaping questions. There were always people who wanted to quiz him about the All Blacks' failure and what he, himself, intended to do in the future.

He had played for Grammar Old Boys before going overseas and he had many friends in the club, including the president, Andy McBeath, who came to see him from time to time. Andy was aware of the stress and indecision his friend was undergoing and did his best to persuade him to return to rugby, perhaps in a coaching role.

So persistent was Andy that, although the wounds of South Africa were still bleeding, Fred finally agreed to coach the Grammar senior team. He enjoyed this new position, even played a few games, and slowly his passion for rugby began to return.

Another turning point came in 1957 when the Auckland Rugby Union was seeking a new selector-coach. Fred was approached and, after considerable discussion, was appointed for a term of three years.

'We didn't have a lot of talent in my first two years,' he says. 'I was struggling a fair bit and results weren't that wonderful. But in 1959 I had recruited some new players and we had begun to make some real progress.

'When we played Southland for the Ranfurly Shield at Invercargill, it was their last defence of the year and naturally they wanted to hold on to the trophy until the following season. They were a really good side and we weren't given much of a chance.

'Wilson Whineray was captain that day. He had not long returned from All Blacks duty and I played him at No. 8, a position he really liked. Halfway through the second spell when the score was 10–9 in Auckland's favour he moved down a lineout, tapped each player on the shoulder and asked them to give him everything they had until the final whistle.

'Wilson's influence worked like magic. The boys won the lineout and for the rest of the game they played out of their skins. We even scored another try to make the final score 13–9.

'Our three tries were all scored by players from the Marist Club, Steve Nesbit, Terry Lineen and Paul Little. Southland failed to cross our line, all their points coming from penalty goals.'

That night the shield was hidden under the bed of Auckland manager Ron Burk so he could keep a watchful eye on it. Hearing of this, a local photographer

After lifting the Ranfurly Shield from Southland in 1959, Fred's team took some time out at Franz Josef Glacier on their way back to Auckland. Fred is pictured in the back row, eighth from left.

took a photo which was published the following day. Because of one of those unfortunate misprints which the press commits from time to time, the caption under the photo read: 'For safe keeping Auckland manager Ron Burk keeps the "sheila" under his bed.'

The team had a good laugh over that one. And when Ron's wife in Auckland received a clipping from an anonymous sender a couple of days later she had a good laugh, too.

'I've often heard it said that if Auckland hadn't picked up the shield in that final challenge I would have been dumped,' says Fred. 'That would have been a real pity because only I knew just how much Auckland was on the improve. I expected great things from them in 1960 — and I was right. They delivered, and for two more seasons they continued to deliver, 25 times to be exact!'

Before the Southland game Fred had told his players that if they won the shield they could take things easy for a day or two. They were on tour and their next game against Westport in Greymouth was not a shield challenge. But he didn't mean them to overdo things and he was furious when he discovered that one of the older members of the squad, who should have known better, was 'leering up' at night with two of the youngest players. He ordered them to cut it out and he expected his order to be obeyed.

'There won't be any more chances,' he warned them, 'so stop acting like a lot of tarts. It's not just enough to be shield-holders — from now on I expect you to behave like shield-holders. So let's get on with it!'

When he found the older player had again taken the young guys out for another night on the town, he acted swiftly and decisively. He woke the duty-boy at six in the morning and said: 'Go round and get everybody out of bed — we're training at 6.30.'

The duty-boy opened his mouth to say something but Fred got in first: 'Don't argue — just do it!'

It was a frosty winter morning and as cold as ice with the rain pelting down. Greymouth was in the grip of a biting wind from the Southern Alps known locally as 'The Barber' because it cut to the quick.

'I could hear them squawking as the duty-boy woke them and told them to get out of bed,' Fred says. 'I wasn't too pleased either, because I always stripped and trained with the team.

'Two in particular were loath to get out of their warm beds so I went to their room and told them: "Get up and train or you'll never play for Auckland again" — and they knew by the look on my face that I meant it! As I left their room I heard one of them say: "What will this mad bastard do next!" As a matter of fact I was in a bit of a quandary myself.

Fred doesn't regret his actions. 'I've never been sorry for what I did that night because it helped to establish discipline for the future. They knew my rules and three players deliberately broke them. Unfortunately, the whole team had to pay for the stupidity of a few, but that's the way it had to be. And I knew I had got to their heads.

'To teach him a lesson, I dropped the older player for a couple of games and for some time he carried a chip on his shoulders. But in the end he was man enough to tell me that, although he thought me a hard taskmaster, he also considered me fair and just. I admired him for that and 50 years later I was pleased to have him at my ninetieth birthday celebration in the Auckland Town Hall.'

Not long after Auckland had won the shield, a new halfback was appointed. Des Connor was a Brisbane schoolteacher who showed such dazzling skills he was selected to play for Queensland against the touring 1957 All Blacks when he was just 21. He later played 12 games for the Wallabies. He was coaxed to New Zealand by Tom Morrison, an executive member of the New Zealand Rugby Union, who had the wisdom to send him a copy of the *New Zealand Education Gazette* containing a number of tempting teaching posts on this side of the Tasman.

The young man was more than interested. In 1959 he applied for a teaching job at Takapuna Grammar, was accepted, and remained in New Zealand for the next six years. He joined the Marist Club in Auckland. They were not particularly strong that year and he found himself having a hard time behind their scrum. And there was another thing not to his liking — the wet and muddy New Zealand fields which were far removed from the hard, fast grounds of Australia.

Having won the Log o' Wood from Southland, Fred was in the process of rebuilding the Auckland side. He not only selected Connor as his halfback, he also made him captain while his regular skipper Bob Graham was in Australia with the New Zealand Universities team.

With his astute rugby brain, Connor quickly adapted to the New Zealand winter. He practised assiduously to perfect a prodigious punt and before long his handling of the muddy ball could not be faulted. He also developed a reverse pass of such length and accuracy it frequently had the opposition in disarray.

Until he came to New Zealand, Connor had never heard of the Ranfurly Shield, but he soon came to recognise its importance to the rugby-mad public of New Zealand. He also learned that for a province to win the Log o' Wood was a signal honour indeed. And the manner in which a team would defend it to the last breath had to be seen to be believed.

In Connor's first game for Auckland, in which the shield was not at stake, they were beaten by Waikato at Hamilton. 'It was a rotten start to my rep career,' Connor says, 'but I was more determined than ever to adapt to New Zealand conditions and do a lot better.'

In the first challenge of 1960 Auckland repulsed Thames Valley 22–6 before disposing of Counties by 14–3. But in the next challenge from North Auckland they went down by 11–17 and the shield was gone.

Eleven days later it was Auckland's turn for a rematch and by this time Fred Allen had his side up and running — they had had a taste of the shield and they wanted it back.

The North Auckland side, coached by the much respected Ted Griffin, played like men possessed and for well into the second half it was anyone's game. It was Des Connor's magic that finally did the trick. In a move known to the players as 'Aussie', it involved Connor racing across the field from a set scrum before flicking a reverse pass behind his back to Mac Herewini, who would then race down the blind side to feed his wing.

It worked like a charm. Once he had the ball in his hands Herewini drew the last defender before passing to John Sibun. The speedy wing raced for the line and dived across in the corner, making the final score 6–3 in Auckland's favour. It was an historic victory because it was the start of a remarkable sequence of 25 successful defences of the shield. Wilson Whineray, now Sir Wilson, has described the next four years as 'one of excitement, drama and fervour that transformed Eden Park into an oasis of magic'. And when his career was over he also said, 'Those Auckland Ranfurly Shield sides were nearer to 15-man rugby than any other teams I played in.'

As crowds flocked to Eden Park as never before, the coffers of the Auckland Rugby Union filled to near overflowing. Ranfurly Shield games are invariably filled with drama and suspense, but none more so than the final challenge of the season from Canterbury.

The crowd converging on Eden Park was so vast that the bus conveying the Auckland team was unable to reach the ground in time for the kick-off and the game was delayed for 30 minutes.

In the first half Canterbury had the better of things and led at the break by 18–14. There was nothing between the two great rivals in the second spell until, with time up on the clock, a scrum went down near midfield. Whineray again called for a supreme effort and to the delight of every Aucklander the home side won the ball against the head. Halfback Connor shot the ball left to Herewini, who put his foot to it and deftly placed it halfway between the Canterbury halfback and fullback. The ball bounced perfectly and in a flash Waka Nathan, the 'Black Panther', had it in his hands and was racing, unmarked, for the goal-line.

'Behind the posts, Waka'. Waka Nathan heeds captain Wilson Whineray's (8) instructions.

'Behind the posts, Waka, behind the posts,' yelled Whineray on Nathan's flank, for he realised in a flash that three points for a try would not be enough.

'I heard Wilson loud and clear,' Waka later said, 'but I was already on my way towards the uprights. I had looked both ways and, apart from Wilson, there wasn't a player in sight.'

Everything now depended on the conversion and Mike Cormack's nerves were ready for the challenge. The fullback struck the ball perfectly and it sailed dead centre across the bar. The score was 19–18 and the shield was still in Auckland's hands.

Two of the Auckland squad never saw that great rugby moment, which is indelibly printed in Eden Park history. A few minutes earlier there had been trouble in a lineout and Kel Tremain had been knocked unconscious by the Canterbury All Blacks forward, 'Tiny' Hill. When the Auckland flanker was carried off on a stretcher, Fred Allen had gone with him while the doctor examined him. Tremain had just regained consciousness when he and Fred heard a mighty roar swelling from 45,000 throats. 'Someone burst into the room,' said Fred, 'and yelled that Auckland had scored. It was an unbelievable moment.'

On 31 August 1963, it all came to an end when Wellington relieved Auckland of the trophy by 8 points to 3. Each side scored one try that day, the difference being in the kicking of Wellington fullback, Mick Williment, who converted the challenger's try and added a penalty goal.

Today Des Connor recalls those Ranfurly Shield days under the guidance of Fred Allen as the most enjoyable of his career. When his old mentor turned 90, Des flew from Australia to help celebrate his birthday in the Auckland Town Hall.

'Fred was a remarkably astute person,' said Connor. 'Before I played for his Auckland team I had never encountered anyone like him. He was someone who, irrespective of rank or record, would bawl you out if you deserved it. He had no favourites. He was also the first coach I had struck who knew how to get the absolute best out of his players. And he had that special capacity of telling you exactly where you were going wrong.'

During one shield game the Maori utility forward Albie Pryor started flitting around among the backs. After the game Fred gave him the full treatment.

Halftime team talk. Fred delivers the message supported by his great friend and assistant Johnny Simpson.

'No more of that showboating, you black so-and-so,' said Fred. 'You get your bloody head down and shove like the others, or you'll find yourself out of a job.'

'Aw, c'mon Fred,' replied Albie. 'It's dark inside that scrum and I get frightened in there.'

Sometimes it was hard for Fred to keep a straight face.

Albie was one of the rugby's great characters. He also had a fearsome reputation as a tough competitor and when he eventually switched from playing to coaching one of his famous sayings was: 'I don't condone fighting on the field but I've seen one good punch clean up a game!'

'Albie was never a dirty player but there were times when he could be pretty vigorous,' says Fred. 'When a touring Maori All Blacks team was playing a test in Tonga, Albie got a bit over-enthusiastic and was ordered from the field. He'd no sooner reached the sideline than the King of Tonga, who'd been watching the game, instructed his immediate recall and ordered the referee to be replaced!

'So Albie ran back on to the field and a new ref was found. Which goes to show that you didn't mess around with the King of Tonga when he was enjoying his footy!'

The manner in which Fred handled the Auckland Ranfurly Shield side from 1960 to 1963 was a triumph that put him on the road to greatness. All eyes were now on him and every rugby fan in the country, as well as the press, wanted him to be part of the All Blacks coaching regime.

In 1964 the New Zealand Rugby Union found room for him on the All Blacks selection panel of Ron Bush, Des Christian, Les George and Neil McPail, where he also helped with the coaching. The following year Fred served another term on the panel and in 1967 they moved him up a notch, appointing him chairman of a three-man panel comprising himself, Ivan Vodanovich and Les George.

His rise to the top continued and before long he found himself coach of the most feared rugby team in the world — the mighty All Blacks.

For Fred Allen, the wheel had turned full circle.

Family Man

Fred meets a beautiful girl at a regatta picnic on Kawau Island and invites her to come dancing.

Earlier in his life, not long after his discharge from the Army, Fred was selling ANZAC Day poppies in Queen Street when Norma Murray came down from her first-floor dress-designing business to put a few coins in his collection box.

'Even now, all these years later, I can remember thinking how neat and attractive she looked in one of those simple shifts she and her workers used to make,' Fred says. 'It was white and decorated with flowers — bright Hawaiian-type flowers.

'Oddly enough, although she made quite an impression on me that day, we didn't speak again until years later. We sometimes passed on the street and used to nod and smile at each other but that was about it. I suppose we were too busy. I think Norma was friendly with someone at that stage and, of course, she was also heavily involved in her own business.

'As for me, I was just starting a business and going on rugby tours as well. I hope this doesn't sound like big-noting but when you're an All Blacks captain there's never a shortage of girls.'

Fred's next meeting with Norma was at the Kawau Island summer retreat of the Royal New Zealand Yacht Club in the Hauraki Gulf. He'd helped crew a friend's yacht, the A-class keeler *Iorangi*, to the picnic and Norma, 18 months younger than him, had crewed on a launch belonging to a family friend.

'We saw a great deal of each other that weekend and got on so well that we arranged to go dancing when we were back in Auckland. We both loved dancing and music and before long I proposed to Norma and she accepted. It was the best move of my entire life.'

They married in 1957 and bought a four-bedroom home in Allum Street, Kohimarama, where they brought up their daughter Marianne and their son Murray. That large, welcoming house soon became Party Central for the All Blacks.

'After big matches we always celebrated at our home,' says Fred. 'Norma and I provided most of the food and drinks because the rugby union never splashed money around in those days. But we didn't mind in the slightest because we had such marvellous times. And what was even more important to me, those get-togethers greatly strengthened our bonding as a team.

'Our champion barbecuer was flanker Ian Kirkpatrick, nine times captain of the All Blacks, but he had tough competition from players such as Waka Nathan and Albie Pryor.'

Fred smiles. 'Yes, those guys were great at cooking steaks,' he adds, 'and even better at making them disappear.'

One of Fred's best friends was Auckland businessman Roly McCrystal. He was quite a bit older than Fred and for a while was like a father to him — the kind of father Fred had never had. Fred often

Fred and Norma on their wedding day, 1957.

Fred and Norma with children Marianne and Murray after the 1967 All Blacks tour.

stayed for weekends with Roly and Maida McCrystal in their family beach house at Manly Beach on the Whangaparaoa Peninsula and whenever the weather was favourable they went on fishing trips.

One day Roly pointed out a property a few metres along the road from his own place. It was a double section with two ex-army huts on it. He told Fred it would be a great buy.

'I knew he was right, but I didn't see how I could afford it,' says Fred. 'I was just a young man with hardly a penny to spare. But I somehow scraped the money together and put a deposit on the place. It's something I've never regretted.'

Not long after they'd bought the property, Norma's brother, Duncan, an architect and builder, transformed the two army huts into a small but comfortable holiday home. Norma, Fred and the children now divided their time between their Kohimarama residence and their waterside bach on the Whangaparaoa Peninsula. It was a happy time.

Sometime later, after selling his shares in the farm near Gisborne, Fred replaced the bach with a new, two-storied house which years later was to become his much-loved permanent home.

The sale of the shares also allowed other luxuries — so while the building work was under way he and Norma were supervising the construction of a Corsair launch. They had the interior built to Norma's design and they named her *Sundancer*. Norma, who had now joined Fred in his business venture, Fred

Fred and Norma's pride and joy, *Sundancer*.

R. Allen Ltd, in Airedale Street, loved cruising and fishing as much as he did. Life for the Allen family was now idyllic.

'Our neighbours along the beach described Norma as The Pied Piper of Manly,' says Fred, 'and that's exactly what she was — a magnet to the kids. She was absolutely marvellous with them. I couldn't count the number of times I've seen seven or eight children dancing in a line behind her down to the beach.

'She'd look after them for the whole day, playing with them, swimming with them and feeding them from a big basket of goodies she'd taken with her. She made sure they all had fun.

'And it wasn't just those children who enjoyed her company. Quite a few of the All Blacks regarded her as a special friend — a sort of surrogate mother, I suppose you might say. She was someone they could turn to for motherly advice.

'I remember one or two who came knocking on our door at night. No, they didn't want to talk to their coach — it was the coach's wife they wanted to see. I think they felt a woman might better understand their problems with the opposite sex. And some of these problems were serious, I can tell you.

'Norma was a really talented designer and she also did a fair part of our cutting, but it wasn't a fulltime job because we now had two children to look after. Marianne and Murray always came before work. Norma ran them to school in the morning and then left our factory about 2.30 in the afternoon to pick them up after school. She was always with them when they came home, which so many mothers aren't doing these days. Caring for the children came naturally for Norma. Before going into business she had been a nurse.

'I've always been proud that we gave Marianne and Murray fine educations, including years at Diocesan and St Kentigern.

'In many ways Norma was much the same as my mother Flossie — soft-hearted and giving of herself — and I always reckoned that, for her, the kids came first, then the dogs, then the Burmese cat and then me!

'Some people I have met might say she had her priorities right,' Fred laughs, 'but I have been a very lucky man to have had a wife like her.'

When he was a youngster Roly McCrystal's son, Barry, spent a great deal of time with Fred.

'My first memories of Fred were when he was about 25. He had just come out of the army and was living with his mother who had moved up to Auckland to be with her sons. He spent a lot of time at our house in Remuera and I vividly remember a scary incident there one Guy Fawkes night there.

'My parents had spared no expense to make this a memorable occasion and they'd invited a large crowd of friends and local residents to share the fun.

Fred with one of the latest designs from Fred R. Allen Ltd.

Fred's job was to let off the fireworks on our tennis court and before he started I heard him say to my father, "I won't be able to hang around after the display, Roly. I've got myself a date and she's very nice."

'At first all went well as Fred set off jumping jacks, sparklers, Catherine wheels and rockets. But after only 10 minutes a spark from a match he was striking flew into the large box of fireworks — and in a split second we had the biggest and most spectacular display of fireworks you'd ever seen. There were bangers, rockets, Roman candles, you name it, all shooting across the tennis court with people scampering for shelter in all directions. It was very lucky no one was hurt.

'After recovering from the shock, my father went over to Fred and said, "You young bugger, you certainly made sure you wouldn't be late for that date!"'

Whenever there was a boxing match at the YMCA Fred went with Roly and young Barry. 'The problem,' says Barry, 'was that I always sat next to Fred, who would swing and sway with the punches as though he was in the ring himself. I had to put up with a decent pummelling and the next morning my right side was always a bit sore. But it was worth it because we all enjoyed those fights so much.

'I could hardly blame Fred for getting so excited. When it came to sport he was one of nature's great enthusiasts.'

Date with Destiny

In 1966 the All Blacks have a new coach, a new captain and a new blueprint for the future.

Fred's pathway to destiny changed dramatically in 1966 when the sporting media trumpeted the news — 'Fred Allen All Blacks Coach'.

Fred was quietly elated. This was the moment he had dreamed of — even from as far back as the ill-fated tour of South Africa in 1949. He was well prepared for the challenge. During the spectacular tour of the Kiwis Army team in 1946 he had absorbed a vast amount of knowledge. And three years later in South Africa he had learned a great deal more about winning rugby — although some of it was not to his liking.

It was because of these two apprenticeships — success with the brilliant Kiwis and defeat by the uncompromising Springboks — that he now had the knowledge and experience to coach at the highest level.

There was another reason for his promotion, one that the selectors could scarcely overlook. His coaching of Auckland during its record 26-match tenure of the Ranfurly Shield between 1959 and 1963 had been brilliant and consistent.

But perhaps his greatest attribute was the fact that his heart beat loud and strong for the game he loved — and for his players. And in the final analysis it

Brian Lochore prepares to feed halfback Chris Laidlaw in the third test against the Lions in 1966. Fred's selection of Lochore as his captain for this series raised a few eyebrows.

would be this unyielding devotion, together with his honesty and integrity, that would bring him success and fame.

From the moment he was appointed coach, Fred knew how important it was to have the right captain — a man who would be cooperative with him in moulding a group of talented players from all walks of life into one harmonious unit.

'I was never in doubt,' he says, 'because there was one man I had been studying for some time and I saw in him the qualities of leadership I had been looking for. I felt that, given the chance, he would become a great captain and I also knew that he would support me one hundred per cent in the type of rugby I intended to promote.

'My selection of Brian Lochore came as a shock to the rugby public because I had Colin Meads, Kel Tremain, Ken Gray, Chris Laidlaw and Ian MacRae, all outstanding players with tons of experience at international level. But somehow I found myself unable to go past this honest, down-to-earth Wairarapa farmer.'

The All Blacks manager, Charlie Saxton, described the appointment as a 'sublime' choice. 'The key to success is teamwork,' he said, 'and Brian Lochore will be right behind Fred in what he wants to do. They will be a great combination.'

However, the most surprised person was Brian Lochore himself. 'It was difficult for me to accept that Fred wanted me ahead of his senior players,' he would later write. 'He had some outstanding men at his disposal, any one of

Kel Tremain takes on the Lions in 1966. His support for new skipper Brian Lochore proved invaluable.

whom would have been an excellent leader.

'I was a bit apprehensive — until the most wonderful thing happened, something I shall never forget.

'Before I arrived in the dressing room to prepare for the first test against the British Lions, "Bunny" Tremain (who was bitterly disappointed at missing out on the captaincy) addressed the troops, saying I needed and deserved everything they could give me — and demanded they give it.

'When I learned about that support from every player, I felt relieved. It was exactly what my confidence needed.'

Lochore's wife, Pam, says that her husband was taken aback by his selection. 'It was not something Brian had anticipated, but if Fred Allen thought he could do it, he would just get to work and do it.'

Before Fred's first test as coach against the Lions in 1966 he had a restless night. It was one of many that would follow in the years ahead. But there was no need for undue concern and, when the All Blacks swept to victory by 20 points to 3, Fred was relieved, his players were satisfied and the rugby-mad New Zealand public was elated.

The second test at Wellington was much closer. But in the end, assisted by a splendid try by Colin Meads, New Zealand again emerged triumphant to the tune of 16–12.

By the time the third test at Christchurch was due, Fred's All Blacks had begun to function more as a team and, looking disciplined and efficient, they won a third victory by 19 points to 6.

They now had the measure of the Lions and the fourth test in Auckland was practically a foregone conclusion. A capacity crowd at Eden Park screamed themselves hoarse as New Zealand outplayed the tourists by 24 points to 11.

Although he has always maintained that games are won by 15 men and the speed of the ball, Fred has never overlooked the importance of forward power. It is no coincidence that the majority of photographs taken during training sessions show him at work with scrums and lineouts.

'If you're getting done over in the forwards,' he says, 'you're losing the game. That's one of the reasons I used the same eight players in all those four tests — Ken Gray, Bruce McLeod, Jack Hazlett, Waka Nathan, Kel Tremain, Brian Lochore and the Meads brothers, Colin and Stan.

'I enjoyed working with that pack and even though there had been some scepticism at first from three or four of the veterans, when they saw how much I valued them, and how much I relied on them, they soon came to understand what I was trying to achieve.

'I was exceptionally proud of those eight men and I still rate them one of the finest combinations ever to wear the All Blacks jersey.'

The 4–0 whitewash of the Lions was an auspicious start for the new coach and, by the time the 1967 season arrived, Fred and his team were in excellent heart and ready for the next challenge.

They looked forward with relish to the first game, the Jubilee Test in Wellington, a one-off clash with Australia organised as part of the New Zealand Rugby Union's seventy-fifth anniversary celebrations. It was a gala occasion in front of a capacity crowd of 50,000 people, including hundreds of past and present All Blacks, test referees and prominent administrators.

Played at Athletic Park, this test marked the baptism to international rugby of a young North Auckland player named Sid Going who would prove in the years ahead to have no superior as an elusive, try-scoring halfback.

It was also the final test appearance of the great Maori flanker, Waka Nathan. This outstanding forward was one of the first chosen for the forthcoming European tour, but a serious injury to his jaw, maliciously inflicted in an early game, prevented him from taking his rightful place in the test XV.

The Wallaby captain in the Jubilee Test was Ken Catchpole, regarded at the time as the greatest halfback in world rugby. But one man does not make a team and it was obvious from the kick-off that the All Blacks were the superior side. After a scintillating display of handling and passing they romped home by 29 points to 9.

The All Blacks wing Tony Steel scored two tries while Davis and Tremain each scored one. Fullback Williment landed four conversions and two penalty goals, and Herewini contributed one dropped goal.

Fred was pleased with the number of tries scored because of the open, running rugby his All Blacks had played. But the time had now arrived for New Zealand to face a much sterner challenge — two warm-up games in Canada followed by an arduous tour of the British Isles and France.

Now, the pundits said, we'll find out just how good a coach this Fred Allen really is. There's a great deal of difference, they declared, between playing at home and playing in strange countries on the other side of the world.

The New Zealand team for the fourth test against the 1966 Lions. Fred's All Blacks swept the tourists 4–0. He used the same eight forwards (listed in bold) for all four tests.
Back row: John Major, Malcolm Dick, Ian MacRae, Tony Steel. Third row: Gerald Kember, **Jack Hazlett**, P. Long (masseur), **Bruce McLeod**, **Waka Nathan**. Second row: Paul Scott, **Ken Gray**, Mick Williment, **Colin Meads**, **Stan Meads**, **Kel Tremain**. Front row: Les George (selector), Ron Rangi, Ron Burk (manager), **Brian Lochore** (captain), Fred Allen (selector), Chris Laidlaw, Des Christian (selector). In front: Lyn Davis, Mac Herewini.

Playing with Fire

There is disbelief and dismay when the new All Blacks coach reveals his plans for the future.

The day the 1967 team to tour Canada, the British Isles and France was announced Fred Allen dropped a bombshell. The social room at Athletic Park in Wellington was packed, as it always was on such an occasion, as union chairman Tom Morrison read the names of those who had made the team. When the babble of emotion had subsided, coach Fred Allen, who was also chairman of the selection panel, stepped up to the microphone.

'This will be one hell of a team,' he said, 'but it won't be playing the type of football you're used to seeing these past few years. This team will run with the ball at every opportunity and it will win by scoring tries — not by kicking goals.

'Rugby is basically a running, passing game so our number one priority will be to attack at all times from all parts of field. And if we get it right, the game will benefit immensely because wherever we go spectators will come to watch.'

The assembled press scribbled furiously — the All Blacks coach was actually planning to change the winning patterns of a world-beating team! Surely not! What on earth was he thinking! He was, they wrote, playing with fire! The room buzzed with disbelief, and in a matter of hours newspapers the length and breadth of New Zealand were voicing grave misgivings about Fred Allen's intentions.

Few in the room that day were aware of other concerns troubling Fred — serious concerns that have been swept under the carpet for 44 years. A few days before the team announcement was due, Fred had been contacted by Tom Morrison, chairman of the New Zealand Rugby Football Union, suggesting that three of the country's finest players, Colin Meads, Ken Gray and Bruce McLeod, be left out of the touring side. The implication was that the NZRFU wished to avoid any embarrassment that might be caused by the overly rough play of these three forwards who were extremely adept at the highly effective rucking game.

Appalled by this attempt to influence the selection panel, of which he was convener, Fred ignored the thinly veiled directive. 'I knew the people who were behind this move,' he says. 'It had nothing to do with them and I wasn't going to let the strength of an All Blacks team be undermined by Tom and his cronies.

Colin Meads and Ken Gray about to embark on the 1967 All Blacks tour. Fred came under pressure not to select Meads, Gray and Bruce McLeod.

Colin, Ken and Bruce were three of the best forwards in the world and as far as I was concerned, they had never done anything illegal. I was buggered if I was going to leave them at home.

'But as far as certain people in the NZRFU were concerned it was a black mark against me and I've always known that by disregarding their suggestion I did nothing to help my career.'

There was a great deal of truth in that last statement as we shall later see.

The first stage of the 1967 tour, which took the All Blacks through America to Canada, was not without incident. It could, in fact, have ended in disaster. During the stop-over in San Francisco, a number of All Blacks, including Sid Going, Mac Herewini, Colin Meads and Fred Allen, were strolling down the main street late one evening when a group of men were tossed out of a night club just metres in front of them. They had been arguing vehemently about the merits or otherwise of the Vietnam War and on the footpath they carried on their feud with increasing intensity, and even louder profanity, in front of the All Blacks. Suddenly, every man in the group drew a revolver and started shooting. In a matter of a few seconds three of the gunmen lay on the pavement, badly wounded.

Fred, who had helped many a wounded comrade during the war, rushed forward to assist the injured men. That was all very noble but when the police arrived with six-guns in their hands, the All Blacks were deeply concerned that their coach might be mistaken for a gunman and receive a bullet for his trouble. But Fred went steadfastly about the task of attending the wounded and helping to load them into the ambulances. Only when the injured, one of whom would shortly die, were on their way to hospital did he return to the horrified All Blacks waiting nearby.

The All Blacks had actually been scheduled to tour South Africa in 1967, but the visit had been cancelled because of the unrelenting ban on mixing races.

The New Zealand union had successfully sought agreement from the International Rugby Board as early as 1962 that teams visiting there should be fully representative, that is in New Zealand's case, include Maori. This was the basis on which planning for the 1967 tour proceeded. But in 1966, the South African Rugby Board president, Danie Craven, told the IRB the conditions could not be fulfilled. As a result, New Zealand cancelled the tour and with the willing help of the British and Irish unions, went there instead.

Prime Minister Keith Holyoake championed in Parliament that 'as we are one people we cannot be fully and truly represented by a team chosen on racial lines'.

The New Zealand Rugby Football Union agreed and immediately postponed the scheduled South African tour. Because of this sudden cancellation, a new tour was arranged to Canada, the British Isles and France, a tour that was to create rugby history as one of the most successful ever undertaken by an All Blacks side.

So now it was time to leave America and start the rejigged tour at Vancouver in Canada.

British Columbia, Vancouver, 14 October 1967

The huge Empire Stadium in Vancouver was the venue for the first game of the tour. Playing under lights, a rampant All Blacks side ran in nine tries, all brilliant team efforts, to win by 36 points to 3.

Fred's promise of winning games by scoring tries (worth only three points in those days) was already being redeemed. And what gave him even more satisfaction was the fact that the night's outstanding player was 'Fungus' McCormick, who notched up three of those tries.

It was a scintillating display of fast, open rugby and when the final whistle blew, the president of the British Columbia Rugby Union, Graham Budge, turned to Fred Allen and wrung his hand. 'This is the greatest lift rugby in this city has ever received,' he declared.

New Zealand 36: Tries by McCormick (3), Dick (2), Hazlett, Kirton, Birtwistle and Thorne; 3 conversions and a penalty goal by McCormick. **British Columbia 3:** Try by Lorenz.

Eastern Canada, Montreal, 18 October

Four days later, the second game against Eastern Canada, played in the University of Montreal Stadium, was contested in a sea of mud after incessant rain. It made little difference to the All Blacks' skilful passing and handling, and again they romped home by a huge margin, 40 points to 3.

The three points came from a penalty goal kicked by the Eastern Canada fullback Peter Norris, brother of Aucklander Dave Norris, one of New Zealand's most durable athletes and administrators. Peter was on sojourn in Canada, part way through a course of study at Western University.

New Zealand 40: Tries by Williams (2), Kirkpatrick (2), Steel, Tremain, Hopkinson and Muller; 2 conversions and 4 penalty goals by Kember. **Eastern Canada 3:** Penalty goal by Norris.

Four hours later the team boarded a BOAC plane from New York to London. They were on their way to the British Isles and France where the main events were about to begin.

It was in Canada that Waka Nathan had a bone to pick with British officialdom. He was indignant when he saw a large portrait of Nelson-born Ernest Rutherford on show at a trade exhibition with a sign describing him as one of 'Britain's greatest scientists'.

'The Poms had tried to nick him just like the Aussies nicked our Phar Lap and pavlova,' says Fred. 'And Waka wasn't having any of that.

'The organisers got the shock of their lives when the Black Panther arrived in their office to tell them in no uncertain terms that Rutherford might not have been much of a footballer but he was "a damn fine Kiwi".

'They had no intention of arguing with a guy like Waka so they hurriedly changed the sign.'

Pitbull Terrier

Fred creates further controversy when he selects a second-string fullback for the European tour.

Minutes before the 1967 All Blacks squad was due to be announced, rugby executive Ces Blazey spotted that one player too many had been selected — 31 instead of the permitted 30. One had to be dropped — and quickly!

Blazey immediately advised Tom Morrison, chairman of the New Zealand union, who in turn broke the disturbing news to the selection panel of Fred Allen, Ivan Vodanovich and Les George.

'Everyone in the room was anxiously waiting to hear the selections,' Fred recalls, 'when Tom came in and pointed out that we had chosen one player too many.

'How the hell could that have happened? It made us look a bit stupid. But we had to make an immediate choice because everybody was waiting. We looked at all the options and finally came to a decision that one of the two fullbacks on the list should be deleted. The other selectors were strong for the current All Black, Mick Williment, who was certainly an excellent footballer. But I had my mind set on the Canterbury player, Fergie McCormick — he had so much guts and heart. And there was a ferocity about his play that no other fullback possessed.

'Tom said, "What now Fred?"'

'I had the final say, so I replied, "Williment's out, McCormick's in."'

'When the team was read out, with Williment's name omitted, the whole room gasped. I saw the look of amazement on people's faces. It didn't go down well at all.'

The news of Williment's omission astounded the New Zealand public. The 6 ft 2 in Wellingtonian had played such brilliant football since the retirement of the great Don Clark that he was regarded as a certainty — by everyone except Fred Allen, who saw in the nuggety McCormick the answer to his long-held dream of open, attacking rugby.

'So I got my second decent hammering from the press,' says Fred. 'Sports writers everywhere were saying that I would rue the day because of Williment's fine all-round play and magnificent goal-kicking.'

One of the most stinging comments was written by Brian O'Brien, editor of *Sports Digest*: 'Fred Allen has made an irresponsible, suicidal selection — one of the most inexplicable decisions in the entire history of rugby selection.'

It was the same in the British press. Peter Laker of the *Daily Mirror* really attacked Fred Allen:

> *Mick Williment has been sacrificed with the ruthlessness that is typical of New Zealand rugby — an unprecedented step which could establish 1967–68 as the most vital season in the history of the game. His omission must be regarded as a sporting miracle for the British Isles.*

There was another beauty in *The Times*:

> *Williment's omission from the All Blacks is like rice without curry … this pleasant chap used to play for Blackheath so he knows conditions over here intimately. His omission will bring sighs of relief in England and will load McCormick with exceptional responsibility.*

'They were stupid to write that crap,' says Fred, 'because Fergie made short work of that thing they called "exceptional responsibility" — whatever that means.

'The reason I chose him was because of all the tough matches he'd have to face — especially in Wales. That's where you need tremendous courage, aggression and strength to go with your ability.'

Fred's decision was not made on the spur of the moment. He had been studying McCormick for some time, ever since his amazing display for Canterbury against the touring Lions in 1959. That day, a capacity crowd witnessed one of the most brilliant fullback displays ever seen on Lancaster Park. Canterbury's 20–14 victory was largely due to a fearless performance by the 20-year-old McCormick, whose anticipation and deadly tackling completely shut down two of the world's greatest wingers — Tony O'Reilly and sprinter John Young.

'I realised that day that McCormick had exceptional talent,' says Fred. 'And he was bloody tough, so tough in fact that when we were having our shots in England before we went across to France, the doctor couldn't get the needle into his backside, the muscle tissue was so hard.

'The doc had a few goes, but it was no use, the needle just wouldn't go in and he finally gave Fergie his shot in his arm.

'I never had the slightest doubt that he was the man for the job. I knew he was a pretty rough diamond, but I also knew he'd never give in, no matter what. Off the field I couldn't fault him either. He proved himself a thorough gentleman. And as for his goal-kicking — well, he answered that for himself!'

The stocky 5 ft 7½ in Canterbury fullback was such a spectacular player that everywhere the All Blacks went he earned himself a different nickname. His full name was William Fergus McCormick and his fellow All Blacks called him 'Fergie McFungus'.

Others had different ideas. One reporter in England called him the 'Rock of Gibraltar'. Another in Scotland tabbed him the 'India Rubber Man'. In Wales he was the 'Pitbull Terrier'.

'But he wasn't like a piece of fungus,' says Fred, 'he was anything but. He could set a game alight when he decided to run. He became totally involved in every game he played and his determination to protect our try-line was unbelievable. He was short and stocky and his upper-body strength was phenomenal. He was also a deadly tackler, but the qualities I admired the most were his unrelenting commitment and his courage under fire.

'He actually won several games for us because of his individual skills. And he finished up top points scorer of the tour.'

'I'd been a bit of a tear-away in my youth,' says McCormick, 'but Fred and Charlie Saxton both treated me like a man and Fred left no doubt in my mind that he believed in me.

'Above anything else he had faith in me. He had selected me on trust and I was determined to justify his faith — I was inspired by it. That's what Fred Allen was like. He was a reader of men. That's what put him above all other coaches. He knew exactly what was going on in my head, just as he did in everyone else's.

'I must admit he sometimes took me to task about my retaliation on the field. It was my natural instinct to retaliate when someone was roughing me up. But Fred wouldn't wear that sort of thing. He didn't like it at all. He told me to cut it out because the time would come, he said, when it would lead to something nasty, something illegal that could cost us a game.' "And besides," Fred added, "it's not rugby."

'Maybe I got my aggro from my parents. Maybe it's in my genes. When I worked as a slaughterman I never avoided a confront-ation. My father Archie was an All Black who had twice been the heavyweight boxing champion of New Zealand. Perhaps that had something to do with it.

'Because of the advice Fred gave me I came home from the tour a much better man. He taught me self-respect and gave me a new confidence in my life, and I've been thankful ever since.

'It's the same with all Fred's players. That's why they respect him so much. That's why they go to see him year after year.'

Herald journalist T.P. McLean, critical at the start, ended up one of McCormick's most ardent admirers: 'His resolution in the face of the enemy was equal to that of the great George Nepia,' McLean wrote.

Fred rated Fergie McCormick 'an exceptional talent'.

'He played as though he was prepared to protect the try-line with his life.'

Fred adds: 'In the first test against England, Fergie started slowly, but then he really hit his stride. He had pulled a couple of rib cartilages during training and was in pain during the game, but he still converted all four All Blacks tries in our 23–11 win.

'After the game the doc advised him to take six weeks off, but Fungus was having none of that. I know for a fact that he kept quiet about the pain because his burning ambition was to play against Wales the following Saturday.

'He kept telling me he was okay — but he wasn't. In the end I called an old friend, Wales and Lions centre, Dr Jackie Matthews. He gave Fergie a thorough examination and told him bluntly, "You're stuffed you know, Fergie, this will take weeks to heal."

'Fergie just glared at Matthews as though he were his worst enemy. And when I told him he had to rest he gave me a similar look. I got a surprise on the Thursday when he showed up for training, although he didn't do a full routine — only a light run.

'In the end he was so insistent I let him go on. It was one of the biggest decisions I ever made — and one of the best — because Fergie played one of the best games of his life. In the wind and rain he never put a foot wrong and his contribution of seven points was vital to the winning of the game.

'Before he went out they wanted to give him a jab of painkiller, but Fergie told them he'd never had anything like that in his life — and he wasn't going to start now! The reporters were outside the room, wanting to know what was going on. They'd heard of his injuries and I think they'd written him off. But they didn't know Fergie very well, did they!'

Fergie was pretty sore for a few days so Fred rested him for the first game in France and by the time the test came round he was almost back to full form. He excelled himself at Colombes as the All Blacks overcame the Tricolours 21–15 by contributing nine points — three conversions and a penalty.

In the final match of the tour against the Barbarians at Twickenham, 'Fungus' was back to his brilliant best. Twice during the game he saved what looked like being certain tries. On the first occasion he ran down speedster Gerald Davies at an angle from behind and then he magically did the same thing to sprinter Keri Jones. On each occasion the crowd rose to applaud him.

The game was won in the final minutes when winger Tony Steel scored a magnificent try alongside the corner flag. When Fergie coolly converted from the sideline it brought up his 100 points on tour.

Alex Veysey summed it up in the *Dominion* newspaper when he wrote:

The 1967 tour produced in Fergie McCormick a player to take his place among the greatest of New Zealand rugby stars. It was a personal triumph for him, just as it was for the men at the top, Charlie Saxton and Fred Allen.

The manager and coach placed such confidence in McCormick that he in return gave them utter loyalty and devotion in his onerous duties. They let him know that he had their trust and McCormick reacted with such warmth that there developed between these three men a friendship which will never fade.

Fergie's brilliance continued throughout the 1968 season. In the tour of Australia he scored 110 points in just eight games. Then, in a three-match home series against France, he was again one of the stars in an All Blacks clean-sweep. This time he notched up 28 of New Zealand's 40 points.

Another milestone was reached in 1969 when the All Blacks won both tests against Wales. In the second, at Eden Park, Fergie established a world record with 24 points — five penalties, three conversions and an amazing long-range dropped goal.

During his All Blacks career, which ended in 1970, this remarkable footballer played 307 first-class games, scored 56 tries, kicked 453 conversions, 313 penalties and 9 dropped goals for a total of 2050 points.

During the 1970 All Blacks tour of South Africa, when Fergie McCormick was again fullback, he was involved in an incident which literally 'changed the face of rugby'.

It occurred during a clash with Sid Nomis when Fergie's elbow caught the South African speedster in the mouth so severely that a number of Nomis's teeth were loosened — and two actually fell into the hand of referee Dr Wynand Malan.

Fortunately, Malan was a dentist. He immediately straightened the loose teeth and pocketed the other two which he later successfully replaced in Nomis's gum.

To protect Nomis's teeth before the next test Malan moulded him an ingenuous tooth protector of plastic and rubber.

'Up until then,' Nomis said later, 'no one had used a guard to protect his teeth. So in a way I started the whole mouth guard thing.'

Battling the British

Fred's blueprint for 15-man rugby creates an immediate impact in England and Wales.

The All Blacks got away to a splendid start on British soil by romping home in their first three matches before the first test against England.

North of England, Manchester, 25 October 1967

To make sure of this first game Fred Allen selected what he considered to be his best forward pack — Lochore, Nathan, Meads, Strahan, Williams, Hazlett, McLeod and Muller. The home side was no match for these men from New Zealand and the game ended 33–3 after the All Blacks had notched up six tries, three conversions and three penalty goals.

Five of the tries came directly from set scrums or lineouts. The clear message to the English was that the All Blacks intended to retain possession, run with the ball and do the basic things correctly — just as they had done in Canada.

New Zealand 33: Tries by Birtwistle (2), Williams (2), Going and McCormick; 3 conversions and 3 penalty goals by McCormick. **North of England 3:** Penalty goal by Chapman.

Brian Lochore leads the All Blacks out against North of England at Manchester for the first match of the European section of the 1967 tour.

Although they had won by a considerable margin, Fred was disappointed with the All Blacks showing. Some of them, he thought, had been sluggish so he lined them up and put them on the scales. Just as he had expected, almost everyone was overweight through eating too much in the past few weeks.

The biggest jump in weight had been made by Arthur Jennings, who had put on more than a stone to reach 16 stone. 'That can't be right!' a concerned Jennings said. But it was.

Of the other forwards Jack Hazlett was up 9 lb to 15 st 9 lb, Bruce McLeod was up 6 lb to 15 st and John Major and Brian Lochore had both put on five pounds. A gasp went up as Ian Kirkpatrick, listed at 14 st 12 lb, tipped the scales at just under 16 stone.

The backs were mostly within reasonable range of their old weights, although Ian MacRae, Wayne Cottrell, Sid Going, Phil Clarke, Chris Laidlaw and Bill Birtwistle had all put on extra poundage.

As far as Fred was concerned, this called for drastic action. So for the next couple of hours the All Blacks, dressed in extra jerseys, wondered what had struck them. The Needle's training sessions were always tough, but this was the daddy of them all.

When it was over Fred weighed them again. Meads, Kirkpatrick, Smith and Going had each lost five pounds while Laidlaw and Clarke had both shed almost half a stone. The most surprising variation came from the team's heaviest man and most enthusiastic eater, Brian Muller, whose playing weight was 17 stone. When the big forward was first weighed he had gained exactly one pound and during the rigorous training session he had lost exactly the same amount.

Midlands, London and Home Counties, Leicester, 28 October

Ronnie Dawson, who had captained the 1959 Lions in New Zealand, predicted an All Blacks upset when, three days later at Leicester, the All Blacks met a far more formidable combination. Dawson based his opinion on the fact that the Counties XV contained no fewer than 10 internationals — all the eight forwards as well as two backs, Hearn and Webb.

The home side fought with grim determination and at times there were incidents not pretty to watch. But at the final whistle the score was 15–3 in the All Blacks' favour.

New Zealand 15: Try by Dick; 3 penalty goals by McCormick; dropped goal by Herewini. **Midlands, London and Home Counties 3:** Try by Lloyd.

Fred and his team were shocked by a tragedy which occurred just four minutes after the start. When the English centre Danny Hearn crash-tackled the New Zealand second-five, Ian MacRae, with alarming violence he suffered one of the most serious injuries that have occurred during an All Blacks game.

Describing the incident, MacRae said: 'I felt it alright — it nearly cut me in half. It left me with broken blood vessels in my hip and massive bruising.

'There was a crunch just as I passed the ball. For a moment I wondered whether it was Hearn or me who had been hurt. Then I saw him lying on the ground and it was obvious he was badly hurt.'

The Warwickshire player had suffered severe spinal injuries when his head struck MacRae's left hip, injuries that would leave him paralysed for the rest of his life. The All Blacks were deeply concerned at such a tragic accident and after the game a group went to see Hearn at the hospital. But only captain Brian Lochore was allowed into the ward.

Despite being a paraplegic, the young Englishman, a 25-year-old teacher of economics, resumed his career and also went on to coach rugby from his wheelchair. MacRae carried on playing and was named one of the five top players of 1967 by the *New Zealand Rugby Almanack*. The wonderful outcome of the tragedy, however, was the comradeship that developed between these two men — a friendship that lasted for decades.

Hearn came to New Zealand in 1969 to spend time with MacRae and his wife Marilyn in Napier. He was guest of honour at a special meeting of MacRae's rugby club and was taken to several games. Hearn told his host he must never feel bad about what had happened. 'I lined you up for a crash-tackle to stamp my mark on the game and there's no way you could be blamed,' he said.

When the MacRaes headed to the United Kingdom on holiday in 2005 they made a special detour to spend time with their friend at his new home in Ireland. Even after 38 years, the bond between these two fine men was as strong as ever.

There was another serious injury when All Blacks flanker Waka Nathan suffered a broken jaw because of a blatant foul. The perpetrator was veteran English international Budge Rogers! Incredibly, Nathan had also broken his jaw on the 1963–64 tour of Britain and France.

Not realising his jaw was broken, the 'Black Panther' ignored the pain, played the rest of the first half, and then saw out the final 40 minutes. It wasn't until the following day, when he went for an x-ray examination, that a clean break was discovered. Sadly, the injury sidelined him for most of the tour. Waka had now suffered two broken jaws and there was one more to come — under the most bizarre circumstances.

Fred is 'hands on' at scrummaging practice, Cheshire, 1967. Behind him is a youthful Sid Going.

During his convalescence he was watching the All Blacks at Swansea when he stood up and yelled encouragement to his mates. Almost immediately he wished he'd kept quiet. His jaw had broken again — and he'd done it himself! Once more he ignored the pain and did not visit a hospital until the All Blacks reached France where the jaw was re-wired.

The surgeon's comment was: 'Looks like you were shouting a bit too vigorously, young man.'

South of England, Bristol, 1 November

The third game in Britain was played in a howling wind and a sea of mud. The South of England team contained four international forwards, Dovey, Pullin and Rollett, as well as Watt, an enormous man 6 ft 6 in tall and over 18 stone.

After a gruelling first half, the All Blacks led by 5 points to 3 but halfway through the second spell they began to get a grip on the game, and in the last seven minutes they notched up eight points. Their superiority was based on fitness and discipline and they ran out winners by 16–3.

New Zealand 16: Tries by Steel, Kirton, Going and Birtwistle; 2 conversions by Kember. **South of England 3:** Penalty goal by Rutherford.

The British press was impressed. 'The men from New Zealand have given the game a new and exciting perspective,' said the *Daily Mail*. 'If they continue to produce rugby of this calibre there will be sell-out crowds wherever they appear.'

Fred Allen was more than pleased with the way his men were playing. All four tries in this game had been scored by backs. They were attacking from all parts of the field and retaining possession for as long as possible, just as he had forecast. They were passing with precision, they were skilful and elusive and they were doing it with spell-binding flair.

They were playing as Fred had taught them to play. Yes, there were mistakes but, in spite of these, they were turning the old, forward-dominated rugby on its ear — and the game would never be quite the same again.

What pleased Fred immensely was the fact that as the tour progressed, and the All Blacks kept winning, the early criticism of both press and public was beginning to subside, and every Doubting Thomas was being forced to swallow his words.

England, Twickenham, 4 November

Heavy rain fell the night before the long-awaited clash with England on the most hallowed ground in the British Isles. Although the downpour eased shortly before kick-off, the field was wet and soggy and the day was overcast. The injured Waka Nathan, who would most certainly have been in the team, was replaced by Graham Williams.

When the teams lined up for the national anthem, the Queen came down from the stands to meet the New Zealanders. Escorted by captain Lochore, Her Majesty walked along a red carpet specially rolled out because of the conditions underfoot to shake hands with each player.

The huge crowd knew they were in for thrilling football when, seconds after the kick-off, New Zealand ran the ball from deep inside their own half. This was the type of rugby they had been promised. This was what they had come to see.

The first try came after seven minutes. Led by Colin Meads, the All Blacks forwards chased a loose ball, scooped it up and got it to Davis on the left. The flying centre drew Rutherford, the English fullback, before passing to Kirton who dived across midway between the goalposts and the corner flag. McCormick made no mistake with the conversion (5–0).

Apart from the odd fumble with the slippery ball, the All Blacks were doing everything right. Fast following up by forward Williams, who wisely kicked ahead, saw winger Birtwistle win the race for the ball as it rolled over the line. Just one yard from the corner flag, McCormick was again on target (10–0).

Now it was Laidlaw's turn. When the English forwards hooked a ball from a scrum right on their own goal-line, the New Zealand halfback, showing great initiative, dived clean through a mountain of muscle to touch the ball down (13–0).

There was no slackening. Seven minutes before halftime, Lochore ran onto a pass from Laidlaw at top speed and made useful ground before sending Kirton over in the corner. Another brilliant kick from McCormick brought the score to 18–0.

With only 30 seconds remaining before the break, England got on the scoreboard with a superb try which Fred Allen later described as the finest of the match. Several players handled the ball before centre Lloyd touched down to the left of the posts. Fifty thousand elated Englishmen were still applauding wildly as Rutherford added the extra points (18–5).

Halftime came with the All Blacks 13 points ahead. But Fred Allen, who knew full well the pitfalls of complacency, was still far from happy. Unless his men, now tiring slightly on the wet and holding ground, could keep up the pressure, the game could well swing against them.

There was no need for Fred to worry. The second half had barely begun when the fired-up All Blacks scored again. It was a glorious passing movement with several players handling before winger Dick raced in at the corner. Once again McCormick raised the flags (23–5).

Halfway through the spell, the gluey ground and the speed of the game were beginning to tell. The zip had gone out of both sides and the football was lacking its earlier sparkle.

The next points went to England when Larter kicked a penalty after an All Blacks infringement, and the home team added further points when Lloyd made another thrilling run to cross for his second try (23–11).

When the final whistle blew with the score unchanged, the crowd rose as one to applaud both teams — the All Blacks for a superb display of rugby and the England XV for a glorious fight against a superior foe.

New Zealand 23: Tries by Kirton (2), Birtwistle, Laidlaw and Dick; 4 conversions by McCormick. **England 11:** Two tries by Lloyd; conversion by Rutherford; penalty goal by Larter.

In the wet and slippery conditions, the New Zealanders' discipline had been outstanding in their scrummaging, handling and backing-up. And once again it had been tries — five glorious tries — all scored by backs, that had won the day.

In the changing room a proud Fred Allen told his men: 'You scored five tries to England's two because you executed the basics of rugby better than they did.'

West Wales, Swansea, 8 November

Two hours before kick-off, the town of Swansea was a sea of excited fans, all 40,000 struggling to reach the stadium and find their seats. West Wales opened the scoring with two penalty goals by Rees, the Welsh fullback, one a majestic effort from 60 yards.

This put the crowd in a buoyant mood until Grahame Thorne received the ball in the All Blacks 25 and, beating man after man, raced more than 70 yards for a sensational try which Kember converted.

In the second spell it was anyone's game and with 15 minutes left on the clock West Wales led 14–13 — until another bewildering run by Thorne ended in his second sensational try.

It was now a matter of stamina and willpower and when Sid Going darted over near the corner flag, and Kember again converted, the game was won, All Blacks 21, West Wales 14.

New Zealand 21: Tries by Thorne (2), Meads and Going; 3 conversions and a penalty goal by Kember. **West Wales 14:** Try by Williams; conversion and 3 penalty goals by Rees.

Wales, Cardiff, 11 November

Torrential rain and a howling wind could not diminish the volume and fervour of the beautiful Welsh singing which filled Cardiff Arms Park and the precincts beyond. As the All Blacks in their room under the stand listened to the rapturous outpouring of Welsh song they could feel the unbridled emotion of an entire nation about to give their all for the land they loved — and they knew that overcoming such passion would not be easy.

Fred was both surprised and delighted when Gale, the Welsh captain, won the toss and decided to give the All Blacks first use of the wind. 'They've made a huge mistake,' he told Lochore. He had made only one change to the team that had defeated England. Gray, who had been injured before the first test, returned to the front row in place of Hazlett.

Ten minutes into the game one of the Welsh centres was caught offside in front of the posts, handing McCormick an easy penalty goal (3–0).

The All Blacks went further ahead when Laidlaw, MacRae, Davis and Birtwistle combined in a brilliant passing movement which ended with Birtwistle crashing over in the corner. McCormick added the extra points with a magnificent sideline conversion (8–0).

Seven minutes into the second half Wales opened its account when Barry John took a long pass from a set scrum and dropped a neat field goal (8–3). New Zealand increased its lead when a Welsh player fumbled a catch which Davis snapped up, and amid general confusion raced in for a try near the posts which McCormick converted (13–3). At this point the All Blacks were gaining the ascendancy and, for Wales, the end seemed in sight. Fred Allen's prediction about the wind was being justified.

Still the Welsh fought back and were rewarded when the All Blacks were penalised at a ruck with only 13 minutes left on the clock. Gale slotted the kick to make the final score 13–6. The old foe Wales had been defeated. Things had gone exactly as Fred Allen had planned.

New Zealand 13: Tries by Birtwistle and Davis; 2 conversions and a penalty goal by McCormick. **Wales 6:** Penalty goal by Gale; dropped goal by John.

Three players were instrumental in the defeat of Wales. One was fullback Fergie McCormick, who played in spite of injuries, and the two others were Chris Laidlaw at halfback and Earle Kirton at first-five. In the atrocious conditions the partnership of this pair was a constant thorn in the Welsh side. The understanding between them was quite remarkable and they gave what could only be described as a flawless exhibition.

McCormick retains two special memories of that unforgettable day which, he says, will remain with him for the rest of his life. Both memories concern Fred Allen.

'The first is the sight of Fred, elated after the victory, walking ankle deep — immaculate tailored pants, polished shoes and all — through the middle of the churned up mud-heap that was Cardiff Arms Park that day to hug his players. They meant everything to him.

'That night so many people were milling around our hotel that Fred finally found me a bed in the management suite so I could get a few hours sleep. But at six in the morning I suddenly woke to find myself staring into Fred's piercing eyes. They were willing me to wake up. In one hand he had a bottle of whisky, in the other a jug of milk and two glasses.

Colin Meads looks to secure lineout ball for the All Blacks against Wales at Cardiff Arms Park, 1967. New Zealand won 13–6.

'"Wake up, Fergie," he said. "Christ, this is no time to sleep. We beat Wales yesterday and it's time for you and me to have one."

'And have one we certainly did — a toast to our victory over Wales and a couple more to the future of New Zealand rugby.

'It was one of the proudest moments of my life.'

The famous Bill Shankly, who coached the triumphant Liverpool soccer team from 1959 to 1974, was among the many British big-names not surprised by the clean-sweep victory of Fred's All Blacks. He later said admiringly: 'I want men who will go through a wall of fire, break a leg and still come out shooting. That pretty well sums up Fred Allen. He was a fearsome man to tangle with. Just ask his players.'

Facing the French

When the All Blacks complete their tour without defeat Fred Allen is recognised as the greatest rugby coach in the world.

The moment the All Blacks set foot in France in November 1967, the French newspapers began pouring out thousands of words about the 'Marée Noire' — 'The Black Wave'. . .

Few people back in New Zealand knew just how strong rugby had become in the republic, or realised the strength of the French side which contained so many players of genuine world class. Now the All Blacks were about to find out.

South-East Selection, Lyon, 15 November 1967

What came as a surprise to Fred in this first game on French soil was the scrummaging power of the French forwards. It was the most potent the All Blacks had experienced on the tour so far.

But of much greater concern was the manner in which such brilliant forward play would suddenly change into something dangerous, involving lethal assaults on All Blacks players. This lack of discipline was clearly evident in the French

Ian Kirkpatrick has slipped the ball to Sid Going during the All Blacks' 32–19 win over France B at Toulouse in 1967.

attitude and it was to reach its climax when Colin Meads was kicked in the head, quite cold-bloodedly for all to see, during the test at Colombes 10 days later.

Sid Going played a courageous game. In the rain and soft ground he had much to contend with, but his resolute tackling and his dazzling running from the base of the scrum often had the opposition on the back foot. Two others who stood out were Kirkpatrick for a fine all-round exhibition and winger Steel who came right into his own and was rewarded with two excellent tries. An interesting game ended with the score All Blacks 16, South-East selection 3.

New Zealand 16: Tries by Steel (2), McLeod and Kirkpatrick; 2 conversions by Kember. **South-East France 3:** Dropped goal by Camberabero.

France B, Toulouse, 18 November

The All Blacks took an early lead and were ahead 18–3 at halftime. But five minutes after play resumed, the French were back in with a chance, the result of a try by Plantefol and an easy penalty by Villepreux. From this point the home side, especially the forwards, played with such fire that the New Zealand pack found themselves going backwards and Lochore had to call on his men for supreme efforts on several occasions. These were the situations in which Colin Meads excelled and his presence played a large part in weathering the onslaught. In the final quarter of an hour the All Blacks were again in control and the game ended 32–19 in their favour.

New Zealand 32: Tries by Williams (2), Kirkpatrick, Going and Dick; 4 conversions and 2 penalty goals by McCormick; dropped goal by Cottrell.
France B 19: Tries by Lux and Plantefol; 2 conversions and 3 penalty goals by Villepreux.

French South-West Selection, Bayonne, 22 November

The thorn in the All Blacks side was Welsh referee P.E. Dickenson. As one reporter wrote 'He gave the impression of having taken the field with preconceived ideas about the play of the All Blacks, and saw himself as an instrument of correction.' He spent much of his time lecturing the All Blacks on their supposed faults, which incurred intense displeasure from Kel Tremain, who was leading the team in the absence of Lochore and Meads. With 10 minutes to play, the All Blacks were behind, but they rallied magnificently to pull the game out of the fire in the final few minutes, 18–14.

New Zealand 18: Tries by Dick, Tremain and Kirkpatrick; 3 penalty goals by Kember. **South-West France 14:** Try by Latanne; conversion and 3 penalty goals by Dehez.

That evening Fred and several of the team, having been given free entry because they were All Blacks, decided to visit the local casino. Fred placed his chips on number 18 because that had been their winning score a few hours earlier. When his number came up, Fred again chose 18, and so it went on four or five times without a miss. When he had won close to a thousand francs, he wisely called it a day and donated his entire winnings to the team fund. It paid for many a cold beer in the days ahead.

France, Colombes, 25 November

So great was the interest in the French test that 30 photographers from various branches of the media were at the ground when the national anthems were played.

Fred and his co-selectors had made two major changes from the side that had beaten Wales two weeks previously. Ian Kirkpatrick, who had started his first-class career only one year earlier at the age of 20, had been chosen in place of Kel Tremain. But an even bigger surprise was the inclusion of Sid Going in place of Chris Laidlaw who had been one of the stars of the tour. Going justified his inclusion by scoring the first try of the game, and it was one of his many elusive breaks that sent Kirkpatrick in for another.

The first points came after only four minutes when McCormick landed an easy penalty goal (3–0). Play had hardly resumed before Kirkpatrick suffered a broken nose while tackling Campaes, but he stubbornly refused to leave the field.

When the French won the ball from a lineout, Gachassin took a quick drop at goal and the ball just cleared the bar, making the score 3–3 after eight minutes of play. Minutes later misfortune again hit New Zealand. While Meads was on the ground, his scalp was ripped open by a deliberate kick from a French boot. Journalist T.P. McLean described this vicious act as the 'most disgraceful foul' he had ever witnessed. After Meads' head had been bandaged and play had resumed the French fullback Villepreux was one of several players who bravely dived on to a loose ball. When they were back on their feet two of Villepreux's ribs had been badly strained.

After 24 minutes the irrepressible Going scored a try which McCormick failed to convert (6–3). It took the French just two minutes to equalise when Villepreux, in spite of his injured ribs, was successful with a difficult penalty (6–6).

The game had now developed into a brutal battle and during the many stoppages more than 30 photographers swarmed on to the field for close-ups of bloody noses and bleeding heads. When the game finally restarted it was again New Zealand's turn. After a classy passing movement, MacRae put Steel over for a fine try which McCormick converted from near the touchline (11–6).

When Muller was penalised for a late tackle Villepreux landed his second penalty from a long way out (11–9).

Ten minutes into the second half the All Blacks were penalised when a French prop was injured during a set scrum. Villepreux put his team ahead with a third penalty (11–12). The French held their lead for 14 minutes before Going made another telling break. He burst round the side of a scrum before handing on to Meads who sent Kirkpatrick in for a try. McCormick converted to again put New Zealand ahead (16–12).

Now the pressure was really on. McCormick made an attacking run right to the line where the ball was jolted from his grasp. But the bounce beat the

French defenders and the ball was pounced on by both Dick and Williams — with Dick touching it down for the try.

McCormick again converted and in less than five minutes the score had shot up from 11–12 against to 21–12.

With less than 15 minutes to go, the French again fought back, but the best they could manage was a dropped goal by Campaes and the final whistle went with the All Blacks in front 21–15.

New Zealand 21: Tries by Going, Steel, Kirkpatrick and Dick; 3 conversions and a penalty goal by McCormick. **France 15:** Try by Campaes; 3 penalty goals by Villepreux; dropped goal by Gachassin.

By scoring four tries against France, the All Blacks had managed the same number as their predecessors, the 1953–54 All Blacks, had scored in five tests. It was a further tribute to the vision of Fred Allen.

The French part of the tour was now complete and it was back to the British Isles for games in Scotland and Wales — and finally against the Barbarians at Twickenham.

Scottish Districts, Melrose, 29 November

This was a far more pleasant game than any the All Blacks had played in France. It took them a while to strike their rhythm and at halftime they led 10–6. The second half belonged to the All Back halfback, Chris Laidlaw, who played a spell of rugby that can only be described as masterly.

He was bitterly disappointed at not being selected for the French test and was now more determined than ever to show his worth. Be that as it may, the fact remains that this day he was the star. He fed his backline with prodigious passes and the three tries scored by winger Birtwistle were in no small measure due to his magnificent play.

It was also pleasing to see the return of Waka Nathan after his long spell recovering from a broken jaw. Waka celebrated the occasion by scoring a try, his first of the tour. A splendid display of running rugby ended with the score All Blacks 35, Scottish Districts 14.

New Zealand 35: Tries by Birtwistle (3), Thorne, Laidlaw, Hopkinson and Nathan; 4 conversions and 2 penalty goals by McCormick. **Scottish Districts 14:** Try by Gill; conversion and 3 penalty goals by Blaikie.

Scotland, Edinburgh, 2 December

Ten minutes after the kick-off, Chisholm received the ball from a smart scrum heel, pivoted and, to the wild applause of 60,000 spectators, dropped a neat goal. Scotland 3, All Blacks nil. Ten minutes later the Scottish backs were caught offside and McCormick slotted an easy penalty from close range (3–3).

Not long afterwards came the first try. A brilliant passing movement executed by Meads and Gray finished with the ball in the hands of MacRae who used every ounce of his pace to reach the try-line wide out (6–3). Five minutes later the Scots were penalised and McCormick, from 40 yards out, kicked a magnificent penalty goal to make the halftime score 9–3. It was a useful lead.

The only points in the second half came from a glorious All Blacks try. It was another brilliant Kirton loop-around that did the trick. Having passed to MacRae, Kirton tore behind him to take the ball again, rip through a gap and give Davis a clear run to the line. The raucous Scottish crowd tried their hardest to put McCormick off his kick, but Fergie made no mistake and the All Blacks were home 14–3.

New Zealand 14: Tries by MacRae and Davis; conversion and 2 penalty goals by McCormick. **Scotland 3:** Dropped goal by Chisholm.

Four minutes before fulltime a hush had descended over the packed Murrayfield when Irish referee Kevin Kelleher called a halt and ordered the world's greatest forward, Colin Meads, from the field. It was a ruling that sparked anger and bewilderment around the world.

Racing from different angles, Meads and the Scottish halfback, David Chisholm, had been chasing a loose ball. Both men arrived simultaneously and as Chisholm bent to scoop it up, Meads stretched out to kick it ahead. Meads' boot made contact with the ball which struck Chisholm's chest. The halfback was unhurt.

The referee immediately blew his whistle,

A disconsolate Colin Meads is dismissed from Murrayfield, 2 December, 1967.

spoke to Meads and pointed to the sideline. The All Blacks then watched in total disbelief as their key forward, head bowed, trudged from the field. It was the first time since 1925 that a player had been ordered off during a test.

Having beaten England, Scotland, Wales and France, Fred's All Blacks were now looking forward with confidence to doing the same to Ireland. That would make them the first team ever to win the Grand Slam — beating all four home nations on one tour. But a foot-and-mouth epidemic was sweeping through the British mainland that year and more than 442,000 cattle were slaughtered at a cost of about £370 million. The Irish dare not risk letting players who might have been inadvertently exposed to the disease into their country.

The tour's itinerary was rearranged and, instead of going to Ireland, the All Blacks would play the Barbarians at Twickenham before departing for home. But before that match there were three to be played in Wales.

Monmouthshire, Newport, 6 December

One player in the Welsh side, Keith Jarrett, of Newport, caused the All Blacks a great deal of headache for the reason that this 19-year-old prodigy, given the right conditions, could kick goals from more than 70 yards. Four minutes from the start he had his first shot 65 yards from the posts. He had the distance with plenty to spare, but the ball just grazed the outside of the right-hand upright. That early miss, however, didn't prevent the golden boy from landing four penalties in the first half to give Monmouthshire the halftime lead of 12 points to 6.

Playing things tight in the second spell to minimise the chance of further penalties, the All Blacks scored some magnificent tries, including an outstanding effort by Earle Kirton in which he ran 40 yards and beat five opposition players. The final score was All Blacks 23, Monmouthshire 12.

New Zealand 23: Tries by Kirton, Steel, Tremain and Muller; conversion and 3 penalty goals by McCormick. **Monmouthshire 12:** 4 penalty goals by Jarrett.

East Wales, Cardiff, 13 December

Twelve hours before the game was due to begin, snow was more than a foot deep on Cardiff Arms Park. The match was cancelled but the All Blacks manager, Charlie Saxton, generously agreed to reschedule it four days later. The reaction of the Welsh Rugby Union, not to mention thousands of fans, was one of sheer delight. It was typical of Saxton's sportsmanship and his willingness to do anything he could for the welfare of rugby.

But, unfortunately, his generosity paved the way for the only game the All Blacks failed to win.

The most interesting point about the match was that East Wales was the only side which played the attacking game from beginning to end. The Welsh backs continually had the tourists in trouble with short, dangerous kicks ahead on the greasy surface and the forwards were magnificent. They gave nothing away in the tight scrums and this allowed their captain, Gareth Edwards, to swiftly feed his backs.

In the lineouts they often confused the New Zealanders with their variations. Even in the rucks the tourists were denied their usual superiority. It was anyone's game and the All Blacks were fortunate to come out of it with a 3-all draw.

New Zealand 3: Try by Steel. **East Wales 3:** Try by Wilson.

Some jocular criticism was levelled at coach Fred Allen after the game. On the Friday evening before the cancelled match, Fred had spoken to eight senior Welsh coaches for one hour on his methods of coaching and training. Because the game then was postponed for four days, this had given the Welsh ample opportunity to study Fred's words of wisdom.

During the second half of the game, when the All Blacks were trailing 3–0, legendary flyhalf Cliff Jones, a selector of the East Wales team, who was seated not far from Fred, leaned across and said: 'We've made good use of what you had to say, Freddie.'

His effort to bait Fred Allen was not entirely successful. 'The game's not over yet, Cliff,' said Fred, 'You may have spoken a bit too soon.'

Barbarians, London, 16 December

Sixty-nine tries in 16 matches — 45 of them by the backs — that was the remarkable record of the 1967 All Blacks as they ran on to the field at Twickenham to do battle with the British Barbarians in the final game of the tour.

In the four internationals the Men in Black had scored 13 tries to three — undeniable proof that Fred Allen's revolutionary methods, ridiculed when first announced, had come up trumps.

'Now they're all copying Fred Allen,' wrote the *New Zealand Herald's* London correspondent.

The great flanker Waka Nathan was invited to play in the Barbarians' team as a mark of respect for the big Maori's ability and the courage with which he had endured his jaw injury throughout the tour. Waka was naturally delighted — until Saxton, the All Blacks manager, rejected the idea of a current All Black playing against his own team.

'This game is an international representative fixture,' Saxton said, 'and this aspect would be severely weakened if an All Black turned out for an opposing side. I recognise the honour the appearance would have meant for Waka and I would have liked to have given him the opportunity. But, as All Blacks, we must retain our identity as a team group.'

After just four minutes play, the Barbarians' fullback and captain, Stewart Wilson, fielded a clearing kick from Laidlaw and dropped a beautiful field goal. Seven minutes later Kirton equalised with his own perfectly struck drop kick.

Tired after their strenuous tour, the All Blacks were making numerous handling errors and several scoring chances went begging. Halftime came with the score 3–3.

Eighteen minutes into the second half, Barry John kicked ahead from a maul and Lloyd sped through to dive on the ball for a try which put the Barbarians ahead 6–3.

Play see-sawed from one end of the field to the other and with time running out it looked as though the All Blacks' unbeaten record was about to be smashed. Then, with one minute of time left on the clock, the All Blacks took a quick tap penalty well inside their own half.

First to the ball was McCormick who set up an attacking movement. When the All Blacks switched the ball back to the right, Steel came tearing through the middle, took it at pace, ran straight at the last defender and, although off balance, managed to unload to MacRae who scored. All Blacks 6, Barbarians 6.

Now the match depended on McCormick's kick which was within easy range. But when the ball slewed outside the uprights, the home crowd screamed with delight and a draw seemed certain.

But three minutes into injury time — and in typical Fred Allen fashion — the All Blacks again ran the ball from their own 25 before Laidlaw kicked it ahead. But Wilson's return punt failed to find touch and Lochore was waiting in exactly the right spot to field it neatly.

Sensing a chance, the New Zealand captain set sail for the Barbarians' line. He made valuable ground, and when his way was blocked he passed infield to Kirton who veered swiftly inward. Then, just when he was wanted, the speedy

Steel came hurtling through to take a beautifully judged pass and roar ahead for the winning try.

McCormick's conversion, which made the final score 11–6, brought him his hundredth point in Europe and made him the top points scorer for the tour.

New Zealand 11: Tries by MacRae and Steel; conversion by McCormick; dropped goal by Kirton. **Barbarians 6:** Try by Lloyd; dropped goal by Wilson.

It was a nail-biting finish to a superb game, one of the most sensational encounters in Twickenham history. And as the All Blacks carried Lochore and Meads shoulder-high from the field the vast crowd broke into song with 'Now is the Hour' followed by a rousing edition of 'Auld Lang Syne'. It was a fitting tribute to a great team, an unbeaten tour and a host of wonderful memories.

That evening every tavern and swanky hotel in London, and indeed throughout the rest of England, was packed with crowds paying homage to what had been a magnificent exhibition of rugby. And while the champagne flowed at the Savoy Hotel, Fred Allen was delighted when the president of the British Barbarians, Brigadier Glyn Hughes, honoured Brian Lochore with honorary membership of that exclusive club.

'If anyone deserved such an accolade it was Brian,' says Fred. 'What a player — what a captain!'

In the 17 matches they played in Canada, the British Isles and France the All Blacks notched up no fewer than 71 tries, an average of more than four a game. And in the four all-important test matches, they scored five tries against England, four against France and two against both Scotland and Wales. Such prolific try-scoring in test matches between these countries had not been seen before.

Just three years previously, after the All Blacks of 1963–64 had beaten Wales by a penalty goal and a drop goal to nil, the coach, Neil McPhail, had exclaimed in frustration, 'It would have been great if we had scored just one try!'

The great, unbeaten tour was aptly summed up by T.P. McLean: 'New Zealand, through this team, became not only the most successful rugby nation in the world but also the most truly dedicated to the playing of rugby of the right sort.' An even greater tribute was paid by Barbarians president Brigadier Glyn Hughes:

The best disciplined side I've ever seen — the side which built success on sound fundamental principles and not on a lot of fancy gimmicks. They showed us, the inventors of the game, how to run with the ball — and that's what rugby is about.

An amusing incident occurred towards the end of the tour when the All Blacks hooker Bruce McLeod, minus his All Blacks blazer, went into the London branch of the Bank of New Zealand to cash a cheque. It was a crossed cheque and the teller, though extremely polite, was firm. 'I am sorry sir,' he told McLeod, 'you do not have an account here and this is a non-negotiable cheque. We can't cash it for you.'

McLeod protested vehemently. But senior tellers, junior accountants and the accountant himself all offered the same answer: no account — no cash!

'But,' said McLeod, 'I'm a New Zealander. I'm an All Black.' The word in every response was still 'sorry'.

'Who' demanded McLeod, 'is the big narner around here?'

The manager, of course, he was told.

'Then fetch him,' McLeod ordered.

This, they advised him, was not possible. The manager was lunching with two New Zealanders in the cafeteria upstairs — two very important New Zealanders — All Blacks, no less. At that precise moment, down the stairs came the manager attended by All Blacks hooker John Major and prop forward Alister Hopkinson.

The accountant explained to the manager that a man purporting to be an All Black was insisting on cashing a cheque in spite of the fact that he had no account at the bank. The manager turned to his two All Blacks guests. 'Do you recognise this gentleman?' he asked.

'Never seen him before,' said Hopkinson.

'He's an imposter,' said Major.

The mischievous pair were scarcely able to keep straight faces as they watched McLeod's increasing discomfort. He appeared, they said later, close to exploding.

When the accountant hurried away to call the police, the pair thought it time to relent before things got out of hand.

'It's okay,' they said to the manager, 'he really is one of us and besides we want the big, ugly bugger in the scrum on Saturday.'

The manager was a good-natured fellow. He called his accountant back and told him to give McLeod his cash.

Problem Pupil

Fred's run of test triumphs comes close to being derailed by a man he once mentored and coached.

In the first two tests of the 1968 season against Australia, Fred encountered a problem he had helped create. That problem was the new Wallaby coach, Des Connor, the former halfback who had played such a vital role in Auckland's record tenure of the Ranfurly Shield. During his time under Fred, Connor had meticulously studied Auckland's potent attacking style. He knew Fred's methods threatened serious trouble for the Wallabies, and he had prepared a counter plan.

'That boy had rugby in his blood — as a player and a tactician,' says Fred. 'I have never seen a footballer with more intelligence. He caused us a lot of trouble on that Australian tour and, to his credit, we had to change our game plan to suit.

'In both tests Des introduced shortened lineouts and a 3-2-1 scrum formation. These tactics gave the Aussies extra defenders which greatly reduced the amount of running rugby we'd hoped to play. It also knocked a lot of speed out of the games and spoilt them as a spectacle. It wasn't the sort of rugby I enjoy.'

Apart from two tests, the All Blacks played nine provincial games in Australia, winning them all by huge margins. The top score was a 74 points to nil drubbing of Tasmania in Hobart.

But the two test matches were entirely different propositions. Connor had drilled his squad extremely well with the sole intention of shutting down the All Blacks open, attacking style of play.

His tactics, especially in the second test, came perilously close to succeeding.

Australia, Sydney Cricket Ground, 15 June 1968

In the twenty-fifth minute of the game Brian Lochore, after colliding with Kirton, was in agony with a broken thumb. He courageously played on but when he also tore a hamstring he had no option but to leave the field. This proved a mixed blessing because his substitute, Ian Kirkpatrick, played sublime rugby and scored three magnificent tries.

For much of the time the test was violent and ridden with casualties. Muller's left eye was heavily bandaged with blood seeping through, both McCormick and Strahan had cuts on their eyebrows but shrugged off attention and the Australian centre, Brass, suffered a dislocated shoulder.

The game ended with a 27–11 victory for the All Blacks, but as a spectacle it fell well below expectations.

New Zealand 27: Tries by Kirkpatrick (3), Kirton, Steel and Laidlaw; 3 conversions and a penalty goal by McCormick. **Australia 11:** Try by Cardy; conversion and 2 penalty goals by McGill.

Thirteen minutes before the final whistle a most unfortunate incident occurred. In an endeavour to remove the Australian halfback, Ken Catchpole, from the New Zealand side of a ruck, Colin Meads seized him by one leg to pull him away. When Catchpole screamed, Meads let go but the damage had been done. Muscles in Catchpole's groin had been severely torn and he was carried off on a stretcher.

Australia, Brisbane, 22 June

The All Blacks were decidedly lucky to win the second test. Admittedly, they were without the services of three star players — Lochore and Gray with broken thumbs and Tremain with a strained leg — but this did not excuse their below-par performance. They simply did not play with their customary skill and intelligence.

Colin Meads, Kel Tremain and Fred during a training run in Australia, 1968.

Nor were they helped by the referee, Mr Kevin Crowe, being over-enthusiastic with his whistle. The pattern was set when he awarded 14 penalties in the first 10 minutes!

The score see-sawed throughout the game with numerous penalties for infringements and, as the end drew near, it looked as though it was going to be Australia's day. Then, with just two minutes to play, a sensational decision by the referee deprived the Wallabies of victory. Terry McLean described it as follows:

Davis had the ball now, going hell for leather. Thorne was outside him, also at speed. The defence was confused. For a minute fraction of time, the two men sped onward. It seemed that if Davis passed to Thorne, there must be a try at the corner. But Davis did not pass to Thorne who was now of no help to anyone. As he ran, without the ball, he was wilfully obstructed by Cardy, an act so deliberate as to warrant an extreme penalty.

Attention switched back to Davis. Alone and in doubt, Davis speared a punt toward the corner flag. A moment after his kick, he was hurled to the ground by a fierce tackle from Honan.

The ball bounced short of the goal-line and carried into the in-goal area where it was picked up and forced down by Pope.

Enter Mr Crowe who followed the ball until he observed it pitching within the in-goal area. Then he blew his whistle and, raising his left arm above his head, began running along the goal-line towards the goal posts.

The tremendous gasp from the crowd sounded like forty thousand cannons simultaneously firing — for here was Mr Crowe, between the uprights, signalling a penalty try for New Zealand. But those three points were still not enough for victory. Everything now depended on Fergie McCormick slotting the conversion.

Thousands held their breaths as the fullback moved forward. Straight and true, the ball sailed over the cross-bar and the match was New Zealand's, 19–18.

Interviewed after the game, referee Crowe said: 'I awarded the try because in my view Davis, had he not been tackled by Honan, would probably have scored.'

He made no mention of Grahame Thorne being deliberately taken out of play by Cardy. That was by far the worse foul.

New Zealand 19: Tries by Thorne, Lister and a penalty try (Davis); 2 conversions and 2 penalty goals by McCormick. **Australia 18:** Try by Hipwell; 5 penalty goals by McGill.

On their way home the All Blacks stopped off at Fiji where a match had been arranged between an All Blacks XV and a President's XV.

'Why the NZRFU decided on this name change I have no idea,' says Fred. 'All I know is that it has never been declared an official game and does not count in test records.'

Everywhere the team went after landing at Nadi airport they were mobbed by chanting crowds, all anxious to hang leis around the necks of their famous visitors. Villagers came from all points of the compass and scores of small boats journeyed from distant islands to be at the game.

Although the main field at Buckhurst Park, Suva, was built to give viewing to 10,000 spectators, such was the interest that when the All Blacks ran on to the field, the place was overflowing with a record crowd of 25,000.

The game, a victory to the visitors by 33 points to 6, was notable for the magnificent performance of a young Grahame Thorne who crossed for four of his team's seven tries. The only points the Fijians could manage were two penalty goals.

No one was more surprised at Thorne's performance than Colin Meads.

'Thorney had been shopping in the sweltering heat all morning,' he said, 'and was late for lunch. So he downed a beer. Imagine — late for lunch and then quaffing a beer — before a game!'

When he heard that bit of news, Fred Allen was far from pleased. But when he saw Thorne gliding through the Fijian defence time after time he felt a certain compassion for the young man — although he did warn him not to come at that pre-match stuff again.

T.P. McLean called Fiji the 'Shangri-la of the game'. Colin Meads was equally enthusiastic. At the airport before they left he told the huge crowd: 'I have never known such wonderful people. I'm going home to tell our folk all about you and I hope this will be the beginning of many matches between our two countries.'

The team left for New Zealand in high spirits with Kel Tremain leading one of the side's favourite songs, 'Ten Guitars'. It had been a wonderful experience and one they would remember for the rest of their lives.

A fortnight after the All Blacks arrived home, a powerful French contingent arrived for a New Zealand tour which included test matches in Christchurch, Wellington and Auckland.

It was a tour marred by violence and ill-feeling on both sides, with play frequently deteriorating to a point where severe injuries were suffered.

France, Christchurch, 13 July

The game began at a hectic pace and in the ninth minute Lacaze drop kicked a goal from 30 yards out. Twenty minutes later McCormick equalised with a penalty. Villepreux retaliated with a 25-yard penalty goal and five minutes later McCormick again equalled the scores with an easy shot from 15 yards before putting New Zealand ahead from 25 yards.

Then it was Villepreux's turn again, but this time he was facing a massive kick with a wet and muddy ball 45 yards from the posts. The fullback struck the ball with perfect rhythm and the Lancaster Park crowd sent up a mighty cheer as the ball cleared the cross bar with feet to spare. It was one of the great goals of the tour.

It was anyone's game right to the final minute. And the two men who deserve the greatest praise were again halfback Laidlaw and five-eighths Kirton.

When he received the ball from a scrum just five yards from the French goal-line, halfback Puget attempted to pass to fullback Villepreux for a defensive kick to touch. But Laidlaw, the All Blacks half, was too fast. He darted round

The irascible Mr Iracabal ... French prop Jean Iracabal tangles with Colin Meads and Kel Tremain in the first test of the 1968 series.

the scrum and deflected the ball away. As it rolled along the ground Villepreux took a fly-kick at it and it flew into Thorne's chest before rebounding into the in-goal area. Players from both sides went after it, but Kirton was there first to dive and touch down.

That was the try — that was the match, 12–9.

New Zealand 12: Try by Kirton; Three penalty goals by McCormick. **France 9:** 2 penalty goals by Villepreux; dropped goal by Lacaze.

France, Wellington, 27 July

The game was notable for the 'impossible' penalty goal achieved by Villepreux from a distance of more than 70 yards. When the French fullback signalled he would attempt such a kick, a murmur of derision and disbelief went through the crowd of nearly 50,000. But when the ball kept soaring on and on to finally cross the bar high up and dead centre the sniggering turned to cries of astonishment. And as for Villepreux — he leapt in the air, hands above his head, in absolute delight.

Because of the French tactics, the game developed into a contest of kicking and punching. On several occasions referee Pring called the captains, Puget and Lochore, together and instructed them to cool things down.

But when the thuggery continued, Lochore said to the referee, 'We've had enough. If you don't stop these jokers from what they're doing, I'm going to let my players go!'

In the years ahead B.J. regretted those remarks, but he was sick and tired of seeing his players being knocked around. He later wrote: 'That second French test was the dirtiest match I have ever played in. I saw Laidlaw kicked in the head, McLeod kicked in the head and Meads kneed in the face. I must also say that I saw actions from upset All Blacks which were regrettable.

'Scrums and rucks were made to order for the game's thugs and their skipper Marcel Puget was being a right little ratbag, stupidly abrasive, yapping like a terrier, stirring up trouble. My players were coming to me and telling me they could not go on just absorbing it. I calmed them down as long as possible until I had to do something about it.

'It was not a good thing to say to a referee and John Pring did not take it kindly. But it was that or, undoubtedly, the game would have blown sky-high.'

The second half was not much better than the first and it was a disgraceful statistic that the time for injury stoppages and arguments amounted to more than 20 minutes. Except for Villepreux's unbelievable kick, it was a test match best forgotten. All Blacks 9, France 3.

New Zealand 9: Three penalty goals by McCormick. **France 3:** Penalty goal by Villepreux.

Before the test, the last street flyer put out on *Dominion* newspaper billboards carried the bold words, 'France to Win — Veysey.' That was distorting the truth somewhat, because all that sports editor Alex Veysey had said was that he believed the French had 'a great chance' of beating the All Blacks.

When someone snatched one of the flyers and hung it in the All Blacks dressing room, Fred got quite a start when he entered. He stopped dead in his tracks, glared at the flyer and actually put one hand over his eyes as if to protect them from the 'glare'.

He began by pointing to the poster and telling his audience how the reporters were saying the All Blacks were going to lose. For the next 10 minutes he was in full cry about how such a thing was not going to happen.

He told them they were on their home soil in front of their home crowd. He told them how well they had trained during the week. He told them they were fighting fit and free of injury and he finished by instilling into them the fact that they were, without doubt, the better team.

'All you have to do now,' he said, 'is follow the plan we have worked on and give me your very best. Do that, and I'll be a happy man.' And by the time he had finished every man in the room had a look on his face that spelt trouble for the opposition.

Then Fred slowly turned and pointed to the poster. 'And now,' he thundered, 'tear that bloody thing down!'

France, Auckland, 10 August

The day was sunny and, as expected, the third test began at blazing speed. Tries were narrowly missed as the ball sped from one end of the field to the other. The first points came from McCormick's boot (3–0) and the second from a brilliant try by Going who scuttled round a scrum, outwitted several defenders and touched down with the greatest of ease. McCormick converted and with only 19 minutes gone New Zealand was ahead 8–0.

The All Blacks increased their lead when, from a lineout, the ball sped along the chain to Cottrell who steadied himself and dropped a fine field goal (11–0).

Then came another piece of Going magic. Around the scrum he glided once again, past Billiere, past Lux, past Spanghero and over the line to thunderous applause. McCormick added the extra points and New Zealand was ahead 16–0.

In the first minute of the second half Villepreux had his one and only shot at goal. But in desperation he muffed the kick and it scarcely rose above grass level. But the French were not done with yet. When a throw-in passed over all heads and hands, the ball went to Carrere, who accelerated swiftly before handing on to Spanghero. Then on to Dourthe. Then again to Trillo — and suddenly he was over the goal-line for a splendid try. Villepreux again missed and the score was 16–3.

Spurred by this success, France struck again — and when a group of players from both sides crashed across the goal-line it was Carrere who had got to the ball first. Villepreux, who was having a shocking day, missed again (16–6).

The French were now playing with Gallic flair and seemed certain to score. But Dourthe had another idea. When he received the ball in front of the All Blacks posts he dropped an easy goal. With the score now 16–9, and the French gaining, the atmosphere at Eden Park was electric.

At the next lineout some relief came when referee Murphy penalised the French for obstruction, and from 23 yards Fergie the magnificent slotted the goal (19–9).

French halfback and captain Marcel Puget gets the message from referee John Pring during the 1968 series. All Blacks captain Brian Lochore is on Pring's side.

With minutes on the clock France struck again. And this time it was all due to Villepreux who tore down the blindside, passed infield to Lux, took it back when Lux was blocked, then magically gave it back when Lux was in the clear, tearing towards the goal-line for a glorious try (19–12).

And that was it. Time ran out and one of the greatest tests of recent years was over.

New Zealand 19: Two tries by Going; 2 conversions and 2 penalty goals by McCormick; dropped goal by Cottrell. **France 12:** Tries by Trillo, Carrere and Lux; dropped goal by Dourthe.

In the dressing room before the game Fred Allen had fired up Sid Going with the words: 'Sid, you can do it today. You can score today. I want you to score today!'

'I thought about Fred's words,' Going said later. 'I thought about them all the time. When Fred Allen drums something like that into you, you're not likely to forget it.'

Two-try hero Sid Going snipes against the French in the second test of the 1968 series at Eden Park. His two tries that day made Fred a very happy man.

A Dream Destroyed

Fred's long-held dream of winning a test series against the Springboks in South Africa is cruelly sabotaged.

On 15 June 1968 an event took place which helped change the course of New Zealand rugby history — and not for the better!

It was the day a packed Sydney Cricket Ground nervously awaited the first test match of the year between the All Blacks and the Wallabies, two of the finest teams in the world. Behind a table in the All Blacks dressing room stands the New Zealand coach, Fred Allen, glancing round the room, measuring each player with his eyes, staring deeply at some and not so deeply at others.

Behind him sits a reporter, Alex Veysey from the *Dominion* newspaper in Wellington. He has been granted permission to attend by Duncan Ross, the manager, and Fred Allen himself.

The coach raps on the table and steps forward. It is time for him to speak. And this is a condensed report of Veysey's article which appeared in the *Dominion* early the following week:

'I've approached a lot of games very frightened,' he says, quietly. A few brows furrow — they hadn't heard him say anything like that before. *'But I'm terrified by today's game!'*

Every head in the room shoots up, even the oldies are grabbed. Pinetree

Meads, Kel Tremain, Ken Gray and Bruce McLeod, sitting together, all stare at the coach. Now he has them where he wants them — so he grinds out his points, sometimes needling, sometimes wheedling, sometimes loosing a shaft, sometimes firing a load of buckshot.

He is a master of timing. He never allows his control to drift. He wants to bring a team that's floating high on a cloud of victories back to bedrock reality.

The heads sink during one of the woodwind passages so he introduces a barrage of percussion, his right fist pounding the table-top. *'Pinetree!'* The heads shoot up again. 'They were using a sack of sawdust for rucking practice yesterday. D'you know what they called it? *They called it Piney!'*

Pinetree stares and nods. Just one, hard perfunctory nod. 'Kel! Tom! If you miss Catchpole today, you're for it!' Two more heads lift, four eyes stare. The heads nod. 'Chris!' And now comes a thump for every syllable: *'Work on your forwards!'* And then comes a bit of needle: 'I don't want any of those funny kicks of yours.' And now a bit of soap: 'You're going to be the architect of this test.'

Then he swings round to big Muller: *'Jazzer! No pushing!* That's the referee's problem, not yours. I want a try from you today, Jazzer.' He turns to face Kirton: 'Conshie, I'm not saying you can't kick, but give us more of the double today. I used to think Mac Herewini was the greatest doubler I'd seen, but you'd leave him for dead. *As long as you run hard!*

'Pinetree, and you too Sam. You're the guts of our scrum, the real guts. They'll be getting at you really hard, Pinetree. And Sam, don't forget there's another fellow pushing for your place. You're there to win us the ball. So get up high and pull it down. Even if you hit your own blokes with your elbows — *Get it down!*

'Don't make any mistake. Today they plan to rip us over. Jazzer, Ken, Pinetree! My God, if they whip you over you'll have me to answer to.' The long, cold stare is telling. And so it progresses as each forward is given the message.

Then he turns his attention to the backs. *'Stainless!* Get in there, no one's holding you back, *Thorny!* We've got other good wingers, you know. You've got the ability to beat a man, but you've got to go flat stick — *all the time!'* And so it goes on — one by one he gives them the message.

In the end every man, except one, has been given the treatment. No one stands unpunished. All heads are down — except Sam Strahan's. He stares, desperately serious — at nothing. The hush in the room is thunderous.

Then comes a quiet appeal to the captain, Lochore. It ends with the words, 'Brian, I'm relying on you for strength and leadership today and I know you won't fail us.'

And when it's all over the coach walks from the room and leaves the gladiators in silent thought.

One of the most famous photos taken of Fred Allen. The inner sanctum of the All Blacks during a training run at Wellington College in 1968. Listening to the famous team talk here are, from left, Kel Tremain, Ken Gray, Sid Going (hand on head) and Brian Lochore.

Once again, Fred's talk has motivated his players to a point where they will play their hearts out for him — and for New Zealand. But there were others back in New Zealand who were far from pleased. They felt the coach had made a serious error in allowing a newspaperman into the room — and they intended to use it against him.

At seven the following morning, Australia time, the All Blacks manager, Duncan Ross, was roused from a deep sleep by an urgent phone call from Wellington. On the line was the chairman of the New Zealand Rugby Union, Tom Morrison, in a high state of indignation. His anger, along with that of other senior administrators, had been triggered by the first-hand report of Fred's talk which had appeared in the morning paper.

Morrison told the manager that Veysey's presence at the team talk had contravened 'traditional practice' and that Allen's address should never have been made public. It was a disgraceful thing to do, the chairman said, and he instructed Ross to pass his intense displeasure on to Fred Allen.

When Ross relayed Morrison's criticism to Fred, the coach was annoyed for three reasons — firstly, because Morrison had not spoken to him personally; secondly, because of the chairman's overly belligerent attitude; and, thirdly, because Fred had surmised that Veysey was attending the meeting for a background story, as opposed to writing a word-for-word article.

Alex Veysey, on the other hand, had always believed that if Fred allowed him to be present at the talk he could write freely about it. 'I openly took notes in front of the players on what was, for me, a most enlightening study of motivation in action,' he said.

When Fred tackled Veysey, who was staying in the same hotel, the reporter showed him a copy of the article and Fred had no hesitation in giving it a 'qualified pass mark'.

There was not one word in Veysey's story that could be of the slightest use to an opposing side. It was merely a graphic description of a coach's intense passion as he psychologically conditioned his players to give of their best for their country.

'It wasn't about moves, or tactics or anything like that,' says Fred. 'All those things had been taken care of in the previous weeks. It was about self-belief and confidence, about dedication and courage. It was about patriotism and your country, and what the game meant to everyone back home.

'I knew how those players sitting in front of me were feeling with the minutes ticking down. I'd been through it myself a hundred times. Fear and anxiety were striking at the very heart of most of them and I wanted to bring them back to reality and convince them that they were the best.'

Fred was openly annoyed at being taken to task in such a belligerent manner. He could see nothing wrong with what he had done. He had always been friendly and open-handed, always willing to spread the word and give advice. He scoffed at the growing custom of holding secret training sessions and he allowed all and sundry to attend his training sessions. 'You can bet your bottom dollar they never saw anything I didn't want them to see, or hear anything I didn't want them to hear,' he said.

Fred and Alex Veysey had a drink together and it was at this stage that Fred 'opened up his heart,' as Veysey later wrote. It was clear to the reporter that Fred was extremely anxious to erase the bitter memories of the 1949 tour and had his heart firmly set on leading a team to South Africa in an attempt to defeat the Springboks on their home soil for the first time. But for some time now his relationship had been rocky with a small group of top administrators and he was growing increasingly tired of their interference and pettiness, some of which was clearly malicious.

'It just didn't make sense,' says Fred. 'I'd been entrusted to coach the All Blacks and we hadn't lost a game. Why would they want to harm a winning coach who was now even better equipped to carry on than ever before?

Fred with fellow All Blacks selector, Ivan Vodanovich. Vodanovich took over as All Blacks coach after Fred's premature retirement at the end of 1968.

'The situation finally reached a point where I wasn't going to let them walk all over me. So I told them to stop interfering with the coaching. I told them to get on with their business and let me get on with mine.

'Nobody had ever spoken to them like that — and they didn't like it. But I wasn't going to hold back any longer. I'd had enough of their bickering and back-stabbing. That's not the way I like to operate.'

'When Fred Allen and I parted that day,' wrote Veysey, 'I had no doubt that at the end of the season he would tell the New Zealand Rugby Union enough was enough.

'That would be an extremely sad thing for New Zealand rugby, Veysey added, 'because Fred Allen is clearly the man with the knowledge, skill and experience to defeat the Springboks in South Africa in 1970.'

The *New Zealand Herald* rugby writer T.P. McLean had earlier voiced a similar view to Veysey's:

It would be impossible to overestimate the contribution to the great success of the All Blacks tour of the three leaders of the party — the manager, C.K. Saxton, the coach, F.R. Allen, and the captain, B.J. Lochore.

At the beginning Fred Allen encountered some resistance within the team toward the gospel he so vigorously preached of running rugby as the basic element of the tour.

He overcame this by strength of character and by demonstrating, with singular clarity, the superiorities of attacking over defensive rugby.

To a student of psychology, Fred Allen was a fascinating subject. As a hard taskmaster on the training field, he was severe to the point of ruthlessness but while awaiting matches he was consumed by a quiet nervousness.

Most fascinating of all, he was never anything but totally indifferent to all the great praise which was being heaped upon him as the greatest coach of his time.

Nothing else mattered to him but the team and a good performance from it — and by demanding as much of himself as he did of his players, he set an example of a truly remarkable kind.

It may go against the democratic grain of New Zealand rugby, but one cannot help saying that it will be in the best interests of the game if Fred Allen is despatched to Australia with the All Blacks team in May.

And furthermore, he must surely be assured by the New Zealand Rugby Union's annual meeting of a sufficient tenure of office, both as selector and coach, to enable him to prepare the All Blacks for the proposed expedition to South Africa in 1970.

And every other sporting writer in New Zealand was of the same opinion — Fred Allen was clearly the man for the job in 1970.

Whether or not Veysey knew of the other concerns on Fred Allen's mind we do not know, but Fred himself has never forgotten that day in 1967 when the team to tour Canada, the British Isles and France was announced.

'I've always known that by refusing the underhanded proposal to exclude Meads, Gray and McLeod from the team I did nothing to help my future as the All Blacks coach,' he says.

'For months the antagonism came from a small clique inside the council. It was obvious in their attitude towards me and, in view of what I was now achieving, I found that very strange.

'I was always wondering what was coming next. Just look what happened when I allowed Alex Veysey into my team-talk in Sydney. Bloody toll calls from New Zealand the following morning to tick me off — to tell me how to run the All Blacks, who had never lost a game.

'They never had the guts to speak to me directly. I got it all second-hand. They wanted to get rid of me, alright, there's no doubt about it. That's why I resigned. I wasn't going to carry on in that sort of atmosphere.

'Several papers suggested I was dumped, but that was not the case. I formally advised them I would not be standing as All Blacks coach the following year. And that's a fact. I voluntarily gave up coaching, but I could never give up my love of the game.

'One of the things I have always cherished is the fact that there wasn't a man in the All Blacks who wanted me to go. When they realised what I intended to do, the entire team presented me with a cup to celebrate our achievements together.

'That cup is the most precious I have. And many in that unbeaten team have been among my closest friends throughout the years.'

Fred admits that not going to South Africa was one of the major disappointments of his life. 'We'd have had a royal chance of beating them,' he says.

'My guys had developed to a point where they were all playing exceptional, 15-man rugby which would have been most effective against the Springboks on their hard, dry fields which would suit our style of play — not like Britain where we had to contend with rain and mud and slippery grounds. I'm positive we could have done it.

'Louis Babrow, the great Springbok centre who had watched several of our games in Britain, agreed. I had some long talks with him. "If you took this team to South Africa, Fred," he told me, "you'd beat us for sure."

The much-treasured jug presented to Fred by the 1968 All Blacks after he told them he was finishing. The inscription reads: 'To Needle. In appreciation from the 1968 All Blacks in Australia.'

'The old brigade of Colin Meads, Kel Tremain, Brian Lochore, Ken Gray and Bruce McLeod would still be going strong and we had some great young guys coming through to join them, players like Ian Kirkpatrick, Bryan Williams and Sam Strahan.

'Then we had Sid Going, the most improved man in the squad. He'd benefited greatly by playing in the big stuff, and he'd developed into a world-class, running halfback.'

When the news broke that Fred Allen had resigned as All Blacks coach, no one was more disappointed than his captain and friend Brian Lochore. Brian had always envisaged the All Blacks staying together, with Fred as coach, for a couple more seasons, at least.

Brian had known of the problems Fred was having with the union, but was unaware of just how much they were weighing on his mind. He also shared the same view as Fred, that if ever a team was equipped to defeat the Springboks on their home soil, the '67 team, with two or three additions, was the one to do it.

But, sadly, it was not to be and in 1970 the All Blacks went to South Africa without the one person who should have been with them. They won every provincial game but lost the test series 3–1 — the first at Pretoria 6–17, the third at Port Elizabeth 3–14 and the fourth at Johannesburg 17–20. They won the second test, in Cape Town, 9–8.

Brian Lochore returned home an unhappy man. In his biography he stated:

We failed in what was the most fiercely burning ambition of my time — to beat South Africa in a series in South Africa.

Were I to believe the judgement of the manager Ron Burk that the tour was a success because of the clean sweep of the provincial games, how could I explain the deep depression I felt at the end of the tour?

An All Blacks series defeat of the Springboks on their home soil now looked as far away as ever.

It took another 26 years before New Zealand gained its first series win against the Springboks in South Africa. Coached by John Hart, managed by Michael Banks and captained by Sean Fitzpatrick, the 1996 All Blacks won the first two of a three-test series to cement their place as one of the finest teams in the history of the game.

A Question of Trust

Fred always helped the press, but woe betide any journalist who departed from the truth.

One reporter whom Fred trusted implicitly was legendary Welsh fullback Vivian Jenkins who became equally famous for his sports reporting after he retired from the game in 1939.

After gaining blues for rugby and cricket at Oxford University, he concentrated on rugby and played for Wales, the Lions and the Barbarians. He had every attribute required for the fullback position. He was rock-solid on defence, brilliant on attack and capable of kicking goals from well past the halfway mark.

He was also interested in the welfare of the game. When touring with the Lions in 1959 he had seen Don Clarke kick six penalties at Carisbrook to just shade the visitors' four tries 18–17 when tries were worth just three points. To him, this was rank injustice, so he proposed raising the value of a try to encourage more positive, attacking tactics. He also campaigned for a law to restrict direct kicking into touch and was the first to lobby for the introduction of the differential penalty. All three of his submissions made it into the law book.

His wife Sue predeceased him in 1984 and after her death he spent the

English winters in New Zealand where his many friends included Fred Allen.

At the end of the All Blacks' unbeaten 1967 tour, Jenkins conducted a lengthy interview with Fred which was widely read by the rugby public. Here, in full, is his article, which appeared in Britain's *Sunday Times* of 17 December 1967:

You've had a wonderful tour and everyone knows how much you and manager Charlie Saxton have contributed to it. What other reasons would you give for the team's success?

We've had a very well balanced side of 30 players and all but four or five of them have been fighting for a place in the international side. Competition, as always, leads to great effort and better results. Also we've had an outstanding captain in Brian Lochore. I rate Wilson Whineray as the finest captain New Zealand has ever had, but Lochore is now right on his heels.

Some people are saying that this is the greatest team that has ever come here. How do you feel about that?

That's very high praise but I think it's stretching it a bit. We've been a good team in the real sense of the word, with everyone contributing, but I always feel the greatest side I ever saw was the 1937 South African one in New Zealand with the 1950 Lions in New Zealand coming next. Still, we've seen quite a bit of one member of that 1937 Springbok side, Dr Louis Babrow, while we've been over here and he says that we are a better side than his was. We think that a great compliment coming from him. The pattern of play has changed in the meantime, of course. There was much more emphasis on scrumming in those days and the Springboks were supreme at it. Now it is the speed of the loose ball and driving forward play that counts. Maybe we could beat them at that. I believe the 1951–52 Springbok side in Britain was also an outstanding one but, of course, I never saw it play.

Could we now turn to the present tour? Which have been your hardest matches?

All our matches have been tremendously hard, even though you might not think so from the scores. East Wales gave us a real fright on Wednesday, and we were very happy to get away with a draw. We missed Colin Meads in all that mud, but I don't want to make excuses. East Wales played wonderfully well, and I wouldn't wish to take anything away from them. West Wales, too, gave us a very hard game at Swansea, and our first match against Midlands and Home Counties at Leicester

East Wales wing Frank Wilson scores ahead of Grahame Thorne in the 3–3 draw at Cardiff, 1967. The draw was the only blemish on Fred's 37-match record with the All Blacks.

was also a tough one. Otherwise the French have impressed us most. We were astounded at the tenacity of their tackling and how big and hard — and fast — their forwards were. We couldn't have seen the best of the French when they came to New Zealand. They were short of several of their leading players. When you meet them in Paris, at full strength, it's a different proposition altogether. Their inter-club knock-out championship, I'm sure, is a great driving force.

How do you rate the present standard of British rugby?
It is definitely improving. Your players are now making a much more positive approach to the game than in recent years. They are realising that, apart from just going out and enjoying the game, they must have coaches who know what they're talking about and who can impart their knowledge to others. Any touring team which comes to this country in future will find it much tougher going. I doubt if anyone will go through unbeaten.

What do you think of our international teams?
Unfortunately, we didn't play Ireland (because of the foot-and-mouth scare) but the three other countries were very tenacious and took a lot of beating. England had one or two forwards who were a bit long in the tooth, I thought, and should bring in some younger men. But their backs seemed the most prepared to chance their arm and run with the ball. It's

time the Welsh team started to think along the same lines. They have some brilliant backs. Why not let people see them? As for Scotland, their midfield tackling against us was terrific and they should develop into a good side.

Now to your own speciality — coaching. What is the most important factor in this?
Discipline, every time. You must have discipline to breed respect. Without respect from your players, you might as well toss it in and let somebody else have a go. It's like the army. The sergeant-major is in charge and everyone must know it. Even if you're doing the wrong thing it's better for 15 players to be doing it together than for everybody to be doing something different. The coach, in other words, must take complete charge. I don't believe, for instance, in letting players talk during a training session. They can talk before it, and talk after it, but while it is going on they work. I won't stand for chit-chat at any price.

In New Zealand you have competitive rugby at all levels, and every team down to the eight and nine-year-olds has a coach. Also all players are expected to turn up for training in mid-week. I hear of a junior player who was dropped from his team because he went to a Beatles concert instead of turning up for training. Is this typical?
Yes, that would be fairly typical of our approach to rugby. It's a team game and if one player doesn't turn up why should a coach waste his time taking the other fourteen? It's like a cog on a bike. If one's missing, the whole thing breaks down. It's vital to have a full muster at training. I'm also quite sure that every team, not just the firsts, should have a coach. In New Zealand we often have former All Blacks coaching quite junior teams, schoolboys included. But the best player doesn't necessarily make the best coach. It's a question of personality, communication and dedication.

Can you describe a typical All Blacks training session?
Normally, we go out for a couple of hours, or just under. We spend the first twenty minutes warming up, by which I mean mainly running round the field. I'm a great believer in this, and not so much in exercise, because the chaps are apt to pull muscles which they don't normally use. We make no use of the ball at this stage. After the warming up I let them play a little soccer or touch rugby, just to get any bruises out which they may have collected. Then, when they've forgotten their aches and pains, I grab them and get really stuck into the training. The great thing then is

to keep them moving, with all the basic skills thrown in, up to exhaustion point. We don't have many special moves, but do try them out from time to time.

Which of these have served you well on the tour?
Chiefly, the 'loop,' as you call it, but what we call the 'double'. This involves one of the inside backs passing to the man next to him and then doubling round for a return pass on the outside This has brought Kirton and McRae, in particular, vital tries. The crux of the move is that the man who receives the first pass must really involve his opposite number by going in to take the tackle before returning the ball to the original passer. Just passing, without neutralising an opponent, achieves little. Another playing move has been to bring Brian Lochore out from No.8 to act as an auxiliary first-five, or flyhalf, at set scrums. He can then make play either to right or to left, or go on his own. This induces uncertainty in the minds of the opposition. We also tried to counter the 'wonky' lineout, as I call

Earle Kirton scores the second of his two tries against England at Twickenham, 1967. Bill Birtwistle is in close attendance.

it, of only a few men by driving through, instead of getting the ball back. But this shortened lineout isn't really rugby. It should be stopped.

Can you give us any advice about rucking? We don't seem to be able to match you at this.
Your players don't seem to position their bodies low enough when they are going into a ruck. They should start bending when they are 10 or 12 yards away so they can get underneath the opposition and over the ball. Also the front two or three men should get on their feet once they are over the ball so that the rest can have a firm platform on which to shove. But speed to the ball, after the set-piece, is still the most important factor.

133

You said before you left New Zealand that you would win by scoring tries, not kicking goals, and you have certainly lived up to it. Up to yesterday you had scored 69 tries, with only 10 against. Does this please you?

It does indeed. Charlie Saxton and I have been striving for years to bring running back play back into New Zealand rugby and now, at last, we seem to have achieved something. Even in wet conditions we have been moving the ball. I am a great believer in retaining possession of the ball, instead of giving it away by kicking. Far better, if need be, to take the tackle and win the ball again from the ensuing ruck. Your forwards have to fight hard for possession and don't want to be trudging to the far side of the field when a player's kick fails to find touch. They just hate it.

Changing the subject — which of our players over here have impressed you most?

Well, I think Stewart Wilson is just about your best fullback. His goal-kicking may have been off-target at times, but his general play has been first-class. We were also very much impressed by Lloyd of England in the centre. He played a grand game for Midlands and Home Counties against us at Leicester, and one of his tries for England was a beauty. Gerald Davies, of Wales, also looked a top-notcher, though the conditions were against him in our match against East Wales at Cardiff. Scotland's mid-field players were also extremely useful. You seem so well off for halfbacks in Britain. Chisholm and Hastie, for Scotland, were a very efficient pair as were Gareth Edwards and Barry John, of Wales, but if I were coaching John I would make him stand flatter and not so deep. We were sorry, though, that we didn't see Mike Gibson owing to our trip to Ireland being cancelled. I rate Gibson as good a flyhalf as I have seen, including Jack Kyle.

What did you think of Keith Jarrett, the 19-year-old Welsh boy?

He has tremendous possibilities with that goal-kicking of his. I'm sure he could kick goals from 65 to 70 yards in South Africa at those high altitudes. But I think Wales may spoil him if they keep on switching him from centre to wing and back again. They should play him at fullback and keep him there. I gather he wanted to play centre, but I'd have said, 'You're playing fullback and that's it.' In New Zealand the coach decides, not the player.

What about our forwards?

It's hard to pick out individuals, but one man who caused us an awful lot of trouble was this chap Stagg. I was very surprised the Barbarians didn't pick him against us. He had a tremendous game for Scotland at Murrayfield. Apart from his height in the lineout — what can you do against a man who is 6 ft 10 in? He also got around the field very well. Wiltshire and Mainwaring, the Welsh lock, are a tip-top pair and the English pack gave us a hard game. 'Budge' Rogers, who was in New Zealand in 1963, is one who seems to keep up his form very well. Reverting to Wales, I feel their selectors are making a mistake in playing Brian Thomas as a prop. He is 6 ft 4 in tall and looks more like a lock to me. Another mistake by Wales was when they decided to play against the wind and the rain after winning the toss at Cardiff. We wouldn't have done that ourselves. I feel that a side battles itself out trying to hold out against the wind, and then hasn't got what it takes to come back in the second half.

You don't think, then, that our rugby prospects in Britain are as bad as some people would have us believe?

Certainly not. These things go in cycles. When I was captain of the All Blacks in South Africa in 1949, we lost all four international matches, and thought it was the end of the world. Our stock, then, was at rock bottom — yet now, in 1967, we're right on top again. Your own turn should come, especially now that you're beginning to take coaching seriously. In another 10 years the entire picture could have changed again.

Fred was a stickler for accuracy. He had no time for writers who played fast and loose with the truth.

That was an early lesson for respected *Rugby News* editor, Bob Howitt, then a young and enthusiastic sports reporter on the *Auckland Star*.

'My first appreciation of Fred's special qualities came way back in 1966 when I interviewed him by telephone,' says Howitt. 'He was in his first year as All Blacks coach.

'I quoted him seriously out of context to achieve the beat-up front-page story sought by the editor of the *8 O'clock* sports edition. The editor was all smiles with my article, but I deliberately avoided Fred Allen for some time.

'He caught up with me in Timaru at a South Island trial game. This hefty paw came down on my shoulder and swivelled me around. He looked me straight in the eye and said, "I give every journalist two chances, son. You've blown your first — don't ever do that again." I gulped. Then Fred, in his fair and forthright manner, shook my hand and said, "Just think about what I've said!"

'It was the best possible lesson for a young upstart. I never again betrayed his confidence and we went on to achieve the best possible working relationship.'

A similar encounter with Fred was experienced by another respected writer, Phil Gifford, then a 19-year-old reporter on the *New Zealand Herald*. Gifford has since admitted that the first time he met Fred, he was so scared he almost fainted.

'Fred was speaking at a men-only function in Auckland,' Gifford later wrote, 'and I was there as a guest of some committee members. After the meeting they introduced me to him and mentioned that I was a reporter on the *Herald*.

'Allen recoiled, froze me with a glare and snapped, "Listen, Snow, you put one word of what I've said here in the paper and I'll have your guts for garters."

'The thought had never crossed my mind, but if it had, I would have instantly withered with fright.

'Since that first terrifying encounter', Gifford added, 'I've been lucky enough to get to know another side of Allen, to be constantly amazed by the perception and wisdom of his views, and to firmly believe that his sensational success with Auckland, and then the All Blacks, sprang mostly from a razor-sharp rugby intelligence.

'And while legendary stories of how tough he could be have great entertainment value, it's a nonsense to suggest he had no man-management skills. The great loose forward Waka Nathan, a sweet-natured, easy-going man, tells a story that illustrates that fact.

'Nathan went through Otahuhu College with Mackie Herewini, a hugely gifted first-five or fullback, who got so tense before a game he sometimes burst into tears in the changing shed.

'These two mates always sat alongside each other before their games for Auckland in the early 60s. "Fred would come up to me," Nathan recalled years later, "and hoe right into me. The papers say you played well Waka, he'd say, but I saw you miss two tackles and drop the ball twice. Now get your lazy butt out there and get things right today."

'I'd sit there and get wild, and then Fred would go to Mackie and all he'd do was pat him on the shoulder — "There's nothing I can say to you Mackie, you're a genius. Just go out and play your own game."

'So Nathan, steam coming from his ears, would tear the opposing backs to shreds, and Herewini would command the backline with supreme confidence.

'Fred Allen had man-management skills alright — the best I've ever seen.'

Scraps of Paper

Days before a game, especially a test match, Fred began to plan the overthrow of the opposition.

Fred's mind worked overtime, and to jog his memory he made scribbled notes on anything he could shove into his pockets — hotel menus, serviettes, envelopes, even pieces of blotting paper. He never showed these jottings to anyone, and he always destroyed them when a game was over. They were for his eyes only and he frequently referred to them before training sessions.

They paid rich dividends. The All Blacks kept on winning and winning because of superior tactics and skill, often in the final minutes of a game.

When renowned English journalist Terry O'Connor was interviewing Fred in a London hotel he saw the coach take a handful of crumpled-up bits of paper from his pocket and throw them into a waste paper basket.

O'Connor was inquisitive and when Fred told him what they were the reporter asked if he could have a look at them. Fred saw no reason why not. They were scribbles Fred had made before the 1967 tests against England and Wales, both of which the All Blacks had won.

O'Connor and his editor were delighted when these small scraps of paper became the basis for a major story in the *Daily Mail* the following day. Samples of Fred Allen's jottings in his neat, distinctive handwriting were:

This is the first test — the one we must have.

Only one chance — this is the day.

Rutherford stands well back and across — deep kick to box.

500 Kiwis have travelled 12,000 miles to support you.

Wales has prepared for this game harder than any other in their history.

Nail flyhalf John first tackle . . . first tackle . . . first tackle.

English coach Rowlands predicts Wales will win.

Welsh are men possessed.

Air of complacency . . . get rid of it.

Run — move them around.

Fred had complete charge of coaching the All Blacks and no one dared interfere, although there were two men to whom he would always listen. One of them was his long-time friend, team manager Charlie Saxton, and the other was his loyal and trusted captain Brian Lochore, in whom Fred had enormous confidence.

There were times when the players came close to hating Fred for the rigorous training sessions he put them through, but he knew how important it was for every one of them to be at the peak of condition because of the heavy grounds in England, Scotland and Wales.

That doyen of sports writers, T.P. McLean, admired Fred's tough, no-nonsense approach which contrasted with that of his predecessors. He was firm in his belief that it was Fred's 'intensive training methods, along with his motivational coaching, that had the most beneficial effect on the players'.

But the most significant comments, the ones which Fred valued the most, came from the All Blacks themselves, many of whom made a point of telling him later in their lives just how much his discipline, hard work, attention to detail and personal motivation had meant to them.

It is said that military generals and international sports coaches have something in common. Both train their squads, drill them and teach them tactics. But in the final analysis, when the bullets start to fly, there is nothing they can do but watch and hope.

Major-general Howard Kippenberger, who commanded the New Zealand 2nd Division at the battle of Cassino during the Second World War, was famous for his battle orders which ended with the words: 'Well, gentlemen, there is nothing more I can do. Now the battle is yours.'

Fred Allen faced similar situations. At the end of his final training session, or perhaps at his team talk, he invariably closed with the words, 'Well, that's it — now it's over to you.'

'Most young men, no matter how hard they try to convey a different impression, are extremely nervous before a big game,' says Fred. 'I've had a number of young players sick through sheer nervous tension.

'Grahame Thorne was one. I felt very sorry for him. He was a player with exceptional talent but he used to get so tensed up in the dressing room he sometimes threw up. Then he'd go out and play like a man possessed. And when he scored a try, he'd vomit again. On more

Fred sometimes left his seat to check on the well-being of the brilliant, but often 'tensed up' Grahame Thorne.

than one occasion I had to leave my seat and go down to the field to help him.

'I've never told anybody this before but one thing I couldn't do on the morning of a big match was eat — not a single thing. I'd just have to wait until the game was over. I got pretty worked up and just before the kick-off I began to worry about the things I might have missed. And I got through a few cigarettes, I can tell. Like all ex-servicemen, I used to smoke in those days.

'But I never let the players know how I was feeling. That wouldn't have done them any good at all.

'I concentrated on one thing. The older, more experienced players would be reasonably calm, but some of the new ones would be pretty nervous. It was my job to build up their confidence and get them all on the same wavelength. It was absolutely essential that they go on to the field believing in themselves

Fred imparts his knowledge on All Blacks front-rowers 'Jazz' Muller, Bruce McLeod and
Alister Hopkinson.

and believing they could win. In my experience, the very thought of winning concentrates a team's mind.

'I have always believed that anything I could say to a team to boost their confidence and calm their nerves immediately before a game was well worth while.

'It is important that the focus of the players should be on the game they are about to play, instead of worrying about their opponents. This business of playing only as well as the other side lets you is bloody rubbish. It's your business to call the tune — and make them dance to it.

'There was a time when British critics didn't believe in coaching. Some maintained that our players were being brainwashed into believing they must win at all costs — even if it involved people getting injured. That, of course, was absolute bullshit.

'If a team of 15 intelligent men — like the great guys I was in charge of — was ordered to win, no matter what, I would expect them to flatly refuse. And what's more, I'd be right behind them. I've got no time for coaches who preach warfare. Some of them get away with it for a while but they don't last very long.

'One of the fascinations of rugby is that it is such a demanding test of body and mind. The small boy who flings himself on the ball at the feet of a raging pack composed of other small boys will not have to suffer many more severe demands of his mental and physical courage during the rest of his life.

'If, because of training and discipline, he can do this unpleasant task without flinching and can actually check the rush he will have added greatly to his courage and self-esteem.

'I have never been embarrassed about speaking bluntly — as a lot of my players found out. In fact, it always worked. If you are candid with your players they will, after a time, be candid with you. And this, take it from me, is a great help to any coach.

'But bluntness wasn't the whole answer. There were times when I had to realise that some players didn't appreciate my directness — so it was sometimes important to be subtle. That's why I developed a little trick which the boys came to call "Fred's white lies".

'If I wanted to ginger them up before a game, for instance, I might say, "Well, I've just met their coach and he tells me his boys think they're sitters today." Some of my team might think, "The Needle's having us on again", but they could never be quite sure. The others would be saying, "Sitters, eh? We'll see who the bloody sitters are when we get out on that paddock!"

'Soon the doubters and the doers in my team would all be thinking the same way and we'd be just that little bit more determined. It helped every time.

'I always had a long talk with the team when we assembled for our first

He might have played his entire career in the backs, but Fred knew a thing or two about scrum training.

training run after a game. I insisted the players come forward with any suggestions they might have about what went wrong, or how to improve our play. I found this a very useful exercise. A lot of valuable ideas come from it.

'At first some of the new chaps were a bit shy about speaking out in front of the others, but they soon got over that and we made a lot of progress about how things should be done next time.

'Those meetings were very important because we talked through each problem until everyone was happy. But I always had the final say.'

The Needle used his own brand of psychology to fire up his players. When he was coaching Auckland, for example, there was the famous occasion of the missing Ranfurly Shield. It was the custom for the team to have the shield with them at each defence but this time it was nowhere to be seen.

Someone asked Fred where it was and he said: 'Canterbury are so sure they're going to take it off us today that they wanted me to loan it to them so they could pose with it for a picture in the Christchurch *Press*.'

The effect on the players was clear to see. 'Cheeky bastards!' they muttered, and they were still seething when they left their hotel and boarded the team bus for Eden Park. Sitting in his usual seat near the driver, Fred was inwardly smiling. He knew where the shield was hidden. And he wasn't going to tell them until the time was right!

Moulding a team often meant stamping on excessive individualism, and during training Fred did not hesitate to single out players he considered were offending. These included stars like Mac Herewini and Albie Pryor. 'I regarded Herewini as a remarkable but sometimes excessively brilliant player. And Albie, despite being a prop forward, hungered for the ball and had a bit too much instinct for the loose.

'There were times when Albie made spectacular runs, and let's face it, he did score tries that few other forwards could emulate. But I often had to remind these two colourful characters that they sometimes needed to curb their individual efforts for the sake of the team. You don't build team-play on individualism. It's the other way round — you build individualism on team play, and that's a totally different thing.

'So I made it very clear to this talented pair that what I required above all else was discipline and teamwork. And, I must say, it worked. When they channelled their talents correctly they both played wonderful football.

'And as far as Mac Herewini was concerned, he could sum up a situation in a split second and place a tactical kick on a threepenny piece. It's a skill we don't see enough of these days.

'Far too often the ball goes straight to an opposing player who immediately sets up a counter-attack. That's bad kicking when there's so much open space.

'There wasn't one occasion, no matter where we were or what we were doing, that I said anything to undermine the authority of any of my captains. With men like Wilson Whineray, Brian Lochore and Bob Graham that would have been stupid.

'But there were occasions when it was necessary to address one or two things at halftime, things I had seen from the grandstand. In those days both teams remained on the field during the interval and if I thought players were making mistakes and needed a shake-up, I'd make no bones about going out and telling them.'

Harold Paton, of the *Auckland Star*, once wrote: 'I can hear him now on the sideline. It was halftime and he was tearing two or three players apart with very strong language.

'But he also patted one bloke on the back and said, "Well done, Mike."'

Pinetree

Fred Allen feels 'bloody scared' when he realises the extent of the problem he's created for himself.

'I'd pitted myself against the toughest, roughest, most dreaded man in the game — Pinetree Meads — and I knew damn well I'd put myself at risk,' Fred says.

'We were in Toulouse at the time preparing for the test against France during the 1967 tour. Colin and I were discussing the merits of open, running rugby and, without considering the consequences, I said that he wouldn't be able to stop me from scoring if he were the only player between me and the goal-line.

'To prove my point I suggested we put it to the test with me starting from the 25-yard line and using only the left-hand side of the field.

'He immediately accepted the challenge and it was decided to test my theory at training the following day. The news quickly spread through the All Blacks camp and before long the entire team was talking about little else.

'That evening the realisation hit me. I had really dropped myself in it — and to tell the truth I was scared. I was about to go head to head with the mightiest forward in the world — 6 ft 4 in tall and 16 stone of sheer rock-hard muscle. And he was pretty fast as well. And to make matters worse he was in superb physical condition whereas I, the coach, hadn't played rugby for years.

'Pinetree' Meads wins a lineout for the All Blacks against France, 1968.

'I went to our manager Charlie Saxton and tried to get him to quietly call the whole thing off without embarrassing me.

'"You know what he's like, Charlie," I said. "He'll break every bone in my body. He doesn't know any other way!"

'"We can't call it off now, Fred," Charlie replied. "Everybody knows about it and you've got no idea the number of bets that have been laid — money, souvenirs, you name it."

'I was stuck with it. I couldn't think of any other way to avoid the confrontation so that afternoon Pinetree and I lined up with the entire All Blacks team barracking from the sidelines.

'I took off down the left side of the field, planning to side-step him because I thought his size would prevent him from moving as fast as me,' says Fred. 'As I neared him I accelerated and stepped to my right. I almost got clear but he just managed to get hold of my jersey and I couldn't shake the big bugger off. But somehow I managed to struggle the last couple of metres to the goal-line.

'As I fell to force the ball, this huge man crashed down on top of me. I felt every bone in my body bend under the impact. I won't even attempt to describe the agony. But I had won the bet and as Pinetree pulled me to my feet he said, "Right Fred, you won that one — now we'll have another go."

'"Like bloody hell we will!" I gasped.'

That duel between two great rugby icons did more than demonstrate their developing respect and friendship. It was also a demonstration of how determined Fred was to introduce open, running rugby into the All Blacks team.

When he had been appointed coach of the All Blacks in 1966 Fred had sensed a certain reservation from Meads and other veteran members of the squad. After all, these were the players who had helped secure such an awesome reputation for the All Blacks. The very name of the team was synonymous with success.

And suddenly here was this new boy on the block intent on introducing an entirely different style of play. Sure, he had a tremendous reputation because, after all, look how he had steered Auckland to a record run of Ranfurly Shield defences and how he had been such an outstanding captain in his playing days. But even so . . .

Fred knew that his first challenge was to win their trust. And he also knew that some of them would find difficulty in coming to terms with the fact that he was a strict disciplinarian, the strongest, in fact, ever to coach an All Blacks side.

'Take the time Colin Meads yawned during my team-talk,' says Fred. 'Pages have been written about the incident — about me threatening to send him home on the bus. Yes, Colin did yawn and, yes, I did single him out and take him to task. But my main purpose was to capture the attention of the younger players. They knew immediately that if I was strong enough to criticise the greatest forward in the world I certainly wouldn't spare them should they ever cross the line.

'I've been repeatedly asked who I consider the greatest player I've ever seen and my answer is always the same — Colin Meads. And it wasn't only his outstanding all-round play that made him so special; it was his courage and his determination to win for the sake of his country.

Those qualities shone through brightly at Colombes Stadium in Paris in November 1967, when the All Blacks beat the French 21–15. During that match Meads suffered a vicious attack while stretched full-length on the ground. A French forward deliberately kicked his head and Meads, seriously hurt, writhed in agony.

His teammates had never before seen him so slow to get to his feet. And when he finally did stand up they saw a huge gash above his left ear.

'And what did Colin do then?' Fred says. 'He plunged straight back into the next lineout, determined to play on for the sake of the team. When the Scottish doctor who had been assigned to us examined the wound in the changing room after the game he found it needed more than a dozen stitches. But all he had in his bag was a bottle of gin — he'd forgotten his anaesthetic.

'But Pinetree just sat there and told him to go ahead and stitch it up. When the needle went in, the big man didn't even flinch — acted as if he didn't give a damn. It was too much for some of the young chaps. One or two came close to throwing up.

'It has been said that I once dropped Colin from a test match,' says Fred Allen, 'but that is totally untrue. But there was one period in 1970 during which I wouldn't have allowed him on the field, had I been the coach.

'Only six minutes into the clash with Eastern Transvaal Colin emerged from a ruck with his arm dangling by his side. He carried on for 20 minutes before going to the sideline for medical advice. He told the doctor who examined his arm that it was hurting, but the doctor didn't think it was broken. He said it was merely a bruise. Colin's attitude was: "Well, if it isn't broken I'm not going off. I'd be a wimp if I did."

'The arm was bandaged and Colin pitched straight back into what was probably the dirtiest game of the tour. He saw the first half out and then, in spite of the fractured arm, played the entire 40 minutes of the second spell.

'When he reached the All Blacks changing room after the game he couldn't

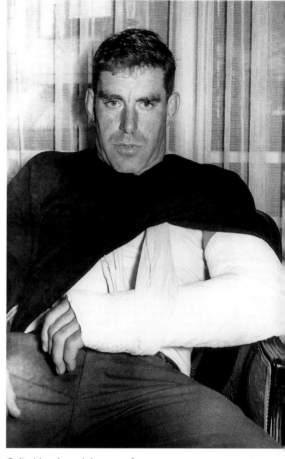

Colin Meads and the most famous broken arm of 1970.

raise his arm to take off his jersey so the doctor cut it away with a pair of scissors. He was taken to hospital and when x-rays showed a complete fracture of his lower left arm they encased it in a plaster cast. But even the heavy cast didn't stop him from training. He was determined to get back on the field as soon as he could.

'To hasten his return he had a protective shield made to cover the area of the break which had not yet fully mended. Then he had to be cleared by the South African Rugby Board because there was the suspicion that he might use the guard as some sort of weapon. In the end he played five games wearing the protective shield, including one test match.

'To my way of thinking that was not a wise thing to do,' says Fred. 'He could have done himself irreparable harm.'

The game in which Colin Meads' arm was broken was one of the roughest ever played. It was a well known fact that Danie Craven, the president of the South African Rugby Board, had encouraged the provincial teams to soften up the All Blacks before the all-important test matches. The more the All Blacks could be intimidated by forward power, the better. It was one of the ploys he had used against Fred Allen's side in 1949.

The Eastern Transvaal XV heeded Craven's message and went to war with a vengeance. The assault on the All Blacks was so bad that Alex Veysey, sports editor of the Wellington newspaper, the *Dominion*, got really carried away. 'The Eastern Transvaal team dragged their match tactics out of a witch's cauldron,' he wrote. There was blatant obstruction, late tackling and barging. No fewer than 12 All Blacks were injured and were unable to compete the following week. Apart from Meads they included Alan Smith, who was bashed unconscious, Alan Sutherland, who suffered a broken nose and Sid Going whose ankle was badly wrenched.

The *New Zealand Herald*'s sportswriter, T.P. McLean, made no bones about the fact that the thuggery was intentional. He was convinced that Meads' arm had been deliberately kicked while he was on the ground.

But in spite of all the mayhem the All Blacks played with skill and determination and came out the winners 24 points to 3.

A further example of Colin Meads' fortitude had nothing to do with rugby. It came shortly after the end of his international career. One night in December 1971 a neighbour came across a crashed Land Rover beside the road a couple of kilometres from Meads' farm. Lying beside it was an unconscious man. It was Colin, who had been thrown from the vehicle when it crashed. The badly injured man was rushed to hospital where he remained unconscious throughout the night. When he came to the next morning he got out of bed and tried to stand up, but fell over, ripping away the attached drip tubes.

Most of the skin had been ripped from his back, but the injury to his spine was far more serious — he had broken some vertebrae. He badgered the doctors to remove the cast which encased him from his armpits to his waist and let him go home. They refused to do so. So he grudgingly wore it for three months until the end of March 1972.

Before the accident he had been nursing hopes of playing for the All Blacks again. There was a tour set down for Britain and France in 1973 followed by a visit to New Zealand of his old foes, the Springboks.

He would be 37 years old but his heart was still in it. Then he got calls from some of his friends, including Fred Allen, who told him to think long and hard before he made his decision, especially about the Springboks.

Peter Bush's classic photo of Colin Meads against the Lions, 1971.

Colin Meads' distinguished first-class career came to an end in 1973. Here, in his second to last match, he leads his President's XV team out to face Ian Kirkpatrick's All Blacks.

It was because of advice from friends like Fred that Colin made the decision to give international rugby away. New Zealand was sad to see him go. He was one of their favourite sons and they would miss him dearly.

But he kept his promise to his Waitete Club and continued playing club and sub-union rugby for the next two years.

On 4 August 1973 he led the New Zealand President's Invitation XV onto Athletic Park, Wellington to play the All Blacks.

Forty-five thousand fans packed the park that day to see their hero in action once again, and they cheered themselves hoarse when Meads' team prevailed by 35 points to 28. It was to have been Colin's swansong, but still they wouldn't let him go. Before a capacity crowd at Eden Park the following Saturday, 11 August, he led an Invitation XV against the All Blacks again, and this time it was the men in black who prevailed.

The score of 22–10 was of no great moment — of far greater concern was the fact that the long and distinguished career of the great Colin Meads was over.

It was appropriate that his final game was on Eden Park, the revered patch of turf on which he had first played in the Roller Mills Shield 25 years earlier at the age of 11.

If ever Fred Allen felt sadness for one of his players it was the legend's ordering off just minutes before the end of the Scottish test at Murrayfield in 1967.

'I was the coach and I saw what happened very clearly,' Fred says. 'Colin, hard and tough as he is, was never a dirty player. He was stretching to kick the ball ahead and when he made contact it struck David Chisholm's body as he stooped to pick it up. It's very clear on the video replay. There was never the slightest intention to injure the Scottish halfback.

'Chisholm, himself, was convinced of this. As the referee was ordering Colin off, the little halfback hurried over to Meads and patted him on the shoulder in a friendly manner as if to say, "No problem, Colin."

'If Colin had intended to kick Chisholm he would have gone right through the little bloke. But, as you can see from the replay, he's leaning back, stretching for the ball. I'm convinced of that and will be to my dying day.

'And another thing that made my blood boil was the fact that an adjudication committee appointed by the International Rugby Board suspended Colin for two matches, Monmouthshire and East Wales, and warned him as to his future conduct.

'The fact that the committee took this action solely on the referee's evidence — and without allowing Colin to appear in his own defence — was, to my mind, shockingly unfair.

'I don't think I've ever been sorrier for someone than I was for Colin that day. It was a crying shame to see the greatest forward in the world walking from the field with his bandaged head bowed in absolute misery. When I went into the changing room and saw him sitting there close to tears, my heart went out to him.

'I'd got to know him very well. He was a tough, unyielding King Country farmer who, by sheer hard work and love for his country, had elevated himself to the top of the rugby world. Now, through no fault of his own, his whole world had collapsed around him.

'Take it from me, they got it horribly wrong.'

The following morning the All Blacks flew from Edinburgh to Cardiff. When they arrived at the airport there were photographers and a small crowd to meet them. One was the great Welsh centre Bleddyn Williams, who immediately sought out Fred.

'How about coming to my place this afternoon and we'll try to cheer Colin up?' he said. 'I'll get a few friends around and we'll have a laugh and a bit of fun.'

'I think that's a very good idea,' Fred replied.

So after they had taken their luggage to their hotel, and had a change and a clean-up, Fred, Tremain, Gray, Lochore, MacRae and Meads took taxis to Williams' house. Several of Bleddyn's friends, including a few of the 1950 Lions, were already there.

'Bleddyn put on lots of bright music,' says Fred, 'and there was plenty to eat and drink. We danced with his two daughters who were about 14 years old and I only wish we had taken some photos of Colin who, for the first time since Murrayfield, seemed to enjoy himself.

'After what he had been through the previous day it did him a world of good, and I made sure that Bleddyn knew just how much we all appreciated his kindness. It was a wonderful gesture on his part and it said a great deal for the spirit of rugby.'

The Flipside

Despite his fearsome reputation The Needle shows a surprisingly tender and compassionate nature.

In the world of rugby Fred Allen was known as a tough, unyielding taskmaster but there were things he did throughout his life which revealed a very different side to his nature. Take, for instance, eight-year-old Nola McGowan, of Manly, Whangaparaoa, who was excited when she learned she'd be accompanying her parents to a family wedding. But there was a niggling worry: Nola didn't have a suitable dress to wear — not one she really liked.

A personal friend of her schoolteacher parents, Bill and Matija, was Fred Allen. On one of Fred's visits he chanced to hear Nola talking to her parents about the possibility of a new dress.

A week later Nola was concerned when she was called out of her classroom to go to the headmaster's office at Whangaparaoa Primary School. What could he possibly want with her? Had she done something wrong?

She was nervous as she knocked on the principal's door. Although he was her father, at school he was very much the headmaster. But as she entered the room, her concern turned to surprise for with him was Mr Allen.

'Hello, Nola,' said the famous All Black, 'I've got a present for you.' Then, from behind his back, he produced a beautiful little dress.

Nola McGowan, now a prominent solicitor in Whangaparaoa, with Fred in 2011, 44 years after Fred had made her dress — and her day.

'I remember it as though it were yesterday,' Nola says. 'It was maroon and waisted and had little buttons down the front with a frill trimmed with black. I was taken to the staff room where I tried it on. It fitted me perfectly. It was magic. I almost burst with excitement.'

Fred, who was off to Canada, the British Isles and France as All Blacks coach two days later, had taken time from his busy schedule to make sure the dress fitted in case it needed altering. It had meant a round trip from Auckland of more than 70 kilometres.

Another magic moment for little Nola came months later when Fred returned from that highly successful tour. He had seen Nola's collection of dolls during his visits to the McGowan household and between games in various countries he had done a little shopping. One of his purchases was an exotic Indian doll wearing a beautiful red sari.

On his first visit to Nola's home after his arrival home, he handed the little girl a neatly wrapped parcel. 'I thought you might like this,' he said.

Nola opened the packet and gaped in wonder. 'When I saw that marvellous doll I couldn't stop trembling with excitement,' she remembers. 'It was such an adorable treasure and even now, more than 40 years later, it still has pride of place in our china cabinet.'

Another treasure from that era hangs today on the office wall of a prominent Whangaparaoa lawyer — a large autographed caricature of Fred Allen in All

Blacks gear. That lawyer is the little girl who was once given a beautiful maroon dress and an exotic Indian doll. Her name is Nola McGowan.

For several years Fred took time off work to attend the annual gala day fashion parade at Orewa College. There he utilised his knowledge of the clothing industry as sole judge of garments being modelled by the girls who had made them during home economics lessons.

After assessing the workmanship and imaginative designs, he presented bolts of materials he had donated as prizes. And it was not only the major winners who were rewarded — he created enough categories to make sure that everyone received an award.

'The girls loved him and crowded round him,' former deputy-principal Matija McGowan explains. 'They thought he was a god.'

A former player, coach, chairman and president of the Suburbs Rugby Club in Auckland, Keith Lawson, was another to benefit from Fred's generous spirit. When Keith was at Avondale College his hero was the Kiwis Army star Fred Allen. He avidly read every newspaper account of Fred's triumphs during the team's tour after the war and was enthralled when snippets of games were screened at cinemas in Auckland.

When the Army Team came to Auckland to play on Eden Park Keith was right there. 'It was even more magical than seeing him on film,' he says. 'Here, right in front of me, was the man who'd inspired me so much he'd clinched my determination to play rugby.'

It was now 1992 and Keith's sixty-first birthday was coming up in a week's time. He had just come out of critical care following successful surgery for the removal of a tumour on his brain and his family was thrilled. It was to be a real home-coming celebration.

Midway through the afternoon the front doorbell rang. Believing it be another family member, Keith opened the door. For a moment he could not believe his eyes. There, standing in the doorway, was the great Fred Allen!

'Hello, Keith,' Fred said, as he shook Keith's hand. 'I've just popped in to wish you a happy birthday.'

'I was shell-shocked,' says Keith. 'I hardly knew what to say. My lifetime hero, whom I'd never met or spoken to in my life, had actually come to *my* home to see *me*. I couldn't believe it. I could never have had a better birthday surprise.

'When I pulled myself together I invited him inside and we talked for at least two hours. The others didn't mind because they could see how excited I was.'

Naturally, Keith wondered how on earth Fred had known it was his birthday.

He later learned it was through a mutual friend at the Silverdale RSA who had told Fred about the wonderful work Keith had done as president of the Suburbs club and how he had once taken the Suburbs senior squad to Argentina. The friend also told Fred how Keith had recently survived a major operation and the family was celebrating at his home on his birthday.

'When Keith saw Fred Allen at the door the look of surprise on his face was unbelievable,' says wife Vera. 'We talk about it to this day. If only I'd had a camera. The warmth and charisma of the man — it was mesmerising.

'It was the best medicine Keith could ever have had.'

When Scottish rugby enthusiast David Mercer was 14 years old he was so badly injured in a rugby accident he was doomed to spend the rest of his days totally paralysed. David's neck had been broken when a scrum collapsed and so severe was his injury that even his speech was affected.

While the 1967 All Blacks were being trained by Fred on a school ground in Edinburgh they saw young David in a group of admiring schoolboys watching from the sideline. He was in a wheelchair accompanied by his physiotherapist.

Fred called a halt to training so that he and some of his players could chat with the boy. Then they carried the youngster upstairs to the lounge of the school pavilion.

'Would you like to see the All Blacks play on Wednesday?' Fred asked the youngster. David's face clouded. He would, of course, nothing could be greater — but it would be impossible to get in.

'Impossible my foot!' said Fred.

The next day David was driven to Melrose to watch the game against Scottish Districts. When he arrived, the All Blacks carried him from his car to the grandstand where he sat with the New Zealand reserves who explained the game to him, and made him feel comfortable.

After the match they carried him back to the car and promised to see him again at the test against Scotland. On the Saturday, true to their word, the All Blacks again met the boy and carried him to a prime seat in the Murrayfield Stadium.

David was overwhelmed with joy. He had mixed feelings about the result — a 14–3 victory for the All Blacks — but he was also pleased by the success of his new friends from New Zealand.

The next day All Blacks manager Charlie Saxton received a letter from the boy's headmaster expressing appreciation at the treatment young David had been given.

The All Blacks felt no need for thanks. With his bright and cheery smile the brave young lad from Edinburgh had made them all feel humble.

Young Reuben Wickstead with Fred's All Blacks cap.

And it's not just people who benefit from the gentler side of Fred Allen's nature — it's also dogs. And that's why, although he is a meticulous dresser, he often has crumbs in the right-hand pocket of his jacket.

That's because, when visiting friends, he always has a biscuit for their dogs. His friends know that when Fred arrives on their doorstep they have to wait until he's finished making a fuss of their animals, and giving them the customary treat — a morsel of biscuit.

There is an aura surrounding Fred Allen which children have always been drawn towards. Fred never fails to offer words of advice and has a legendary soft spot for young people. Not long after he was 'capped' by the New Zealand Rugby Union, Fred was visiting friends who live nearby. He brought with him his newly-acquired cap which he placed on the head of young Reuben Wickstead. The look of admiration and pleasure on the lad's face said it all. And when he had his photo taken with the great coach it was a thrill he will never forget.

Few of the people Fred helped so cheerfully realised that for many years he and Norma were nursing a secret sorrow — the drug addiction of their beloved son Murray.

'He was a great kid,' says Fred. 'He had a strong sense of humour and he made friends easily. We were so proud of him and he seemed set for a wonderful future. What we didn't know, however, was that for some time he'd been hanging out with the wrong people.

'One day he brought three young guys to our house. One look at them was enough for me — they weren't the type I wanted my son mixing with. I knew at once they were the bastards who had tempted him into drugs. I won't tell you what I said to them or what I did, but Norma and I were devastated. For years we sought the best help available, but unfortunately it was too late.'

Sadly, Murray passed away in his sleep. He was only 42.

Ambassador Abroad

An eminent judge pays tribute to Fred for the manner in which he helps and inspires young players.

One of New Zealand's most esteemed judges, Michael J.A. Brown, a former Chancellor of the University of Auckland, was acutely aware of the valuable work Fred was doing for young people both in New Zealand and overseas. Because of his profession, the judge had first-hand knowledge of just how much the great coach was influencing and inspiring young players, not only on the rugby field but in their daily lives as well.

So impressed was the judge that he lent his weight behind a submission recommending Fred be recognised for a royal honour. A section of his statement reads:

> *I record my profound respect for Mr Allen. His astonishing record as a New Zealand sporting icon is legend and needs no further recitation from me. Rather it is his wider contribution to New Zealand, particularly his extraordinary generosity of time and talents with regard to monitoring and inspiring young people that I wish to draw your attention....*
>
> *Because of my own interest in the welfare of young people there have been numerous occasions where I have either observed his efforts or where some act of personal generosity by him has been brought to my attention....*

Throughout so much of the sporting community, which as a country we value, Mr Allen's name and his influence on the lives of literally hundreds of young sportspersons is revered.

Judge Michael J.A. Brown, Auckland.

When Fred's playing and coaching days at international level were over, his willingness to do whatever he could for the game of rugby remained undimmed and when asked for help he never hesitated to pack his bags and travel — even to the other side of the world.

As far back as 1974, when he could well lay claim to being the best rugby coach in the world, he accepted an invitation to the United States to assist a number of unions and clubs in dire need of help. For several weeks he lectured and coached in major cities and it is more than likely that the American rugby team competing in the 2011 World Cup might never have made it to New Zealand had it not been for that visit.

Rugby in the States had come close to disappearing in the 1920s because of the public's overwhelming preference for American-style football. After a few years, however, the game reappeared, especially in the San Francisco area. But its recovery was painfully slow and unless it could be given a major boost, its future again looked bleak.

It was at this stage that Fred was approached by the international firm of Lane Walker Rudkin, asking him if he would go to America on a goodwill coaching tour to see if he could make a difference.

'They knew damn well that I would jump at the chance because of my passion for the game and my desire to see it promoted in the weaker rugby nations of the world,' says Fred. 'So the next thing Norma and I were making arrangements for the running of our business and I was on my way.

'When I arrived in the States I found that a lengthy itinerary had been arranged and for the next few weeks I was extremely busy. The clubs I visited looked after the travel costs and arranged my accommodation, usually in members' homes. Not only were they extremely hospitable people, they were also mad on rugby and that was a plus from the start.

'From the moment I arrived I realised that coaching of quality was non-existent. At the most I'd give it two out of 10.

'From time to time they had players coming over from England, plus a few from Wales and Ireland, but these newcomers weren't coaches and they didn't have the knowledge to improve the standard of play in their new country.'

The Americans, used to a lackadaisical style of training, wondered what

Washington's Capitol Hill forms the backdrop for this training session under Fred's guidance in 1974.

had struck them when Fred appeared on the scene. Every day for the next few weeks he was hard at work running training sessions and mentoring coaches at colleges, clubs and defence academies in cities like Boston, Philadelphia, Washington and New York.

Initially, the Americans were jolted by the unrelenting hard work and discipline imposed by this affable Kiwi. But when their play began to improve in leaps and bounds they came to realise there was much more to coaching than they had ever dreamed possible.

'One day in Washington we were training hard right near the White House,' Fred recalls. 'I was working on a scrum and there was this enormous forward whose back was bent almost double.

'I told him a number of times what was wrong, but he wouldn't take the slightest notice. So I grabbed him by his hair, jerked him upright and told him to listen to what I was saying — and get his bloody back straight!

'He'd been an American grid-iron player and jeez he was big, 20 stone at least. He could easily have pulverised me. But this time he did as he was told and what a difference he made to that scrum.

'When we were going back to the changing rooms he came over, shook my hand and thanked me for my help. It makes a coach feel really good when someone does something like that after you've been flogging them up and down the field for an hour or so. That shows a man's true character and makes the hard work all worthwhile.'

159

Fred's coaching in America worked wonders, a fact that became increasingly clear by the letters of gratitude which arrived in New Zealand on his return home.

Dr Joseph Walsh, president of the New England Rugby Football Union, Massachusetts:

Fred Allen spent four days in Boston and accomplished much more than I believed possible in that short time. His coaching of our union XV showed immediate results and the effects of his work with college students will undoubtedly be seen in the seasons to come. One valuable contribution was his stress on the importance of fundamentals. Now that Fred has said it, the players believe it, and the work of our coaches has become much easier. Fred Allen's visit was an unqualified success.

Joe Regan, coach of the Philadelphia Rugby Club: 'Everyone in Philadelphia thoroughly enjoyed Fred's visit. He expanded our knowledge of the game and his enthusiasm for rugby was contagious. Everyone was impressed by Fred Allen, the man.'

Geoffrey Berry, coach of the Vanderbilt University Rugby Club, was so eager to catch sessions with Fred that he and his assistant flew specially to New York from Nashville, Tennessee. He wrote: 'Fred is a great sport and a tremendous coach. His visit has been a great stimulus to rugby over here. His visit was indeed a great success and he was a fine ambassador for rugby and New Zealand.'

Ben Spillard, Philadelphia Rugby Club: 'The direction and encouragement given to the game by Fred Allen has been of enormous value.'

Ron Bragg, club captain Condor Rugby Football Club: 'Your inspiration and immense contribution brought greatness to our country, and the writer believes all rugby peoples to be forever in your debt. Our club members drink a toast to you and wish you good health and longevity.'

Because American football had such a powerful hold in the United States there was considerable scepticism that rugby would progress no further. But Fred did not agree then and he does not agree now.

'I have always felt that with the right coaching the United States could become a force to be reckoned with on the world stage,' he says. 'They were big, strong men and some were incredibly fast, especially the Black Americans. And they had unbelievable enthusiasm, which was half the battle.'

He cites the fact that in 2010 rugby in the United States had 2300 clubs and 90,000 registered members — an increase of more than 50,000 since the World Cup in 2003.

'They are taking things very seriously,' he says. 'They have appointed former

English captain Nigel Melville as their CEO and have engaged Eddie O'Sullivan, a former coach of Ireland, to look after their international side, the Eagles.

In 1984 Bob Howitt, editor of the popular publication *Rugby News*, came up with a brilliant idea — to select New Zealand's most talented under-21 players and send them overseas to compete against similar age groups in the world's top rugby countries. There was one man, Bob felt, who would be ideal to lead these youth teams on their annual ventures, and that man was Fred Allen.

He contacted Fred who, recognising the potential value for the future of the game, agreed to take charge. When he was advised he would be able to take an assistant, he nominated former All Blacks halfback Sid Going for the position.

For the next five years Fred managed these under-21 teams on overseas tours of Canada, the United States, England, Wales, Scotland, Ireland, Germany and Holland.

The fact that they were not once defeated — and also produced no fewer than 15 All Blacks — was an incredible achievement and yet another demonstration of Fred's extraordinary ability.

Again a flood of mail arrived in New Zealand. Typical was a letter to Fred from Peter Brewster, Nottingham, England:

> *Please accept from me and numerous thousands of Rugby followers my sincere thanks for bringing back to this country Rugby football as it should be played. With their sense of discipline and physical fitness your players represent to me and my generation all that is good in amateur sport.*

When Fred finally decided to stand down, the coaching of the *Rugby News* youth teams was handed over to Peter Thorburn, with Sid Going again second in charge.

In a letter of thanks to Fred, Bob Howitt wrote:

> *On behalf of all of us at* Rugby News *I want to thank you for your mighty contribution to the establishment and success of our youth teams.*
>
> *It was no more than a hopeful concept back in 1984 when you first became involved but now it ranks as one of the most prestigious teams in the country.*
>
> *In your inimitable way you have helped shape dozens of young footballers who are the richer for the experience.*

A further glowing compliment came from another of Fred's admirers, the Governor-General Sir David Beattie, who several times played against Fred in club games. A short extract reads:

Fred Allen is a giant in the game. Success never turned his head and he has always been held in the highest esteem by public and players alike. His influence on both the players and the game has been profound.

Fred was quick to realise that one of the basic requirements for the development of rugby was the enthusiasm and encouragement of youth, and it was for this reason that his dedication to the game has never wavered. That is why, on his regular business trips throughout New Zealand, Fred has always made a point of calling on officials of local clubs, or watching games in the areas through which he passed.

Many letters of appreciation came to his letterbox at Manly Beach, such as the one from Neil Neilsen, King Country selector:

This letter is to convey to you my sincere thanks for the help you have always readily given our country union selectors. At all times you have been available for discussions and at every opportunity you have attended games in our areas and discussed our problems with us.

There was never the suggestion of a let-up. For many years Fred attended every primary schools Roller Mills Shield tournament on the Auckland Domain — keenly watching young players and occasionally offering words of advice.

On many occasions he was accompanied by former All Blacks hooker Arthur Hughes, a close friend who was also an advocate of teaching youngsters the correct skills at an early age.

Fred always left the Domain with plenty to think about — some of it good, some not so good. He had watched a lot of excellent football, and seen a number of promising players. But his main concern was always the manner in which many of the parents and so-called coaches had behaved.

'It was great to see fathers and mothers barracking for their kids,' he says, 'but some of those people really overdid it as they ran up and down the sidelines screaming their heads off. I saw youngsters from eight to 12 being abused by their parents when they did something wrong — and, worse still, when they did something right!

'Now that's sad. I hate to think what that sort of behaviour does to a young fellow's confidence and self-respect. A youngster who is getting yelled at by a parent or a coach in that fashion is even likely to steer clear of the ball to avoid being embarrassed in front of his peers.

'It's good to see kids trying their hardest to win for their school but rugby, especially at this age, must be fun. Those parents should know better. I suspect some of them are trying to relive their own careers through the ability of their children.

'When I was a kid, I was lucky. I had a mother who was there most of the time.

But she didn't behave like some of the people I saw on the Domain. Whenever I did something good, she gave me a smile and a little clap. It was just between the two of us. It made me feel great and it spurred me on.

'And another thing Mum always did was make sure I had a pair of garters to hold up my socks. She used to buy a length of elastic and make them herself. She wanted me to be neat and tidy for the sake of my team.'

Fred has always been a fan of secondary schools rugby, especially the games against Auckland Grammar where for some years the headmaster was John Graham, one of his ex-All Blacks.

'During John's era I never once saw bad sportsmanship or fighting,' he says. 'It just didn't happen in school rugby in those days. But times have changed. Today I see terrible flaws in some of our secondary school players, and that's a great pity. I see arguments with referees, vicious fighting, blatant late charges, socks around the ankles even when players run onto the field — all that sort of thing.

'You might think I'm being petty about the socks but, to me, the appearance of a team says a great deal about the players — and the coach.

'I watched some of that school violence on the evening news and it looked pretty bad. Those young footballers lacked discipline and that's what every youngster must have — discipline and self-control.

'I can tell you here and now that none of those guys I saw slinging punches non-stop would be chosen in any team of mine.

'And besides, it's only a game, remember.'

When it comes to charity events, Fred has always been generous with his time. Here he is with a bowls team made up of great mates 'Tiger' Weir (left), Barry McCrystal and co-author Alan Sayers at the Remuera Bowling Club where money was being raised for the St Joseph's Hospice in Epsom.

Land of Song

The passionate crescendo of sound at Cardiff Arms Park was something Fred had never before experienced.

Fred was enthralled by the Welsh passion for rugby and when it came to the fervour of test matches at Cardiff Arms Park he was blown away. Never before had he seen such emotion in a rugby stadium when a choir led the vast crowd in a rousing rendering of 'Hen Wlad Fy Nhadau' — 'Land of my Fathers'.

When the thousands of full-throated fans joined in that national anthem, and in favourites such as 'Cwm Rhondda' or 'Calon Lan' — and with the sound of singing flowing far beyond the confines of the stadium — the atmosphere was electric.

'That majestic sound is Wales' answer to all challenges,' Fred says, 'and it lives in the hearts and minds of those privileged to hear it for a very long time. Music is at the heart of Welsh culture and every true Welshman believes that the mass singing is worth at least one try to the home team.'

There is a mystic Welsh word 'hiraeth' that cannot be adequately translated into English but it roughly means 'a longing or a yearning tinged with nostalgic memories'. For Welshmen overseas, those memories are of home. They are of Wales.

Fred has always been in awe of the full-throated Welsh fans.

'After several visits to the country, that's something I can thoroughly understand,' says Fred. 'I love Wales and the warmth of its people. They remind me of New Zealand. I've lost count of the number of friends I've made over there. To me it's like a second home. And the men, especially the footballers, are so like our hardy, no-nonsense New Zealand farmers. I've always thought that if I had to live in another country I would choose Wales.'

In Fred's playing and coaching days many Welsh players came from work-hardened, coal-mining families. They were powerful and fearless men who matched his own love of the sport and who, in the main, were as inherently decent as they were talented.

Typical of the players Fred admired was the legendary Gareth Edwards, who won his first international cap at 19 — and a year later became his country's youngest test captain. He was born the son of a miner in the Welsh village of Gwaun-cae-Gurwen and eventually was voted the Greatest Welsh Player of all Time by the Welsh Former International Players' Association.

Edwards captained the East Wales team which came close to breaking the remarkable winning run of Fred Allen's All Blacks during their 1967 tour of the British Isles.

'They played like men possessed and never let up on us,' says Fred. 'They were easily the best opposition we met on tour. I was never more pleased than when I heard that final whistle.'

The legendary Barry John, whose tactical kicking earned him the nickname 'The King', became one of Gareth Edwards' closest mates after switching from Llanelli to join him at the Cardiff Rugby Club. Both these fine backs played pivotal roles in that historic Cardiff Arms contest.

Three days later, in the final match of the '67 tour, the same pair, now wearing Barbarian jerseys, again came close to nudging the All Blacks off their triumphant, unbeaten perch.

Both are revered as heroes in Wales and statues of them, each carved out of a single slab of coal, are on permanent display at Millennium Stadium, which in 1999 replaced the old stands at Cardiff Arms Park.

Fred has the greatest respect for Welsh players of his era, many of whom toiled in dangerous mines deep underground.

'I was lucky enough to be taken to see what their working conditions were really like underground,' says Fred. 'About a dozen of us accepted an invitation to go down a mine in the Rhondda Valley. A couple of others turned down the offer because they were worried that being in a confined space over half a mile below the surface would be too claustrophobic.

'But as for me, I was damn glad I did go because it wasn't just interesting

— it was an experience that helped me understand more than ever why so many Welshmen played with such commitment and fervour. After a week of working in such shocking conditions so far underground, these men found rugby a glorious release. They revelled in the cleanliness of the fresh air, and the wonderful feeling of freedom — and it was all the more precious because they knew that in a couple of days they would again be toiling in the darkness and danger of the pit.'

Fred's group was told to strip to their underpants before being given grey overalls to wear. Then came the obligatory safety talk. One of the possible dangers, they were told, could be the presence of methane gas.

Over the years that lethal gas has killed thousands in Welsh mining tragedies. The worst-ever disaster was in 1913 when 439 men perished in the terrible Senghenydd explosion.

'If we get a gas warning,' said their guide, 'just run like hell.'

'I think he meant like a bloody Welsh winger,' says Fred. 'Those fellas would be away like a shot.'

As the cage descended, the only lighting in the blackness was provided by their hand-lamps and when they reached the bottom, more than half a mile below the surface, they set off towards the coal-face along a low tunnel with a railway track.

'It was very narrow and it seemed as if the sides were pressing in on us,' says Fred. 'There was just enough room for the coal-trucks with only a tiny space on either side.

'The roof was held up by props which looked strong enough, but later we learned that most miners were more anxious about the danger from beneath them, than from above. The pressure of the moisture below the floor sometimes tended to raise its level and that could be a real worry — particularly when you're already bent almost double.'

When a strident alarm warned of an approaching train, Fred's group scrambled, as instructed, to the safety of mini-caves carved into the tunnel walls and waited as a long stream of loaded trucks raced past.

'That was nerve-wracking,' admits Fred. 'The wagons were so huge and noisy and fast. And, what was worse, they seemed much too close.'

Then, crouching almost double, they walked another half mile to reach the miners toiling at the coal face.

'I hadn't expected such an amazing sight,' says Fred. 'A circular-saw type of machine on legs was ripping the coal out of the solid wall ahead and it was gigantic — probably a quarter the length of a rugby pitch. And there were these fellows around it shovelling up the loose stuff and throwing it on to a conveyor belt.

'Then the machine pulled away another great chunk and they were at it again. To think they were doing that six or seven hours a day. No wonder they were hard, tough opponents — men who deserved to be respected.'

Back on the surface, even after scrubbing and scrubbing in the showers, Fred and the others couldn't completely get rid of the black dust. 'It had got into our pores and was still coming out a week or so later,' he says. 'As for our underpants, well it was hopeless trying to get them clean. We just had to throw them away.'

Everything in South Wales is now changed and little remains of the industry which once made Cardiff the largest coal exporting port in the world. In the last 30 years the mine shafts have been either filled in or capped, the old colliery buildings have gone and supermarkets, industrial areas and playing fields have taken their place.

Gone, too, is the same breed of footballer who came from those terrible, claustrophobic mines — tough, uncompromising players who rejoiced in the joy and freedom of the rugby paddock.

'They were men who gave rugby everything they had,' says Fred. 'And now that mining in Wales is almost non-existent, we may never see their like again.'

The stately Angel Hotel in Cardiff, which opened in 1833, is Fred Allen's favourite hotel in Wales. Others who have chosen to stay there include celebrities such as Marlene Dietrich, Gregory Peck and The Beatles. Its convenient situation in Castle Street, nestled between Cardiff Castle and the new Millennium Stadium, makes it a popular base for visiting rugby teams.

It was at this hotel that the infamous Keith Murdoch incident occurred in 1972. The All Blacks were staying at The Angel when they notched their 19–16 win over Wales with Murdoch scoring their only try. And it was there that the career of this immensely strong All Black ended in the most controversial circumstances.

Hours after the game, in the early hours of the morning, Murdoch, who weighed more than 18 stone, felt in need of a snack and decided to inspect the hotel's kitchen fridge. When he was questioned by a security guard, a rowdy argument began and team manager Ernie Todd was summoned.

One report said Todd, siding with the guard, said to Murdoch, 'This time you've had it, Murdoch. You're going home.'

An incensed Murdoch responded: 'If that's the case I might as well make a job of it.' And the next thing, according to teammate Graham Whiting, the security guard was flat on the floor.

It was later revealed that Murdoch, along with the other All Blacks, had been angered during the course of the evening by the belligerent attitude of the

Welsh security guards, who had taken the day's defeat very badly.

The following morning Todd called a team meeting and reminded the players of their responsibilities on tour. He cited the Murdoch incident but said nothing about him being sent home. Murdoch was, in fact, named for the team to play in the following Wednesday's midweek game.

During the next few hours, however, things took a different turn. On the Monday morning, as the All Blacks were aboard a bus ready to take them to training, manager Todd made the startling announcement that Murdoch had been expelled from the tour and was being sent back to New Zealand. Thirty years later, it was learned that the British authorities told the New Zealand union that if Murdoch was not sent home, they would seek a replacement for Todd as manager. And if that didn't happen, they would call the tour off.

That same evening Murdoch flew out from Heathrow Airport, leaving his All Blacks teammates angered and bewildered. Naturally, the press had a field day. 'Wild Man Sent Home' was the glaring headline in the London *Evening Standard*.

Keith Murdoch exits the 1972–73 All Blacks tour in sad fashion.

But instead of returning to New Zealand as instructed, the giant forward slipped off the plane in Singapore and later surfaced in Northern Queensland where, for a number of years, he went bush.

A full year passed before he telephoned his mother in Dunedin to tell her he was alright. She pleaded with him to come home, but he assured her he was better where he was. A year later he did make a fleeting visit to see his mother before returning to Australia.

Throughout the years a number of pressmen have attempted to find and talk with Murdoch, but he has flatly refused to give an interview to any of them.

With his 50 inch chest and massive shoulders, Murdoch could well lay claim to be the strongest All Black in history.

Two Freds — Trueman and Allen — were in the Criterion Hotel in Dunedin the night Keith
Murdoch showed off his remarkable strength.

'He'd certainly get my vote,' says Fred, 'especially after one evening in the Criterion Hotel in Dunedin when I witnessed his phenomenal strength first-hand. I was having a drink with the famous English cricketer Freddie Trueman and Bert Sutcliffe, the world's best left-handed batsman, after we'd been guest speakers at a charity function in the Dunedin Town Hall.

'Keith Murdoch, a friend of the hotel proprietor, was acting as barman and he, along with everyone else in the room, was becoming increasingly annoyed at the offensive behaviour of a red-headed boozer unknown to any of us.

'This guy became so abusive that Murdoch finally said, "Don't worry, I'll get rid of him." He then vaulted his huge body across the bar, spun the red-head around, picked him up by the back of his shirt and the seat of his pants and hurled him through the large double doors at the end of the room.

'Fortunately, the swing doors opened and the poor fella went clean through and landed on the pavement,' says Fred. 'We were all amazed because he was a big man, and to see him picked up like a rag doll, and sent flying through the air, was an astonishing sight.

'Trueman and I went outside to check he was alright. We were relieved when we saw him staggering away, swearing at the top of his voice.'

Keith Murdoch was not always the 'wild man' that some reporters would have the public believe. He was enormously respected by his teammates on the 1972–73 tour of the British Isles and France. They saw him as a loyal, caring person of few words who always carried the heaviest luggage and stayed behind to clean up after festive occasions.

In his book *Beegee*, Bryan Williams wrote: 'Keith couldn't do enough for the team. It was a role he relished.'

Lin Colling, who played alongside Murdoch in the Otago team from 1969 to 1972, described him as 'a terribly considerate team man. Whenever there was a function Keith made sure everyone had a drink and afterwards he was the one who tidied up.'

The coach of that side, Eric Watson, was also impressed by Murdoch's attitude. 'After training on cold, miserable nights he was the one who went round, gathered in all the flags and put them away safely. That was his nature — the team's welfare came first.'

'It's a shame such an excellent team-man let himself down the way he did,' says Fred Allen. 'Had things been handled differently, his life may well have taken a different turn.'

Shock Victory

Fred receives a phone call from Marlborough, and a minor union wins the coveted Ranfurly Shield.

There wasn't a province strong enough to take the Ranfurly Shield away from Canterbury in 1973 — and certainly not a minor union like Marlborough.

That was the view of rugby pundits throughout New Zealand. Even the Marlborough squad shared that opinion. There was latent talent in the side, but what it needed was a massive dose of confidence and self-belief. But how could this be injected?

It was union chairman Pat Dwyer, a member of the New Zealand Rugby Council, who came up with the answer. In Auckland there was a master coach — and if anyone could accomplish such a miracle he was the man.

That evening he phoned the maestro Fred Allen. Could he possibly come down and help Marlborough for two games, one against Buller followed a week later by an all-important challenge for the Ranfurly Shield against Canterbury? Fred, who had just come back from conducting coaching clinics in America, declined the request.

Not one to give up easily, Dwyer rang again the following night. He reminded Fred that he had once played for Marlborough in 1944 when he was stationed at Woodbourne airbase, six kilometres out of Blenheim, during the war. Perhaps he would like to revisit the district and meet some old friends.

This time Fred relented. 'Okay, you've talked me into it,' he said.

The following day he flew to Blenheim, where he stayed at the home of Marlborough manager Jim Fraser.

When he first arrived Fred spent hours with the local team, teaching them things they had never known before — things he had used as coach of his great All Blacks sides that had not been beaten in 37 games. Then, in his team talk before the first game against Buller, Fred slammed into the Marlborough side.

'He began by picking on me,' said All Black Alan Sutherland, 'He really gave me the treatment and I'm certain this had a big impact on all the players.

'Then, one by one, he worked on the rest of the team. I don't know how he'd worked it out but everything he said was spot on.

'He had us so fired up that when we ran onto the paddock we felt 10 feet tall and well-nigh invincible. Buller didn't know what hit them. We hammered them 39–3.'

The Marlborough players were now gaining in confidence as they prepared for the big one the following week — the long-awaited Ranfurly Shield challenge against Canterbury. Unfortunately, Fred was recalled to Auckland for business reasons, but before he left he made a tape recording in Fraser's lounge to be played in the changing room just before kick-off.

Five minutes before they ran onto the field the Marlborough players listened intently to the voice of the man they had learned to trust.

'Last weekend you annihilated Buller. Before the game I took the opportunity to watch the parade and it made me realise just how much your local people are behind you. Today you cannot let them down so now it's up to you. The ball is in your corner. You must make the supreme effort. You must leave this room with a real will to win . . .

*'I am confident in my own mind that, even in the short time I have had with you blokes, there is every chance of you bringing the shield home. Remember — there must be no slacking or short cuts. You must all make up your minds that you are going to play rugby for 80 minutes — **and I mean non-stop** . . .*

'Get right in behind your captain, Ray [Sutherland]. I have had long talks with Ray and he will lead you well. And Alan [Sutherland], you have been an All Black. So get out there and show these people that you are capable of getting back into the New Zealand side. . . .

'Today every one of you is playing for your province and the Ranfurly Shield so attack them from the kick-off. Give them a real arse-knocker. Get those points on the board . . . keep them back on their heels. . . .

Marlborough captain Ray Sutherland (left) with the Ranfurly Shield in 1973. Brother Alan holds the Seddon Shield.

*'Now, good luck to you. I will be anxiously watching and listening to the game and I hope that if you are beaten you will at least know you have done your best for those full 80 minutes. We all know that somebody has got to lose — **just make sure it's not Marlborough** . . .*

'And there's something else I want you to know. When I was with you for two days last week I studied you closely and I am certain that today you are capable of springing the biggest surprise in the history of the shield. You have the talent among you to win this game . . . now just go out and do it.'

When the tape ended the looks on the players' faces said it all. The passion in Fred Allen's voice had again transformed them into warriors. They sat in thoughtful silence for a few moments. Then they rose to their feet and followed their captain on to the field.

Doug Saul, one of Marlborough's coaches, was heard to say: 'That's the first time I've ever come away from a team talk with a lump in my throat — *and I'm not even playing!*'

Before returning to Auckland Fred had warned the speedy Marlborough winger Brian Ford that some time during the game he would encounter the talented Canterbury fullback Fergie McCormick eyeball to eyeball. In preparation for such a confrontation he had spent a long time explaining to Ford how to beat McCormick.

With three minutes remaining on the clock, and the game hanging in the balance, the ball squirted from a ruck and was snapped up by Ford. He broke a couple of weak tackles and set off for the goal-line 70 metres away. Now there was only one opponent between him and the try-line and that opponent was Fergie McCormick, the most deadly tackler in the country. If the flying winger could evade the fullback and reach the try-line the game was won.

As McCormick hurtled across the field to take Ford out of play, the powerful winger remembered Fred Allen's instructions. 'My mind was clear,' he said, 'and I knew exactly what I had to do. I had to throw McCormick off balance.'

A second before they made contact, the flying winger slowed perceptibly — and swerved straight towards McCormick. Taken by surprise, the Canterbury fullback hesitated, uncertain of Ford's intentions. Now completely off balance, he had done exactly what Fred Allen had predicted.

Sensing McCormick's indecision, Ford switched back to overdrive, swerved through the fullback's desperate tackle and raced in for the try as the Marlborough supporters danced and screamed like madmen.

The impossible had happened. The mighty Canterbury had been humbled. And 15,000 Canterbury supporters at Lancaster Park were shattered.

After the Marlborough captain Ray Sutherland had accepted the prized Log o' Wood from Canterbury captain Alex Wyllie he told reporters: 'Fred Allen was with us for only two days but what he instilled into our team cannot adequately be described in words. He taught us the value of cohesive teamwork and you have just seen the result.'

The New Zealand media agreed. A bold headline splashed across an entire page of the Christchurch *Press* summed it up: 'Former All Blacks Coach Behind Shock Win'.

For Fred Allen this was a significant triumph, almost as memorable as any he had enjoyed with his All Blacks. It was also the start of a magnificent winning streak for a rejuvenated Marlborough side. A fortnight after taking the shield they undertook their first defence against Wairarapa-Bush. Again functioning as a team unit, they romped home by 36 points to nil.

The next challenge came from North Otago. It was another one-sided victory for Marlborough by 26 to 9 with Alan Sutherland and his brother Ray both scoring tries.

Then came Wanganui. They, too, were crushed 30 points to 6. And the same fate befell Nelson Bays who went down 29 to 9. Mid Canterbury were next to fail. With Alan Sutherland again leading the charge the final score was 36–9. Then came West Coast, who succumbed 18–nil.

By this time there were signs of weakening in the Marlborough squad. Their string of walk-over victories had brought with it an air of complacency. This cost them dearly in the next challenge from South Canterbury when they failed to cross their opponent's line and went down by 6 points to 18.

The shield had gone and so had a sporting era of which the Marlborough province is justifiably proud.

The Enforcer

Kevin Skinner is a quiet and placid man but the South Africans who toured New Zealand in 1956 didn't think so.

Fred Allen has always had great admiration for the remarkable achievement of his good friend, prop forward Kevin Skinner, in the third test against the touring Springboks in 1956.

'I've never seen anything like it, 'says the Needle. 'In the first and second tests the South Africans had badly injured our two best props and the selectors were at a loss to find a replacement. In desperation they coaxed Kevin out of retirement and in the vital third test not only did he play a fine game, he also straightened out the two toughest forwards in the Springbok pack, the ones who had been doing the damage.

'There was only one way to put an end to the visitors' illegal tactics and Kevin knew exactly what that was.'

By the time the game was over, with New Zealand the victors by 17 points to 10, the powerful Counties forward had indelibly written his name into the history books of New Zealand rugby.

Fred's respect for Skinner began when they were teammates on the tour of South Africa in 1949. 'Our front row combination of Has Catley, Johnny Simpson and Kevin Skinner is still regarded as one of the finest of all time,' says Fred.

It was on that tour that Skinner first encountered the ruthless Springbok psyche. 'They always selected the most powerful, most intimidating front row they could find,' he says. 'The objective, of course, was to get their opponents' front row to buckle and if they could do that, which they invariably did, they had the upper hand.'

For many years Fred celebrated his birthday at his cliff-top home at Manly Beach in the company of his closest friends, two of whom were Kevin and his wife Loretta.

'He is one of the finest men you could ever wish to meet — a family man and a gentleman,' says Fred. 'And, in spite of all the talk that has circulated over the years, he was one of the fairest and cleanest players I had anything to do with.'

Skinner, the youngest of six boys, came up through the grades in Dunedin's Pirates Club to first represent Otago in 1947. Two years later, at 22, he was selected to tour South Africa in the team captained by Fred.

He was also a fine boxer with a powerful punch, as we shall shortly see. He won the Otago heavyweight championship in 1946 and the New Zealand title the following year. 'But rugby and boxing didn't mix,' he says. 'I needed to get my weight up to around 14 st 8 lb for rugby and down to 13 st 10 lb for boxing, my best fighting weight.'

Fred and Kevin Skinner share a drink at the Pukekohe Rugby Club. They have been great friends for many years.

Skinner played 61 games for the All Blacks, including 18 tests. He captained the side against the 1952 Wallabies and his retirement in 1954, when he was only 26, proved an enormous loss to the All Blacks scrum.

By then Kevin, now married, wanted to be with his family and get on with his life. The game of rugby was still dear to him, however, and he kept fit by playing club matches in Dunedin where he and Loretta ran a grocery business.

In 1956 he moved north to Waiuku, just south of Auckland, to try his hand at farming. 'I knew it would be a bit of a gamble,' he says. 'But I was fit and strong and reckoned I could handle it.'

The back-breaking work on the farm kept him in excellent shape, even building up his already powerful frame. But as he went about his daily tasks, little did he know of the drama about to unfold.

Like many great players when their careers were over, he found rugby hard to give up completely and when he visited the local Waiuku club to watch a Saturday game the urge to play was still there. Not surprisingly, the local officials were eager to have a great ex-All Black turn out for their club and they finally persuaded him to pull on the Waiuku jersey.

'I loved those country games,' says Kevin. 'They were nothing like the type of football I'd been used to. And as far as training was concerned — well, they just did a few laps around the field on training nights and then got stuck into the beer. But, without the stress of the big-time, it was all very enjoyable.'

The Springboks had now arrived in New Zealand and, because they were his old foes, Kevin took a great interest in the tour. He had his ear glued to the radio during the first contest at Dunedin which the All Blacks won narrowly by 10 points to 6.

But what concerned him most was the fact that the All Blacks front row had been completely demolished — and by questionable tactics. New Zealand's tighthead prop Mark Irwin, 6 ft tall and 15 st 4 lb in weight, had taken a terrible hammering and was unable to return to the field after halftime. Several of his ribs had been broken. He would not play again that season.

This came as no surprise to Kevin for, since South Africa in 1949, nobody knew better than him just what these tactics were and how they were applied.

Although New Zealand was now one up in the four-match series, the selectors were greatly worried about the enormous strength of the Springbok pack. So one of the selectors, Jack Sullivan, made a trip to Pukekohe stadium to watch Kevin play in a minor union game. He asked Kevin if he would consider turning out for the second test, but Kevin firmly declined. 'I wouldn't last the distance,' he said, 'I'm nowhere near fit enough for test rugby.'

In the second test at Wellington the South African forwards repeated their dominance of the All Blacks front row. This time it was the New Zealand replacement prop, Frank McAtamney, who bore the brunt of their onslaught. The powerful Otago player struggled to cope, but the pressure finally told. He left the field a bruised and broken man as the Springboks evened the series with an 8–3 win.

The All Blacks selectors were in a quandary. They had twice chosen the best props available, but to no avail. Unless the All Blacks front row could be considerably strengthened, it looked odds on that New Zealand would be defeated in yet another Springboks series. With the third test at Christchurch only a couple of weeks away, they decided to approach Skinner a second time. He had done a great deal of training since their last meeting and he was also concerned and angry at the old Springbok tactics that he knew so well. This time, for the sake of New Zealand, he had no hesitation in accepting.

'When I joined the team in Christchurch the atmosphere was unbelievable,' he says. 'You'd have thought the fate of New Zealand rested on this one game.

'But what worried me most was the downcast mood in the All Blacks squad. Some of our guys were clearly intimidated, so I gave a few of them a real talking to. I told them I'd played against some of these Springbok forwards before, and they certainly weren't supermen. All we had to do was lift our sights and get stuck into them.

'The Boks' whole idea was to crash-bang and intimidate. They did this in the lineouts as well as the scrums. They tried you on and you had to let them know you weren't going to stand for it.

'With this team the main trouble was in the lineouts. That's where most of the dirty work had been going on. And not only were they good at it, they were getting away with it. I certainly wasn't going to allow New Zealand to be beaten by illegal play. I'd been through it all in 1949. That's why I made up my mind to do something about it.'

In the first lineout of the third test, prop Chris Koch came through on the All Blacks side. Skinner warned him: 'Do that again, Chris, and I'll belt you.' But Koch ignored Skinner's warning and in the next lineout the big Springbok again barged through, a mile offside. Some spectators reckoned they heard the whack. Fifty-three thousand fans saw Koch go down and stay down.

'He was such a big guy I couldn't miss,' Skinner says. 'I knew I was taking a big risk, but I felt sure the ref would have given me a warning before sending me off. Anyway, it worked, and Koch never tried it again. But he didn't like it — he kept glaring at me. I think he would have liked to have had another go. And I got a lot of pleasure out of seeing the looks on the faces of the other Springbok forwards.

Trouble in Christchurch . . . referee Bill Fright separates Jaap Bekker and Kevin Skinner during the third test between the Springboks and the All Blacks.

'The trouble in the scrums was just as bad. The Springbok prop Jaap Bekker was giving our other prop, Ian Clarke, a terrible time. So Ian and I decided to change over.

'The first thing Bekker did was give me those intimidating looks of his. Then he started making a real nuisance of himself and when I wouldn't budge he deliberately put his shoulder into me as hard as he could. I could see his clenched fist, too, and I knew that he was looking for a chance to pop me.

'So I got in first — a real beaut to the side of his head. He would have gone down if he hadn't had his arm around the hooker. There was a decent scuffle for a while, but the ref settled it down and from then on we had no more trouble.

'I got no pleasure out of hitting these two guys. But for the sake of New Zealand something had to be done before it was too late. I couldn't let them get away with their illegal tactics any longer.

'From what I've read over the years you'd have thought the fighting in that third test had lasted the entire game, but that simply wasn't true. There were only two punches — the one that floored Koch and the one that stopped Bekker.'

But those two punches weren't enough for a number of journalists, especially the overseas ones. They wrote as if Skinner was a cross between a raging Jack Dempsey and a fired-up Joe Louis.

'I only threw two punches to sort things out,' says Kevin, 'but the stories became so exaggerated it was beginning to get to me. So I phoned Fred Allen and asked him what I should do.

'He told me the best way was to write to the press, so I took his advice and wrote to the *Auckland Star*. I asked for an end to those ridiculous stories of fists flying the whole game. The letter to the editor did the trick because the highly exaggerated stories stopped appearing. I was pleased about that.'

Because of his impact on that vital third test, won by New Zealand by 17 points to 10, Kevin was the first man selected for the fourth and final encounter at Eden Park. In a nail-biting struggle New Zealand triumphed by 11 points to 5 to clinch a series victory.

It was the first time the Springboks had been defeated anywhere in the world since 1896.

Kevin left Eden Park a tired but happy man. He had turned the tide in New Zealand's favour, but his right hand had suffered in the process. After the game Don Clarke, the All Blacks fullback, who was another magnificent contributor, swore he saw a large patch of skin peeled back on Kevin's right fist.

'Kevin will always be a hero as far as I am concerned,' says The Needle. 'What he did in that third test took so much guts it's hard to imagine.

'No wonder the guy's a legend. And not only in New Zealand — he's a legend in South Africa as well.'

The crowd at Eden Park for the fourth test totalled almost 61,500, the largest-ever attendance at a test match in New Zealand.

The quiet and unassuming Kevin Skinner was elected to the New Zealand Sports Hall of Fame in 1996.

The Baabaas

Fred becomes the first New Zealand player to lead a British Barbarians XV.

When the Kiwis Army tour of the British Isles was over, Fred and the rest of the team were staying at the Fernleaf Club in London awaiting transport home. They had been told there would be a delay of several weeks because of a desperate shortage of shipping — so many Allied vessels had been sunk during the war.

He was busy cleaning and packing his gear when he received a phone call from the secretary of the famous British Barbarians Rugby Club. They were keen to have him play in their annual Easter tour of South Wales. They wanted him for two matches: the first at Swansea and the second at Newport, where he would also captain the side. It would be, they told him, the first time such an honour had been bestowed on a New Zealand player.

'It came as a wonderful surprise,' says Fred, 'and I was delighted to accept.'

In the first game for the Barbarians at Swansea, Fred found himself up against his own Kiwis captain, Charlie Saxton, who had been asked to captain the Swansea XV. Two other Kiwis in that team were fullback Herbie Cook and five-eighths Ron Dobson.

'We had a tough battle on our hands, but we beat the Swansea side 11–6,' says Fred. 'And a lot of the credit for that belonged to one of our Kiwis players, the Maori centre Johnny Smith, who gave one of his best-ever displays as well as converting one of our three tries.'

Then came one of Fred's proudest rugby moments when on 23 April 1946 he led a mix of international players, including stars from England, Scotland, Wales and Ireland, on to the field at Newport.

Although the Newport side beat Fred's Barbarian team, the outcome of the contest was in doubt up to the very last minute and the game ended 11–6 in Newport's favour. A feature of the game was the fine displays by Fred in the five-eighths and winger Bill Meates from Greymouth. The pair combined beautifully for Meates to score one of the Barbarians' two tries.

Another star of Fred's team was Scotland's gigantic Glasgow-born forward, Frank Coutts who, like Fred, had earned distinction on the battlefield as well as on the sportsfield. He gained promotion through the ranks from private to brigadier and was several times commended for his courage on active service.

It is interesting to note that, again like Fred, he was one of six children who had been raised in humble circumstances — with his father a lowly paid minister with the Free Presbyterian Church of Scotland.

He started out as a pavement-pounding London 'bobby' and bought his first pair of boots out of his weekly wage of £3-30. He became president of the Scottish Rugby Union in the 1977–78 season.

Fred has fond memories of Frank Coutts. 'I remember him chuckling over some of his experiences during the war,' he says. 'At one stage, for instance, he was billeted at Roedean, a snooty, upmarket girls' school where each dormitory bed had a bell with a notice that said, "Ring If You Need a Mistress in the Night".

'A few of the wishful-thinkers rang and rang, just for the hell of it, and Frank Coutts would often call out in the darkness, "Keep it up lads, God loves a trier."'

Another war hero in Fred's team was Tom Jackson, who won 12 Scottish caps between 1947 and 1949. He, too, had reached the rank of brigadier and was mentioned in despatches while serving with the 9th Armoured Division in the Middle East.

'I felt very privileged to be captain of a team with so many born leaders,' says Fred. 'All my players were men of the highest calibre and every one of them was highly respected in his own country.'

A day or two after the Newport game the Kiwis vice-captain Jack Finlay, along with Fred and Herbie 'Cookie' Cook, were officially detailed to attend a function at Fulham Palace, residence of the Bishop of London, Dr John Wand.

The bishop, ranked as the third highest Anglican in Britain, had been

Bishop of Brisbane during the war, and he had great admiration for Australians and New Zealanders.

Before they left for the palace, Cook was in a nervous quandary and said to the manager of the Kiwis, Colonel Alan Andrews, 'What can a fella like me talk about to someone like the Bishop of London?'

Even the colonel wasn't sure, but away the trio went to keep the appointment. They hadn't been long at the function before Cookie found himself shaking the bishop's hand and introducing himself as Trooper Cook of New Zealand.

A steward passed by with a tray of drinks and Cookie helped himself to yet another whisky. 'Care for a drink my lord,' he asked the bishop.

'Er-er, yes thank you Cook, I think I'll join you.' And so a stilted conversation began. It looked like continuing that way until Herbie said: 'You know, my lord, when the colonel told us we were to come here I said to him, "What the hell can I talk about to a bishop?"'

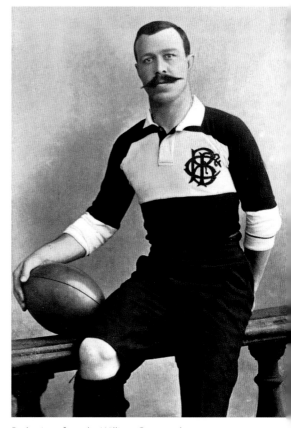

Barbarians founder William Carpmael, pictured here in 1896.

The bishop smiled, clinked glasses with Cookie and said, 'Just say what the hell you like Herbie — and let's enjoy ourselves!'

'That unexpected reply took Cookie completely by surprise,' says Fred, 'and immediately put him at ease. And it did the same for me. He was a great fella that bishop.'

The formation of the Barbarians Rugby Club took place in a most unlikely setting — an oyster bar in Bradford, Yorkshire, in 1890. A 37-year-old Blackheath forward named William Carpmael was touring there with a scratch side. While having a meal in the bar they decided over drinks to form an elite rugby club purely for the enjoyment of the game. They had no ground, no clubhouse and membership would be by invitation only.

Carpmael's dream was to spread good fellowship among all rugby players and his dream became a reality on 27 December 1890 at Friary Field, Hartlepool, when they played the local side. They called their team the Barbarians.

There were two key qualifications for membership: being a good player and a good sport with no discrimination against players of any class, race, creed or colour. They agreed on a simple motto: 'Rugby football is a game for gentlemen in all classes, but never for a bad sportsman in any class.' This matched Fred's philosophy exactly and is one of the reasons why he has always been a keen supporter.

The gear of the British Barbarians — black and white hooped jerseys with the overlapping letters BFC — was first worn in 1891 and in 1925 the club introduced a dark-blue blazer with a pocket badge showing two lambs playing with a rugby ball.

In the years that followed, the Baabaas, as they became known, played just a few games each year to enjoy the camaraderie of rugby. This allowed them to play adventurous, free-running football without the pressure of having to win for their country.

The player with the most appearances in the famous jersey is dashing Irish winger Tony O'Reilly, who represented the club 30 times. He has also scored the most points with a total of 38 tries.

What is generally considered the greatest team try ever scored on a rugby field was in a Barbarians game against the All Blacks in 1973. A ball kicked long and high toward the Barbarians goal-line by All Blacks winger Bryan Williams was fielded by Phil Bennett, who turned and dummied his way past several tacklers.

What happened in the next few seconds was pure magic as the ball sped through the hands of eight dodging, weaving men before reaching Gareth Edwards on the left flank. Edwards took the pass at speed, scorched for the line and dived across in the corner. As he did so Cliff Morgan spoke the immortal words: 'If the greatest writer of the written word in the world wrote the story of this try, no one would believe it.'

The Barbarians gained a New Zealand link in 1935 after a touring All Black, Hugh McLean, brother of writer T.P. McLean, spent an evening with one of the club's founders in England. This led to the New Zealand branch being formed in 1937 after much work by McLean and another All Black, Ron Bush.

'They held their first meetings in the Auckland business premises of Ron Bush and later I had the honour of joining them as a committee member,' says Fred, who has now been a Barbarian for nearly 65 years.

'I had brought my Barbarians badge back from England and I suggested it would be a good thing to have a fernleaf included on the New Zealand version. There was a lot of discussion with headquarters in London, but eventually we were granted permission for the silver fern to be included.

Fred (front row, third from left) has had a long association with the Barbarians Rugby Club. He coached this Baabaas side against the Coronation Shield Districts after the Springboks' tour of New Zealand in 1956. Springboks skipper Basie Viviers captained the New Zealand Barbarians.

'We were all very proud of that badge and it's great to see it embossed in the leadlight entrance door to the new Eden Park clubrooms.

'The first game the New Zealand Barbarians played was against a united Thames Valley side. The sub-union was financially strapped at the time and they decided to put it back on its feet. That's what the Barbarians did — raise money to help those in need.

'Our first clubroom was a house in Cricket Avenue right next to Eden Park. When the financial institutions wouldn't help, two of my good mates, Arthur Hughes and George Nelson, bought the property for £13,000.

'Next morning the *Herald* reported the sale of the house to the two famous footballers. George's wife, Peg, was totally baffled. She knew nothing about her husband buying a property and rang Arthur's wife, Jean, in great concern. "What on earth are they up to?" she asked. "They're not going to live there, are they?"'

The historic old house remained the headquarters of the New Zealand Barbarians for 40 years until it was demolished during the reconstruction of Eden Park for the 2011 World Cup.

'We were all sad to say goodbye,' says Fred, 'but the new self-contained premises on top of the main Eden Park stand are a very impressive replacement.'

The ambience of the huge lounge and bar area, which leads onto two specially designed corporate boxes for watching games, is a combination of the old and the new. All the priceless memorabilia from Cricket Avenue, plus a great deal more, has been installed in the new headquarters.

In pride of place is a magnificent new honours board donated by the widow and son of the late Pat Walsh, a most esteemed All Black and former Barbarian. The logo on the board was carved by former Maori All Black Fred Graham.

There is a modern, well-stocked bar and red leather chairs embossed with the Barbarians emblem. Even the red table mats bear the logo. There are jerseys and leather balls used in famous matches and row upon row of historical photographs.

The new clubrooms were officially opened on 24 June 2010 by the club patron, Bob Sorenson. Well over a hundred members and their wives attended and every person was full of praise for the manner which the entire complex had been prepared.

The joint founders of the New Zealand Barbarians, former All Blacks Ron Bush and Hugh McLean, spent their last days together in the Ranfurly Veterans Home in Auckland. In his heyday fullback Bush weighed 15 st while loose forward McLean was lighter at a little over 14 st. They were big men for those times.

When Fred Allen visited them 'they were shadows of the great physical specimens they once were,' he says. 'But it was great to see these two friends still together being well looked after and keeping each other company in their final days.'

Ron Bush, who played for New Zealand in 1931, died in 1996 and Hugh McLean, who wore the All Blacks jersey from 1930 to 1936, passed away a few months later.

Advice from an Icon

Discipline, respect, team spirit and morale were the qualities Fred Allen demanded from his All Blacks teams.

During his war days in the front line, when Fred was under fire and his life often depended on the quick-thinking actions of his comrades, he had come to realise the tremendous value of discipline, self-respect and team morale, which he now saw as the basic essentials of winning rugby.

'If you can achieve these qualities when you're young,' says New Zealand's most famous coach, 'and retain them throughout your career, the enjoyment and the friendships you make will remain in your memory long after your playing days are over.

'And when you're old, as I am, these memories will become even more precious. That's one of the most wonderful things about the game.

'Always have pride in your team, no matter what grade you play, or how you are faring in a competition, and you will find yourself enjoying the game with a lot of friendly people — and that's what football is all about.

'I've always enjoyed my rugby and so have all the great players I've known. I believe this is very important because, if you don't enjoy the game, you'll never become a first-class player. Footballers who can loosen up and express themselves on the paddock are a great asset to any team. Their exciting running and smooth passing — you can recognise the mood straight away. These are the players who warm a coach's heart.

'The Kiwis Army team after the war springs to mind. It was a team of soldiers who had just come off the battlefield and they had every reason to be happy. And that's the way they played. They spun the ball at every opportunity, and they backed up tirelessly. They were thrilling to watch. Sixty-five years later they're still talked about.

'My Auckland side that defended the Ranfurly Shield on 25 successive occasions had similar qualities. There was a lot of pride in that squad, a lot of discipline — and it showed. And we made sure we had lots of laughs along the way.

'Then there's the unbeaten All Blacks of 1966–68. I don't believe any other team, touring or otherwise, had as much fun as they did, especially during the long tour of Canada, Britain and France. Those players possessed all the qualities I could wish for in a team. They had discipline, self-respect and a strong belief in themselves — and it didn't all happen by chance.

'It was the same with all those sides, and what's more, they thoroughly enjoyed themselves both on and off the field. I'm confident that without that splendid attitude we would not have achieved what we did.'

That view was endorsed by writer T.P. McLean, one of the touring press party:

> *The humour of the 1967 All Blacks explains a great deal of their success. In fortune and misfortune they were sustained as a party by a passionate loyalty, one to the other, by an unfathomable pride in their status as All Blacks — and by a deep sense of humour. They got along with each other and they had a hell of a lot of fun together.*

'A cheerful disposition is a very important thing when you've got more than 30 grown men travelling together for months on end,' says Fred. 'Sure, we had our differences from time to time but we resolved them with sensible, face-to-face discussions and got on with the job.

'I'd also like to say something about speed, because speed is essential for winning rugby. There's an old saying, but it's true: "It's the speed that kills — it kills anyone who doesn't have it!"

'My good friend Bob Scott wrote in his book that the man with blazing speed was the one he feared the most. And Bob should know because of the countless hours he spent defending against some of the fastest players ever to take the field. Bob wasn't a speedster himself but he had his own method of working "a flyer" towards the sideline so he could only come back infield, and

Practice session at Coogee Oval, Sydney, 1947. For Fred Allen and Bob Scott it was always about teamwork.

then, more often than not, Bob would nail him. But, as Bob has told me many times, guys with exceptional speed were his biggest worry.

'The word "pace" makes people think of a wing three-quarter tearing down the touchline, beating one defender after another and diving across for a brilliant try. That's fair enough, but there's much more to it than that. It's not only fleetness of foot that's important — it's also a quickness of mind. That's what I taught during my training routines. The faster the forwards reacted, the faster the midfield backs, the faster the wings, the more intense the pressure was going to be on the opposition.

'I wanted every member of the team to execute everything he did as swiftly and accurately as he possibly could — and not only when going forward. It's just as important when you're on the back foot and the ball is behind you in an awkward place. That's when split seconds really count.

'Another important aspect of pace is the delivery of passes so the receiver can run on to the ball at speed. I can never emphasise this enough. It's an art that can be taught and my players spent hours perfecting the technique. I have

191

always maintained that this skilful passing was a major factor in our success.'

The great All Black Bryan Williams, universally regarded as one of the greatest wing three-quarters of all time, totally agrees: 'Nothing will ever beat speed. You know, after all the changes in world rugby, this statement still rings true, and yet so many coaches espouse game plans that keep the ball away from the speedsters. I just don't get it.'

To fully understand Fred Allen's coaching philosophy we must go back to the days of the Kiwis during which the young lieutenant came under the influence of Major Charlie Saxton, the team's captain. A man of exceptional character, Saxton had been an All Blacks halfback in 1938. During the war he had served with distinction in the famous Long Range Desert Group in North Africa and, when the Kiwis side was formed, he was the logical choice to lead it.

The farther the tour progressed, the more Fred was inspired by Saxton's profound knowledge of the game, and he has always acknowledged that Saxton had a greater influence on his rugby thinking than any other person. As the Army Team was enthralling crowds wherever they played, Saxton was proving to Fred, and to other members of the side, that rugby was a simple game if the correct fundamentals were applied. He referred to these as the three Ps — Position, Possession and Pace.

It was another godsend for New Zealand when the liaison between the pair continued in 1967 when Saxton was appointed manager of Fred's great, undefeated All Blacks side.

'With Charlie Saxton as my manager, and Brian Lochore as my captain, I had tremendous support,' Fred says. 'I was fortunate indeed to be associated with men of such sterling character.'

'When I joined up with the Kiwis the first advice Charlie gave me was to make myself familiar with the basics of the game,' says Fred. 'He convinced me that, if the basics weren't in place, there was no foundation, nothing to build on. The thinking had to be done before the training began.

'Charlie also instilled in me that possession is nine points of the law. First of all you have to get hold of the ball, then you have to retain possession and if you do these things at speed — and that includes passing — you'll be bloody hard to beat.

'He taught us that rugby is a game of passing the ball swiftly and accurately from man to man in order to outflank, or outwit, your opponents. And once you've got your pass away you must immediately back up the ball carrier. It all sounds easy, but it isn't. It only happens after a helluva lot of work. And doesn't matter how brilliant the players are as individuals, the entire team must be committed.

'Each man, forward or back, must understand positional play. He must know his correct position to suit every angle. He must say to himself the whole time: "I must keep in position — I must keep in position."

'And when you kick the ball — if you really have to kick — make certain that you direct it to a spot where it will be the most difficult for your opponents to deal with.

'Then either you, or one of your teammates, must get to the ball first. If you do this, you've got a better than a 60–40 chance of a good result. But if one of the opposition gets there first, nine times out of 10 you're in deep trouble. Success depends on two things — the accuracy of the kick and a commitment to the chase.

'Over the years we've had several All Blacks who could place these kicks to perfection. Mac Herewini of my 1967 side could drop the ball on a sixpence. Jeff Wilson was another. He scored many tries as he raced through to get the bounce. It's a great attacking weapon when it's done properly.

'Defence is just as important as attack — sometimes even more so. So always hold your position because if you're not in

Major Charlie Saxton — a friend, confidant and a man of great character.

the right place at the right time, your team could be in trouble at any second. If you find yourself out of position for any reason, get back into place as fast as you can, even though your legs may be tired and a bit wobbly.

'It's obvious that if you haven't got the ball you can't score tries. So get hold of it — from scrums, rucks, lineouts, broken play — from anywhere you can. And when you've got it — use it. It's up to each player to keep the tempo going.

'That's where fitness plays such an important part. That's why I worked my players so hard. That's why they grizzled so much during the early sessions which sometimes lasted a couple of hours. They'd never trained like that before and some of them didn't like it. But I kept drilling into them — giving them glaring examples — how a game can be won or lost in the last few seconds.

'Take our last game of the 1967 tour against the Barbarians at Twickenham. Defeat was staring us in the face. But three minutes into injury time we ran the ball from our own 25 and scored the winning try.

193

'I see shocking passing today. There's too much fancy stuff, too much passing behind your back, too much flinging the ball without looking where it's going — and the next minute there's an intercept.

'Once that happens there's nothing more demoralising than standing there helpless while an opposition back runs 60 or 70 yards to dot down between the posts — after one of your mates has handed him the ball! Just look at the players' faces when that sort of thing happens. They're not very happy, I can tell you.

'In no way would I tolerate dangerous or illegal play. Every time I saw a punch fly I held my breath, hoping it wasn't one of my blokes. My greatest worry was that someone had lost his cool and would be sent off, which meant we would have to carry on a man short.'

Fred wanted no part of gaining advantage by brutality. He had seen it at its worst and it was loathsome to him. His All Blacks were under strict instructions that if they kicked, punched, gouged or maliciously maltreated an opponent in any way they would be shown the door. And they knew that when The Needle made a statement like that, he meant it!

'While you're engaged in that sort of rubbish,' he told his squad, 'you're not being loyal to your team. And when the referee sends you off, it's not the opposition you've hurt — it's your own mates!'

Always a stickler for discipline in any team he captained or coached, Fred is on the end of a late tackle, against Queensland in 1947. Meanwhile, Johnny Smith keeps the All Blacks movement going.

Fred recognised that rucking was always a difficult area. 'New Zealand forwards were the best in the world at raking the ball,' he says. 'We trained very hard at this, but I insisted my chaps got right over, or in front of the ball, to protect the men on the ground.

'I was never at ease until a team I was coaching had discipline and a winning attitude. In the dressing room before a big game you can sense these qualities. Whenever I had that feeling I knew we would do well.

'I could always tell how the players were reacting to what I was saying because you could bet your bottom dollar that at one stage someone would want to stand out and make a name for himself. That was the reason I hoed into them. Moulding them into a team with a strong mental discipline was the first thing I concentrated on — and the most important!

'And there's another factor about playing 15-man rugby — it's far more entertaining for the spectators and that's very important for the welfare of the game.'

In his biography Brian Lochore wrote:

> *If Fred Allen ever needed a disciple for his belief that rugby was a game for fifteen players he certainly had one in me. His greatest strength was his ability to motivate individuals and have a team function at maximum capacity. Fred opened up a new era of rugby. He wanted us to play a brand of rugby no other team in the world was playing. It opened up my mind — it was a rush of new understanding.*

Newcomers to Fred's squads were in for a shock when they attended their first training session. The discipline and intensity of his training was greater than they had ever experienced before and there were few who, at some time, did not have a love–hate relationship with their coach. But although he made them suffer the pangs of exhaustion, at the end of the day not one of them had anything less for Fred Allen than abiding respect.

When Southland captain Jack Hazlett was selected for the All Blacks tour in 1967, he was blown away by the intensity of his first training run. Something had upset The Needle that day and he was in one of his fiercest moods. After they had been flat out for more than three-quarters of an hour, Hazlett managed to find enough breath to gasp out to Meads, Tremain and the others: 'My God, are all his runs this hard?'

'You're joking Jack,' they replied. 'Most are a bloody sight harder!'

When Hazlett went to bed that night with every muscle in his body aching he wondered whether the honour and glory of being an All Black was really worth it. But before long, as he became fitter than he had ever been before, he realised it was indeed well worth it and during the tour he played in seven of the 17 games, including the test against England.

T.P. McLean wrote:

When Freddie Allen was in charge, training runs were for training. Once the preliminaries are attended to, the players are set about their paces crisply, briskly and, most important of all, continuously.

There's not one moment of let-up. The ball is put through the scrum and among the backs and, as Mr Allen bellows 'Spin, spin, spin,' it is flung from man to man with maximum speed.

Then there is a check, the forwards go in and when the ball emerges by pass or from a heel, it is sent spinning along the backs again, while Allen's voice once more commands, 'Spin, spin, spin.'

By the end of an hour of this relentless exercise the players are on the way to exhaustion. And still the passionate voice urges them to run harder, pass faster and give better support to the ball carrier.

And while all this is going on nothing, but nothing, escapes Fred Allen's eye.

One of Fred's most intensive training routines involved his entire All Blacks squad traversing two lengths of the field. They walked the first two lengths, trotted the second and ran the third, during which each man was to take only two steps before passing the ball. If the ball was dropped at any stage they went back to the start and did it all over again. His players called it 'The Arse Knocker', but it worked, and since the Fred Allen era it is generally recognised that no other All Blacks team has passed the ball so swiftly and accurately.

One day Kel Tremain, puffing profusely after an especially long workout, said within the coach's hearing: 'Allen, you're a bastard.' The moment the words were out of his mouth he realised his mistake.

'Now you can all go back and do it again,' The Needle demanded, 'and you can blame Tremain for calling me a bastard.'

So the entire All Blacks squad trudged wearily back to the goal-line and when Fred gave the word they set out on more lengths of the field, passing the ball as they went.

They won their next game by 23 points and that was the last time any of them said anything derogatory within earshot of The Needle.

Fred's very presence dominated his training sessions. He always changed into rugby gear and ran with his players in order to be closer to the action.

'You can't train a team from the sidelines,' he maintains, 'because from that distance it's impossible to teach them the finer points of passing, or taking a high ball from different angles. But when you're right alongside them you can tell players exactly what they're doing wrong. After a few weeks' practice my players showed decided improvement.'

Although Fred was sensitive and sympathetic to the needs of his players he was also capable of tongue-lashings that could make strong men cringe. No one was exempt, not even the most celebrated players. Even Pinetree Meads, the Player of the Century and certainly not one to annoy, copped his share. However, like all the giants of the game, Pinetree eventually came to respect Fred's integrity and his deep concern for his players. At the All Blacks' last team meeting in London before departing for home, he said: 'We are now all convinced about this business of 15-man running rugby. We must take the idea back to our clubs and show them just how good it is.'

Fred would like to see a few changes to the current laws, the refereeing and the welfare of players.

'If the game is to prosper it must be fair,' says Fred, 'which means 15 men playing 15 men. And for that reason there should be no such thing as red-carding, yellow-carding or sin binning.

'A player should not be sent off in the middle of a game. There should be an appropriate penalty right there and then — even a penalty try if necessary. Then mete out the punishment when the game is over: banish the offender for a couple of years if necessary. But let him stay on the field in order to keep the contest an even one.

'The fans don't pay good money to see a lop-sided encounter — like 15 men playing 14 men, or even 13, which is often the case! It's already turned a lot of people away.

'The scrums also need looking at. The ball should go in dead-centre but today a halfback places it right under the feet of his front row which means that, nine times out of 10, scrums are foregone conclusions. How can that be a fair contest?

'And another thing — quick throw-ins and quick penalties make a big difference to the fairness and the spectacle of the game. It upsets me when I see players deliberately kicking or chucking the ball away to prevent the other side throwing it in quickly.

'The same applies when a player hangs on to the ball, or kicks it away to prevent the opposition taking a quick tap penalty. These offenders are deliberately slowing the game down. They should be penalised far more than they are.

'The repeated collapsing of scrums which sometimes goes on for minutes on end, also concerns me. The public doesn't want to watch that sort of rubbish.

Three of world rugby's great thinkers, New Zealand's Fred Allen, South Africa's Danie Craven and Wales' Carwyn James.

The refs should make up their minds after the first warning, penalise someone and get on with the game.

'And as for some of those goal-kickers — the time they take to line up their kicks is a joke. They concentrate far too long — and lose it. Then, four times out of five, they miss. The best kickers are far more decisive — and accurate. Just a couple of glances at the posts and the ball's on its way.

'Your health and well-being are also important. When you're young and growing, don't overdo things. I see youngsters playing far too much football before they've matured. I see kids playing rugby in the morning and league or soccer in the afternoon, sometimes on both Saturdays and Sundays.

'That's not a good idea. When a growing youngster is playing too many games a week, or overdoing his training, he's using up far too much physical and mental energy. He'll soon become listless and his school work will suffer. Choose one code and stick to it. And when you've done that, learn as much as you can about that sport and let your body and mind develop as nature intended.

'Don't misunderstand what I'm trying to tell you. As you get older, of course you've got to train — and you've got to train bloody hard. What I'm talking about is pushing the boundaries too far when you're young, even to the point where you're running on empty.

'Take it from one who knows. There's a strict limit on the amount of punishment a young body can withstand. Only when you're fully matured will you be ready for serious training, not to mention the hard knocks that go with senior football. Be patient — it's one of the keys to success.

'Our great Olympic champion and world mile record-holder John Walker had this to say: "If you start packing in a hundred miles a week when you're too young, by the time you're 18 you won't want to stay in sport too much longer."

'There's another important factor — coaching. If a youngster is fortunate enough to have a good coach at school, or belong to a club that has a good coach, he's bound to benefit. I think it was John Walker who also said: "I believe that coaches remain the most important people in the sporting world. Without good coaches, you don't have good players."

'If you're lucky enough to obtain a knowledgeable coach, he will spend a lot of time teaching you the basics of the sport, as well as the rules. He'll also study each player on an individual basis in order to know what makes him tick, how to handle him and where to place him in a side.

'These learning days will be some of the most enjoyable of your life. And when you're fully matured, hardened up and ready for the big time, make up your mind to give the game your best shot. Then, when your playing career is over, you can always say, "I did my very best."

'And no one can do more than that!'

T.P. McLean was wrong when he wrote that 'nothing, but nothing, escapes Fred Allen's eye'. Canterbury prop Alister Hopkinson did fool Fred during one rigorous training session.

While the team were doing their customary laps of the field, Hopkinson nipped behind a goalpost as his group passed by. It was a terribly hot day and while his teammates sweated through another lap he stood motionless before stepping out and joining in again.

Fred hadn't noticed that 'Hoppy' had enjoyed his little rest which, on past experience, was just as well for all of them. Had Fred found out, 'Hoppy' would have been well and truly for the high jump. And all the others would have been sentenced to an extra lap or two.

A Staunch Life

The Needle's loyalty to the game he loves is as strong today as it was more than 80 years ago.

Fred has always put the welfare of rugby ahead of any desire for wealth. This attitude became apparent immediately after the Second World War when, as a hard-up young man, he turned down an offer of £4500 to join the famous Wigan League Club in England. It was a small fortune at the time but it was also a pattern he would follow throughout his life.

During his playing years he had several other offers to switch to league, but all were rejected. Later, when he became a famous coach, he received further offers — not to play league, but to coach other rugby-playing nations.

The most tempting came in 1985 and few knew of it until the *New Zealand Herald*'s rugby writer, T.P. McLean, got wind of the fact and wrote the following:

At least twice to my knowledge, Mr Allen has refused what could have been lucrative contracts to coach in South Africa. As a prime example, in 1985 he was the first man approached to coach the Cavaliers, that unfortunate team which was conceived in secrecy and which so much damaged the game in this country.

The offer was $150,000. Mr Allen instantly spurned it. In his view, everything about the tour was anathema.

That was an extremely lucrative offer at a time when New Zealand's annual average wage was $27,000.

In 1985 an All Blacks tour of South Africa had been arranged and the team had been selected. But five days before the All Blacks were due to depart, the tour was cancelled. The High Court in Wellington had upheld an application from two Auckland lawyers to stop the All Blacks leaving the country. Because of apartheid in South Africa, the tour would breach the New Zealand Rugby Union's legally stated purpose: 'the fostering and encouragement of the game of rugby'.

At this stage a number of influential South African businessmen, eager for a tour by New Zealanders, invited a small group of Kiwi players to a meeting in Hong Kong. It was at this meeting, held in the highest secrecy, that an unofficial tour was planned with a New Zealand team to be known as The Cavaliers.

Every All Black picked for the original tour received an invitation. All but two accepted. The reason the others gave was that they relished another chance to defeat the Springboks in a test series in their own country. Not one word was said about the huge financial inducements they were being offered.

The two who declined were the Auckland captain, David Kirk, and wing John Kirwan. Kirk later said he had been offered $100,000. But none of the players who went on the tour would disclose the amount that had been dangled in front of them.

When the New Zealand public heard the news, they felt betrayed. They could not believe that 30 players were deserting their provincial teams in the middle of the season and were sneaking away like fugitives. It was a highly controversial issue at a time when rugby was still an amateur sport.

Fred Allen's inclusion as coach would have given the Cavaliers enormous credibility. But Fred, like Kirk and Kirwan, found the concept abhorrent and refused to be involved.

It was later revealed that Brian Lochore had also been asked to coach the rebel side. But he, too, had flatly declined.

The much respected headmaster of Auckland Grammar, John Graham, himself a former All Blacks captain, wrote a scathing letter to the NZRFU accusing the rebels of betraying every school, club and province for which they had played. He called for lifetime banishments.

The Prime Minister of New Zealand, David Lange, was outraged. 'The Cavaliers represent nothing but their own self-interests,' he said. 'To travel to South Africa at a time of heightened racial violence, after hundreds of deaths, is insensitive in the extreme.'

The Cavaliers' management team of Colin Meads (coach), Andy Dalton (captain) and Ian Kirkpatrick (manager). A big, six-figure offer was not enough to lure Fred to join the side.

It was a short tour of only 12 games, including four against the Springboks. In the midweek games, the SARFU referred to the visitors as the 'New Zealand Cavaliers', but in the four games against the Springboks they were advertised as the 'All Blacks'.

The South African union treated the Springbok games as tests and rewarded their players with caps. This aroused the ire of the NZRFU because the tour was unsanctioned and the All Blacks name and jersey were forbidden.

The first pseudo 'test', in Cape Town, was lost 15–21 but the second, at Durban, was narrowly won by the Cavaliers 19–18. The third clash in Pretoria was lost 18–33 and the fourth at Johannesburg was a third defeat for the Cavaliers 10–23. Once again the South Africans had proved unbeatable at home.

Fred was hardly surprised. 'There were some wonderful players in that Cavaliers side,' he says, 'but everything was far too underhand and secretive, and the pressures hanging over the players would not have helped. You can't play your best football when you've got those sorts of problems on your mind.'

The rebels returned home expecting severe punishment. But after lengthy discussion they were declared ineligible for one match because they were not in New Zealand by a required date, and suspended from another. That ruled them out of a forthcoming one-off test against France, and the first of a three-match series against Australia.

More than 20 years passed before David Kirk, by then CEO of Fairfax Media in Australia, admitted that it was not easy to turn down the tour especially in view of the $100,000 offer.

'Every New Zealand rugby player wanted to play the Springboks in South Africa where we had never won a series at that time,' he said. 'But we wouldn't have been representing anything, or anyone — and, besides, there was the stench of money under the table.'

Fred recognises that professionalism in sport was inevitable. 'It brought a number of changes which I don't exactly like,' he says, 'but I don't agree with critics who say that our current All Blacks are soft because of the money they get. There were times when I could have done with two or three of today's forwards, especially in South Africa. Most of them are bigger and fitter than in my day. And the speed of some of those big guys is amazing.

'Today, as professionals, they train for hours and have the benefit of sophisticated gym equipment. We had far less time for training because of our fulltime jobs. We had to fit it in whenever we could. We used to do a great deal of stamina work on the roads, or around golf links, or paddocks.'

The huge changes since Fred's day are illustrated in a clipping from the *Auckland Star's* sports edition, *8 O'clock*, dated 7 October 1967:

Fred Allen's 1967 All Blacks aren't going to get rich on their allowance while they are on tour. They will receive one dollar a day which is consistent with previous All Blacks teams in Britain and touring sides in New Zealand.

Compare this with the incomes of today's players. The superstars earn millions a year and many others earn more than the Prime Minister. In addition there's a bonus of $100,000 for every player in the All Blacks squad should New Zealand win the 2011 World Cup and $35,000 should they lose the final.

One thing the All Blacks did receive before the 1967 European tour was a free issue of clothing for each player. It consisted of two white shirts, one pullover, one scarf, one blazer, one dress blazer, two pairs of socks, two pairs of slacks and six ties.

'But the trouble was,' says Fred, an authority on garment manufacture, 'some of the blazers and slacks looked as though they'd been cut out with a knife and fork!'

'Ban Them for Life'

Fred speaks his mind on the evils of performance-enhancing drugs in sport.

'Athletes who use drugs to boost their performance are bloody scumbags,' says The Needle. 'Fortunately, during my era we never had to deal with these ratbags. It wasn't a factor when I was playing and coaching.

'Now you read about them all the time. They suspend them for a few months and then they're back into it again.

'It makes me angry when I read about rugby players being caught for drug use. Letting the game down is bad enough, but there's another angle to these idiots being on the field — they're a real danger to other players. There's no knowing what they'll come at.

'Some of the dangerous play we've seen during the last few years has been right over the edge, like kicking guys in the head and ripping off bits of testicles. It makes you pretty suspicious. No player in their right mind would do things like that.

'If I had my way the cheats who use banned stimulants would be out for life — first time — if proven guilty. No ifs, no buts! That's what I'd do with them. If the authorities adopted a policy like that the whole thing would soon be cleaned up. Instead they tell us that as long as drugs are available, there'll always be a problem. I won't wear that kind of negative talk.

'They're not being anywhere near tough enough. Most of the time they let these ratbags off with short suspensions. Most of them don't give a damn. When their time is up, they thumb their noses at authority and get into the drugs again.'

'They do it, of course, because of the enormous money on offer today, not thousands but millions of dollars. It would be impossible to determine the number of drug cheats who have become millionaires, mostly in track and field. There are dozens of them earning colossal money right now who've been convicted in the past — some more than once. Some even three times! How can that be good for sport? In fact, it's bloody frightening and if it isn't stomped out it's only going to get worse.'

Fred's concern is shared by other top New Zealand sportsmen including Olympic champion and world-record holder, John Walker, who has stated: 'I do not believe any serious attempt has ever been mounted to remove drugs from sport.'

New Zealand's Athlete of the Century, triple Olympic champion Peter Snell, is equally concerned. In his autobiography he wrote these frightening lines:

The attitude of some Americans to the taking of drugs is very sad. When some kids were asked that if they could take drugs which would guarantee them an Olympic gold medal — but as a result they would be dead in five years — they said they would willingly take that risk. Now that is scary.

In 2009, following an investigation by the respected Cardiff newspaper *Wales on Sunday*, rugby and rugby league were listed among the most contaminated sports in the world when it came to the use of illegal drugs. The worst offender was Wales itself. Since January 2003 no fewer than 40 of that country's players had been sanctioned for drug violations — either for using banned products or refusing to take tests. Thirty-six of these, including two women, were rugby players.

Asked to comment, Welsh coach Warren Gatland expressed shock at the figures. 'The problems are just below the elite level,' he maintained. 'It is the players trying to make it to the top who see the incentives of what professional sport can bring them.'

Illicit recreational drugs are also a problem. Typical of rugby stars who have been caught taking drugs is former Wallaby, Wendell Sailor, whose annual salary was reputed to be in the vicinity of $750,000. After returning a positive test for cocaine, the winger was banned for two years.

British Lions forward Matt Stevens, who claimed his first test cap during

Ben Johnson . . . 'the worst I've seen.'

England's tour of New Zealand in 2004, was another high-profile player suspended from all participation in rugby, also for two years. After failing a test, Stevens admitted taking cocaine and in an emotional televised interview said: 'It's pretty distressing talking about this when you think how much time and effort so many people have put into your career.'

When Stevens was dropped from the English squad he added, 'Now I have thrown it all away with irresponsible behaviour. I want to say how very sorry I am. I want to change my life and hopefully one day win back the faith that people had in me.'

Rugby's list of shame includes international players from several countries and it is to New Zealand's credit that, apart from a few cheats in other sports, the slate is clean.

'That makes me feel really good,' says Fred, 'especially when I read what's going on in other countries.'

Many players refuse to submit to tests. Several members of the Bath Rugby Club have adopted this policy and have been suspended for nine months. In the opinion of many, to refuse a drug test is as good as admitting guilt.

'The worst I've ever seen,' says Fred, 'was Canadian Ben Johnson who won the Olympic 100 metres in Seoul in world record time. Just one look at him with his muscles almost bursting through his skin and it was obvious he was a cheat.

'They disqualified him but later they let him run again. That was a big mistake. He got into the drugs worse than ever and made another fortune before they caught him a second time.'

It is well documented that Johnson's coach argued that taking drugs was perfectly fair so long as their use was discontinued in sufficient time to return a negative result on the day of competition. In his opinion, this was not cheating

— a strange logic indeed when for years he had been filling Johnson's system with performance-enhancing substances to win races, break records and rake in the cash!

In 2006 the world's 100m record-holder, Justin Gatlin, and the winner of the Tour de France, Floyd Landis, both tested positive. Both flatly denied they would ever do such a despicable thing. Not us, they said, we're real champions! We don't have to cheat! Gatlin claimed that a masseuse bearing a grudge had rubbed a testosterone cream into his legs. Landis, whose drug test showed testosterone three times over the legal limit, blamed it on too much Jack Daniel's whiskey.

Four years later Landis hit the headlines again when he opted for an open use of drugs in sport.

'You've got to legalise doping. The testers are so far behind in the testing organisations that there's no way to change it now. Just accept that it's here, that it's not going away and that it's just going to get more complicated. You can't stop it, and you can't fix it. Monitor it and make sure people don't hurt themselves, but you have to accept it.'

When Fred Allen read this, he could scarcely believe it. 'This guy would have to be one of the most dangerous people ever to take part in sport,' he says. 'What he's done is issue a direct challenge to the authorities, telling them they can't beat drugs, so why not make them open slather — then it would be fair to everyone!

'That's about as bad as it gets. And that's why people like Landis, who know nothing about the clean and healthy side of sport, should be out on their arse for good.'

Drug cheats never stop looking for ways to avoid detection. But for sheer audacity the one uncovered at the 2004 Athens Olympics surpassed them all.

When an athlete undergoes a drug test, a urine sample is supplied in the presence of an official witness. In order to deceive this observer, several male athletes wore a lifelike artificial penis which emitted not their own urine but 'clean' urine instead. Attached to the base of this synthetic penis was a thin tube leading to a small reservoir filled with uncontaminated urine hidden in the athlete's rectum.

After the games, one of these lifelike devices was shown to assembled newsmen by New Zealander David Howman, chief of the World Anti-Doping Agency. It had been anonymously sent by mail together with names and dates.

Even hardened journalists were astounded at the lengths to which some athletes were prepared to go in their pursuit of wealth and fame.

'I Can't Let Them Down'

Fred returns to the Passchendaele killing fields and lays a wreath on the grave of a fallen All Blacks hero.

As he neared 90 years of age, Fred Allen had gained such respect that he was approached to make three journeys to the other side of the world — twice in 2005 and again in 2007.

The first of these journeys was to a destination he had visited 10 years earlier — the tiny Belgian village of Passchendaele where he went with other members of the triumphant Kiwis Army team on Anzac Day, 1995. The mission on that occasion was to pay homage to the thousands of New Zealand soldiers who had perished in the bloodiest battle of the First World War.

No conflict in history was ever fought under such terrible conditions as those at Passchendaele and this small village on the outskirts of Ypres has come to symbolise the nightmare conditions of trench fighting. More than 204,800 Commonwealth troops died in that battle, which was fought in three stages. Many now lie in 620 beautifully maintained cemeteries around the town of Ypres.

The slaughter was on a gigantic scale — the Allies suffering nearly half a million casualties and the Germans just over a quarter of a million.

Bob Scott and Fred Allen prepare to lay a wreath at the Menin Gate Memorial to the Missing at Ypres in Belgium, 2007. Fred and Bob were there, along with members of the New Zealand Defence Force, to mark the 90th anniversary of the battle of Passchendaele when almost 3000 New Zealand soldiers were killed, wounded or listed as missing in action in just two hours.

'It is sickening to think that at least 54,000 men just vanished without trace in chest-high water and mud and that more than 90,000 remains have never been identified,' says Fred.

'What a waste of young lives — an absolute bloody waste. And what did it achieve? A load of useless mud, that's what.

'From well behind the front line, the British field marshal directing the battle, a stupid bastard called Haig — Sir Douglas Haig — just kept ordering our boys forward to be slaughtered.

'Yet more than 20 years later, we were doing much the same thing in the Second World War — sending young men to be slaughtered. It's all so bloody pointless!'

It struck Fred as being even worse when he learned from his guide that one of the enemy soldiers firing at the Allies was a lance-corporal named Adolf Hitler who was wounded and temporarily blinded but survived.

'Millions of lives would have been saved if only the little bastard had been killed,' was Fred's comment.

For Fred, that first visit to Passchendaele with the Kiwis was an experience he would never forget. During front-line action in the Pacific and Italy during the Second World War he had seen many men killed and maimed, but nothing came remotely close to this horrifying slaughter.

The first of his three arduous journeys around the world was in 2005 when he was contacted by the Royal New Zealand Returned Services Association who wanted him to return to Passchendaele. He was the soldier they had chosen to entrust with a sacred mission — to represent their 120,000 members at that year's Anzac Day memorial service.

But Fred was not keen to go. He did not want to be reminded yet again of those horrors. But he also knew he could not let the RSA down. He was now in his eighty-sixth year and because of recent knee surgery he felt the long flight on his own might be beyond him.

It was at this point that the RSA agreed to his request to have as his companion his long-time friend, legendary fullback Bob Scott. Bob had also experienced front-line action during the Second World War. His job was driving truckloads of high explosives for the guns at the front. It was extremely dangerous, making him a top target for aerial attack, but he somehow came through unscathed.

Bob had an added reason for feeling emotional about the suffering of the previous generation of soldiers — in the earlier conflict his father was chronically wounded at Gallipoli.

On this second visit to Passchendaele Fred had more time to study the area and visit buildings that had been lovingly recreated after being totally destroyed during the war.

'Everything looked so clean and peaceful that it seemed almost impossible that these buildings were standing on what was once the most horrendous battleground in history.

'Liquid mud was so deep in the places I was now walking that rifles became blocked and unusable and tanks and gun carriages were completely bogged down. Thousands of men drowned in that filth, together with their mules and horses.

'Right where Bob and I were standing there had been soldiers up to their waist, day and night, in stinking contaminated muck, along with the bodies of dead comrades.'

After weeks of the most torrential rain for more than 20 years, the entire area had been churned into a quagmire by the heaviest bombardment of any war. Aerial photographs later showed more than a million shell holes in a single square mile.

Soon after the battle had ended, one of the Allied commanders, General Sir Hubert Gough, visiting the front for the first time, burst into tears: 'Good God!' he exclaimed in disbelief. 'Did we really send men to fight in this!'

One of the most memorable of the new buildings Fred and Bob visited was

Fred and Bob visit war graves just outside Ypres, Belgium, 2007.

the imposing Cloth Hall in the central market square of Ypres. It now houses the In Flanders Fields War Museum and has been listed as a heritage site.

The reconstruction of these buildings, along with many others, was financed by reparation payments from Germany, which also paid for the striking Menin Gate Memorial which, as Fred explains, is a location of particular poignancy. Names of New Zealand and other Commonwealth troops who fell at Ypres and have no known grave are recorded on that Gate. As graves have been discovered the names have been removed from the memorial.

'Bob and I both had this eerie feeling when we walked through the Menin Gate and saw the names engraved of all the New Zealanders and Australians who lost their lives,' says Fred, 'and there were a hell of a lot, believe me.

'We thought of those thousands of Allied troops who marched through on their way to death — and a bloody horrible death it was!'

As a mark of respect traffic is stopped around the arches of the memorial every evening at precisely eight o'clock as 'The Last Post' is played in memory of the British Empire troops who perished in and around the area. This rendering of 'The Last Post' is unexpectedly provided by six buglers of the local volunteer fire brigade.

Tears are invariably shed during these ceremonies of remembrance and Fred recalls that more than once he had a lump in his throat.

One of the saddest parts of the visit was when their guide took them to a crossroads not far from the Gate where former All Blacks captain Dave Gallaher had been fatally shot just 26 days before his forty-fourth birthday. He was the oldest New Zealander to die at Passchendaele.

'Obviously, I never knew the man because he was killed nearly three years before I was born,' says Fred, 'but even so I felt a certain kinship with him because we seemed to have had much in common.

'For instance, he also did the same as me — changing his age so he could fight for his country. The difference was that he pretended to be three years younger than he really was, whereas I pretended to be one year older.'

Dave Gallaher, one of 13 former All Blacks killed in the First World War, captained the Originals, the first team to tour Britain. In the 26 matches he played between 1903 and 1906 he proved an outstanding leader as well as a brilliant player. He was one of 1556 Commonwealth soldiers buried at Nine Elms Cemetery, Poperinge after the Battle of Passchendaele.

Many more Kiwis lie in nearby cemeteries. In two days alone New Zealand casualties at Passchendaele exceeded 4000 men. Dave Gallaher's death was a particularly cruel one for his family back home as two of his brothers had also been killed in action and a third had been chronically injured.

Meeting the Queen outside Westminster Abbey, 2005. The occasion was the commemoration of the 60th anniversary of the end of World War II.

Chatting with Prince William in the Auckland Museum library, 2005.

As they laid a wreath on his grave, Fred Allen and Bob Scott bowed their heads in silent tribute. Then, as they stepped back to salute, they felt a deep surge of kinship with this great man on whose headstone was the silver fern.

Five years after his death, Gallaher's memory was commemorated by the Auckland Rugby Union when they presented a handsome trophy for the winner of the Auckland inter-club championship and every year there is fierce competition for the prestigious Gallaher Shield.

Shortly after returning to New Zealand Fred Allen received a letter from London advising him he had been voted into the International Rugby Hall of Fame. Two other former All Blacks had also been selected that year. One was first-five Grant Fox and to Fred's surprise and delight the third was Dave Gallaher.

'Once again it was pretty tough on the old body but they did everything possible to make my journey comfortable,' says Fred. 'To be joining so many famous players was an enormous privilege.'

But the long flights to the other side of the globe were not yet over. In 2007 Fred received yet another communication from the New Zealand RSA. This time they wanted him to represent them at an Anzac Day service of commemoration and thanksgiving in Westminster Abbey.

'My first thought was "Hell, no, I can't go all that way again",' growled Fred. 'But again I couldn't bring myself to say "no" — not to the RSA. So once again I was off to the airport.

'And the next thing I was sitting in Westminster Abbey in the front row with the Queen.'

Detective Allen

Forty years after a dramatic rescue in the storm-tossed Hauraki Gulf Fred uncovers some surprising facts.

In the summer of 1969 the worst cyclone in living memory swept along the southern shore of the Whangaparaoa Peninsula with frightening speed. From their cliff-top homes, locals scanned the rapidly mounting seas through binoculars and were thankful no boat was out in such treacherous conditions — until their attention was alerted to an object being tossed before the storm, visible only when it rose on the crest of a wave a mile from the shore.

A closer study revealed it was an aluminium dinghy, and residents were relieved there was no one in the boat. Until they saw a small head and shoulders appear just for a second or two above the dinghy's gunwale. There was a child aboard and with the dinghy careering before the wind and waves towards the vertical cliffs south of the Okura River mouth, that child was in grave danger!

Beachfront resident John Melville (name changed for personal reasons) hastened to phone his neighbour Les Vause, whose 18-foot runabout was standing in his driveway, fuelled and ready to launch as the pair had intended to go fishing that evening. In record time they had their tractor started and the runabout in the water. Battling their way out through the huge surf was proving a difficult task until several residents waded into the water to keep the boat's bow head on to the waves to prevent it being swamped.

Although it took only a few minutes to zigzag across the mouth of the Wade River, to Les and John it seemed an eternity.

When they came as close as they dared to the wildly rocking dinghy, they saw a girl kneeling on the floor, her hands gripping the sides. When she saw them approaching, she half-scrambled to her feet and clung to the dinghy's windscreen.

Then the two boaties got the biggest shock of all. Each time the dinghy rolled at an alarming angle they could see three more children huddled together on the floor.

There were four children on board!

They could not come too close for fear of swamping the small craft so John threw a looped line to the girl and told her to place it over the bollard on the dinghy's foredeck. With the dinghy pitching wildly, everything depended on her carrying out that difficult task. After three or four attempts in the howling wind, she was successful. But had she lost her grip as she lent precariously over the windscreen she would certainly have gone overboard. She was a very brave girl when everything depended on her.

With the cliff face against which huge waves were pounding now dangerously close, Les throttled the runabout away from the danger and they began to make progress.

When the strain of the tow proved too great, the bollard on the starboard side of the runabout, with the towline attached, ripped from its socket and went flying through the air. The entire towrope threatened to disappear overboard until they managed to seize it and attach it to a second bollard on the port side. As they took up the strain again, they prayed that the second bollard was more secure than the first.

Fortunately, everything held fast as they slowly moved away from that menacing cliff and made their way back across the mouth of the river toward Arkles Bay.

Word of the ongoing drama had spread rapidly and by the time the runabout with its precious tow neared the shore a large crowd had gathered. This time a dozen helpers waded into the surf to assist with the children and the boat. John waded ashore with a small, frightened boy in his arms.

Neither Les, a former president of the Silverdale RSA, nor John ever spoke about how they had saved those four children from acute danger in a storm-tossed sea. And for almost 40 years neither of these two friends was aware that since that dramatic rescue that small, frightened boy had become a national hero. He was Sean Fitzpatrick, who had become the most-capped All Black in history and captain of the team for five years.

News of Fitzpatrick's dramatic rescue may never have been acknowledged had it not been for the initiative of Fred Allen who lived nearby. It was Fred who unearthed the truth nearly four decades later after hearing rumours of a rescue near the mouth of the Wade River from friends at the Silverdale RSA. They were discussing boating tragedies around the Rodney coast and they told him that four children had once had a very narrow escape when a dinghy had been swept away from Matakatia Beach.

But it wasn't until Fred's friends mentioned the name 'Fitzpatrick' that Fred began to put two and two together. He knew the Fitzpatrick family well because 'Fitzy's' father, Brian, had played for the All Blacks in the early 1950s. And he also knew that Brian and his wife Louise had once owned a beach house somewhere on the Whangaparaoa Peninsula.

So when Fred heard the rumour, and especially the name, he decided to phone the Fitzpatricks' home in Auckland. His call was answered by Mrs Fitzpatrick who confirmed that, yes, Sean had been the little boy rescued from the sea all those years ago. And, yes, there *were* three other children in the boat, two of whom were Sean's sisters, Julie, aged 13, and Anna, 11. The other child was a playmate, Simon Pearson.

Mrs Fitzpatrick also remembered hugging the man who had carried Sean ashore in his arms and thanking him from the bottom of her heart. This surprising fact, Fred felt, should not go unrecognised. So he told his neighbour, a reporter for the local paper, to contact Les or John who may, or may not, be prepared to tell the story. And if the paper wanted further evidence they should get in touch with Julie, the brave little girl who was so instrumental in saving her brother's life.

By then Les Vause had died, but John was still not keen to give the story to the reporter who came to see him. So, through Mrs Kirkpatrick, the reporter contacted Julie, now 50, who described how she and three other children were in the dinghy when it was seized by the cyclone and swept away.

'We were having fun in the boat along the shoreline when suddenly there was this incredible wind and the sea was wild with huge waves,' she said. 'We were blown right out of Matakatia Bay absolutely out of control.

'I was terribly frightened because we were being blown towards a cliff-face against which huge waves were breaking. The three children in the boat with me were also terrified. They were lying on the floor, crying.'

'The little boy was my young brother,' Julie told the newspaper, 'and if those two men hadn't come to our rescue it is very likely that rugby fans would never have heard of Sean Fitzpatrick.'

And if Fred Allen hadn't paid attention to that rumour in the Silverdale RSA the story of a most fortuitous rescue would never have been recognised.

Sean Fitzpatrick

The little boy went on to represent New Zealand in 128 games including 92 tests. A powerful forward with all-round ball skills and an aggressive attitude, he was 1.83 m in height and weighed in at 106 kg. After showing tremendous promise as a member of the All Blacks side that won the World Cup at Eden Park in 1987, he later achieved rugby immortality when he captained New Zealand to its first series win in South Africa in 1996. At one stage he played 63 successive tests for New Zealand, during which he was regarded as the best hooker in the world. Tough and uncompromising, he gave no quarter and expected none in return.

His outstanding career came to an end when a serious knee injury failed to respond to treatment, forcing him into retirement. He made his ninety-second and final test appearance on 29 November 1997 as a substitute in the 42–7 victory against Wales. He was 34 years and 178 days old.

A Fishing Story

'If all men were fishermen there would be no need for
psychiatrists.' — Anonymous

When he could find the time, which wasn't often, Fred loved to go fishing in the Hauraki Gulf.

There are fishing stories and fishing stories, but an event that occurred the day Fred was introduced to Orewa car painter Basil Hollows is well worth telling. Basil was a recreational fisherman who brought to boat fishing a science all of his own. Big snapper and kingfish were his quarry and he was extremely skilful at enticing them on to a hook. Through years of trial and error he had invented new methods of rigging his line for changing wind, sea and tide conditions and his strike rate was phenomenal.

One evening Fred phoned his friend John Melville to tell him he would be leaving Manly Beach at 6.30 the following morning for a day's fishing at Flat Rock, Kawau, should he like to come along.

John asked Fred if he could bring a friend. 'Why are you so keen to bring someone else?' Fred asked, reticent about taking another person, especially a stranger.

'For insurance purposes, Fred,' John replied. 'If this chap's with us, we'll get plenty of fish.'

There was pause and then Fred said, 'Okay, if you want him to come so much, bring him along. But make sure he's on time!'

Knowing how Fred was a stickler for punctuality, John had Basil on Manly Beach right on the tick of six o'clock, just as dawn was breaking.

In those days Fred had a 19 ft Bertram named *Miss Valiant*, a sturdy sea boat, ideally suited for Hauraki Gulf conditions. When Fred left the beach and headed for Kawau he was accompanied by a 14 ft 6 in Sea Nymph with former Auckland rugby rep George 'Gunboat' Nelson and his son aboard. Gunboat and Fred had been friends for a long time. He had been a major during the Second World War and had played with Fred in the famous Kiwis Army team. He was also one of the two men who had raised the money to purchase the first clubrooms for the Barbarians Rugby Club next to Eden Park.

As the two boats neared the halfway point the weather turned sour. A few minutes of this and George yelled he was turning back. The bigger and much heavier *Miss Valiant* was handling the seas well so Fred made the decision to carry on. When *Miss Valiant* reached Flat Rock, Basil Hollows asked Fred if he could show him where to drop the anchor. Basil had lived on Kawau for several years and knew the sea floor around the island like the back of his hand.

So with Fred at the controls, and Basil signalling instructions from the foredeck hatch, they manoeuvred until Basil called for Fred to cut the motor while he dropped the anchor.

The party had been fishing for several minutes before Basil turned to Fred with a question. 'What's the biggest fish you've ever caught, Fred?'

'A 16-and-a-half pounder,' Fred replied. 'I caught it myself round the back of Tiri a couple of years ago.'

'Then how would a 19-and-a-half pounder do?' said Basil.

He was sitting at the stern — his favourite possie — his right hand holding a handline out of sight over the transom. Slowly, he began to play a fish. It had already been hooked when he asked Fred the question.

As *Miss Valiant* pitched in the swell, Basil lifted it over the side and laid it, still kicking, on the cockpit floor. It was a beauty. It had taken Basil only a few minutes to hook, and another two minutes to land, and when they weighed it, it tipped the scales just a fraction over 19 and a half pounds!

Few people have ever seen Fred Allen dumbfounded, but for a few seconds he just sat and stared at the big snapper. For his visitor to have so accurately judged the weight of that huge fish when it was still metres below the surface was one of those marvellous fishing moments that remain embedded in one's memory.

As the weather worsened Fred decided to cross into Kawau Bay and fish in the lee of Rabbit Island until the wind abated. It didn't take long for Basil

Fishing has been a lifelong passion for Fred.

to prove himself a second time. He kept pulling in fish, one after the other, although none was as big as that first catch.

Then, as the wind dropped and the sea flattened, they headed for home. There were lots snapper on board *Miss Valiant* and Basil had caught most of them. And the 19 lb 8 oz female fish, the first one landed, was the biggest of them all.

They cleaned the catch at Fred's beach house which looks down on Manly beach, before Fred asked them inside for a drink. As they chatted about the great day they'd had, Fred called for silence. He wished to pay Basil a tribute.

Fred spoke for a few minutes about excellence in sport, saying he had never seen such a skilled fisherman as Basil Hollows. Then he shook Basil's hand and presented him with a bottle of fine Scotch whisky — a tribute from one sportsman to another. Fred Allen had always been one of Basil's idols and the look of pride on his face as Fred handed him his trophy was good to behold.

On his way home in the car Basil said: 'It's true, you know. There are things in life that money can't buy.'

Apart from rugby and fishing, Fred's other sporting passion was duck shooting. For more than 30 years he and a group of friends, including Warwick Harvey, Roly McCrystal and Roly's son, Barry, went duck shooting near Cambridge on a farm at Te Miro owned by Loma and Dick Cook.

The Hauraki Gulf, off the Whangaparaoa Peninsula, has always been a happy hunting ground for Fred.

'They had really comfortable mai-mais and huge purpose-built duck ponds,' says Fred. 'It would be hard to imagine a better place for enthusiasts like us.'

Barry McCrystal, now a prominent businessman on Auckland's North Shore, has treasured memories of those expeditions.

'We'd get to Cambridge about four o'clock and head straight to the private bar of the Nash Hotel where a number of locals were always waiting for us — mainly because they wanted to have a natter with Fred,' he says.

'Fred never forgot the names of any of those men, or of the shopkeepers and others we met through all those years — and he had a knack of making them all feel special. They would hit him up with rugby questions for hours on end but he was never fazed. His memory for the nitty-gritty details of historic games was phenomenal and they lapped it up.

'They were absolutely rapt when he was expressing his feelings about certain things such as the bad handling of the Keith Murdoch affair, or when he was describing the hours he spent teaching Sid Going to pass without taking a step by making him stand with one leg against a goalpost — and never letting him move.

'Then he'd make Sid turn around to do the same thing and pass the other way. There were so many stories, and each one had the locals spell-bound.

'They loved hearing Fred describe how he startled the Queen with his exploding cigarette. That was during the 1967 tour when he and the non-playing All Blacks were seated directly behind the Royal family during the Scottish test at Murrayfield.

'Jazz Muller, who was on the injured list that day, handed Fred a rolled cigarette which he lit, but after he had taken a few puffs it suddenly blew up. Fred got a hell of a fright, but worse still was the start it gave the Queen. She looked round and gave Fred one of those "I am not amused looks".

'Fred always chuckled when he told that story. "That was typical of Jazz," he said, "he was a practical joker — a real hard case."

'Fred is very competitive, of course, and watching him shoot you'd think he was back in the war. It was the steely look on his face and the way he gripped his gun.

'This intenseness was even more apparent when we went looking for rabbits, hare, quail or pheasants. His demeanour was as though he was approaching an enemy line.

'On one of these hunts we walked down a clay slope, slippery after recent rain. Fred, who was wearing gumboots, slipped and started to slide down an embankment, not realising that mud was getting into the barrel of his gun.

'Back in our mai-mai we waited for ducks to appear and when they finally came Fred took careful aim and squeezed the trigger. We all recoiled as the barrel of Fred's gun exploded and split in four. It looked like a picture from an old Disney cartoon.

'Later, over a drink in our small shanty, we all had a hearty laugh — all of us, that is, except Fred — and I did promise never to tell anyone. I can only hope he'll forgive me for breaking that promise,' says Barry.

'The shanty was divided into two rooms. One was a kitchen-cum-lounge, eight feet by 12 feet, with photographs and cartoons covering the walls. Most of them featured some sort of sport — horse-racing, hunting and, of course, rugby. The bedroom was completely wallpapered with pin-up pictures clipped from men's magazines.

'Fred was the group's chief cook, and very capable he was too. He was great with all our favourites including roast lamb, silverside and steak.'

Fred always took three dogs to Te Miro and when the Cooks saw the third one, a sprightly little character called Miranda, they almost doubled up with laughter. The other two looked fine because they were handsome Labradors, dogs that could be relied on to retrieve, but Miranda was surely a joke.

'I couldn't blame them,' says Fred. 'She was an odd-looking mix of a mongrel, not much bigger than a rabbit, but she was a bright-eyed intelligent little thing and I became very fond of her. The only reason I took her to the farm was to let her have a run around and get a bit of exercise. I certainly didn't expect her to do any retrieving.'

'But when it came to rabbits or game birds we were astounded. The little blighter's nose was amazing and, although we'd seen or heard nothing, she'd suddenly rush into the dense undergrowth and every time she barked out would come a rabbit or a pheasant.

'Before long no one laughed any longer at little Miranda. She had earned our respect and was an accepted member of the team.'

Loma and Dick Cook insisted on plucking the ducks before Fred and the others took them back to Auckland for the big occasion — the annual black-tie duck dinner at the Auckland Club with the main course provided by Fred Allen and Warwick Harvey.

'We'd each invite six people,' says Fred, 'so there were always 14 at the table. After the meal we all enjoyed cigars and a glass or two of port while swapping stories about the past. They were very special evenings, those duck dinners.'

One of Fred's favourite after-dinner stories was about that irrepressible Maori All Black, Ike Proctor, one of the stars of the Kiwis Army team that toured Great Britain.

'We'd been invited to Buckingham Place to meet King George VI and the Queen, and were in this ornate reception room waiting to be introduced. The

Queen was doing most of the talking because the King, who had a severe stutter, liked to leave that to her. I was standing in line next to Ike and heard the Queen ask him where he was from and Ike politely said he'd been born north of Auckland.

'That was fine until Ike went on . . . "We used to eat people like you."

'I nearly jumped out of my skin. I just wanted the floor to open up and swallow me.

'But the Queen just smiled and replied, "I know — Samuel Marsden told me so."

'When the introductions were over, I couldn't get Ike out of Buckingham Palace fast enough. That guy was a real hard case if ever there was one.'

Racing was another of Fred's sporting interests. Although he was never a punter, he loved the sight of thoroughbreds in full stride. One of his first horses was Melodic, which won 18 races, including a Nathans Memorial at Ellerslie.

He tried to register his colours as all black, but permission was refused by the racing conference. But he did call one of his horses Tout Noir (All Black). 'It was no champion,' says Fred, 'but it won a few races and gave me a lot of pleasure.'

On the other side of the Tasman he won a Summer Cup with Hyde and a Queensland Derby with Florissa.

He was later involved in a partnership with another All Black, Arthur Hughes, a leading figure in the racing industry. Arthur served as president of the Auckland Racing Club as well as the New Zealand Racing Conference. In 2005, just a couple of months before his death, he paid Fred the compliment of naming his new racehorse 'Fred the Needle'.

This particular Fred had a fine pedigree and was trained by New Zealand's leading jockey, Lance O'Sullivan, at Matamata's famous Wexford Stables. *Sunday News* racing commentator, Dave Bradford, described his first meeting with the four-legged Fred: 'I looked at his proud head and wondered if there was another horse in all the land which had a bigger name to live up to.'

Killer Nets

'Get rid of the bloody things before someone is drowned,'
was Fred's blunt warning to his local council.

In 2002 Fred Allen played a crucial role in ending a nightmare at one of the most popular family beaches on the Hibiscus Coast.

For nearly four years no one swimming, boating or playing in the water at beautiful Arkles Bay had been safe from harm. Set-nets, as many as five at a time, laid down in shallow water at right angles to the foreshore of this small beach, and left unattended day and night, became potential death-traps.

Concerned parents forbad their children to swim at the once-safe beach. They saw little difference between nets set along the foreshore and nets set across a public swimming pool. Youngsters in small boats were capsized and runabouts were brought to abrupt standstills with outboards badly damaged.

It was a life-threatening situation that should have been outlawed long before it snared its first victim — a 12-year-old boy, over from Brisbane to spend Christmas with his grandmother. The youngster was doing handstands in the water when he landed in a set-net all but invisible in choppy water.

'I was horrified as I watched him struggle,' his grandmother said, 'but fortunately he didn't panic and was able to free himself. But it takes only a few minutes to drown and had he been less confident in the water, there would have been a tragedy.'

A drowned dolphin at Arkles Bay . . . the result of illegal set-netting.

She sought a hearing before the Rodney District Council calling for an immediate ban on set-nets along the foreshore of prime swimming areas. Her confidence that the council would act without delay was badly shaken when one councillor said, 'But nobody's been drowned yet!'

When Fred, who lived nearby, saw where the boy had been trapped he could scarcely believe his eyes. For someone to set nets where children enjoyed swimming and boating, and leave them unattended day and night, was beyond his belief.

'I'd always kept clear of politics,' Fred says, 'but this wasn't politics — this was a community in grave danger.'

Days later Fred was again appalled when a 75-year-old woman, swimming backstroke in four feet of water, was snared in a net with both arms through the mesh. She, too, was lucky to escape. She fought to free herself before being helped ashore by her elderly husband who had waded into the water. When the couple reached dry land, the netters, who did not live in the area, bombarded them with obscenities and ordered them to keep away from the nets.

Still the authorities did nothing and before long a total of 13 swimmers had been entrapped, several lucky to escape with their lives, while dolphins, dogs, penguins and other seabirds had been drowned.

'Don't tell me there are nets set right where kids swim at your best beaches, yet your local council does nothing about it,' wrote a visitor from Canada. 'That

Nets — as many as five at a time — were set at right angles to Arkles Bay beach before fisherman and conservationist Fred Allen entered the picture.

wouldn't be tolerated in Toronto for one second.'

But in spite of hundreds of similar letters to the press and as many petitions, neither the council nor the Ministry of Fisheries moved to rid the community of this life-threatening menace. And, as if this wasn't enough, fish stock from the adjoining Okura Marine Reserve was being plundered in huge quantities.

Fred had always been a keen fisherman and conservationist and the protection of our fishing stock was of great importance to him. He had always obeyed the fishing rules and he expected others to do the same.

When he learned that catches were always retrieved under cover of darkness by a group of itinerant fishermen driving SUV vehicles down to the water's edge, he became even more concerned.

'This wholesale taking of fish night after night without any official check on type or size is a national disgrace,' he told the authorities.

So concerned was he that he joined the Arkles Bay Action Group which was struggling to have a by-law introduced. He made a strong submission before the Rodney District Council to make his views clear and he also helped local papers take up the cudgels. Their stories sparked the interest of national media including TV One which ran a revealing segment on the six o'clock news presented by Judy Bailey.

The episode shows two of the netters angrily denying even possessing nets. But when the television reporter and her photographer investigate further they find several nets stacked in canvas bags at the side of the netters' Stanmore Bay house.

So serious did the situation become that a public meeting was held in the Whangaparaoa Community Hall with Fred as the main speaker.

'It's bloody insane that these netters are wading out from the shore and setting nets between kids playing in the water,' was the crux of his message to a large audience. 'The authorities must act before someone is drowned.'

Fred also stressed the fact that every time the nets were set, the netters were blatantly flaunting every item in the fishing ministry's Set Net Code of Practice.

Because the nets were dragnets, cleverly re-rigged to remain stationary on the surface, numerous boating accidents occurred. When her father's runabout was jerked to a standstill by a net, a visitor from Wellington was hurled over the windscreen into the path of a jet-ski which missed her by inches. The woman was bruised and shaken but escaped serious injury. The boat's propeller, with the net wrapped tightly around its shaft, was severely damaged.

When a Stanmore Bay housewife asked one of the netters why they were being so greedy, she became the victim of a frightening experience. She was tailgated by a large SUV vehicle, driven by one of the netters, over a distance of 14 kilometres from Arkles Bay to Orewa. Fearing for her life because of the driver's intimidating tactics, the woman dialled 111 for help. She was told by the police operator to lock her car doors and drive directly into the forecourt of the Orewa Police Station.

She did so, hurried inside and spoke to the station officer who had already been briefed. He despatched a police car to pursue the departing SUV, siren it down and bring it back. The driver was interrogated at length and issued with a stern warning.

The netters brooked no interference. Anyone who dared to complain was subjected to intimidation, even on their own properties. Residents walking on footpaths were forced to evade vehicles veering to the wrong side of the road. There was a threat to burn down a house and inflict physical harm.

When the netters mistakenly thought the woman owner of a launch had removed one of their nets during the night they threatened to bomb her boat. It was later confirmed that the missing net, illegally anchored by sandbags as they all were, had been washed ashore.

Written complaints of these, and other incidents, were received at both the Whangaparaoa and Orewa police stations on a regular basis.

It would require an entire book to fully record the long and bitter struggle to have the infamous set-nets removed. But finally in October 2006 a new by-law outlawing the nets was passed.

'This wonderful result has been brought about by the efforts of those who campaigned so hard and determinedly,' said neighbourhood watch supervisor Jimmy Haddow. 'And, no doubt about it, it was a fantastic bonus having the support of a man which such immense mana as Fred Allen. When he joined our group it made all the difference.'

The day the by-law was passed, the atmosphere of gloom that had hung over the area for so long disappeared and that evening a joyful community celebrated with a barbecue beach party and danced to the lively music of a jazz trio.

Almost immediately scores of families who had been avoiding the beach were back enjoying themselves in the water. And within a few weeks, to the delight of adults and children alike, the much loved Arkles Bay dolphins, which had been avoiding their habitat for so long, began to return.

The gratitude of the local community was summed up in a letter hand-delivered to Fred's home:

Dear Mr Allen

On behalf of the residents of Arkles Bay, and the thousands of visitors who enjoy our beach each summer, I would like to thank you most sincerely for helping solve a problem which at one stage appeared insurmountable.

We had fought vigorously to rid the foreshore of those life threatening nets and your support at Rodney Council hearings was one of the pivotal reasons for our eventual success. You have the gratitude of us all.

Yours most sincerely
James Haddow
Neighbourhood Watch Supervisor

Saving a Yacht Club

When an historic yacht club is on the verge of extinction Fred steps forward to assist.

'We must do something!' was Fred's immediate reaction when he read the 1997 annual report of the Manly Sailing Club on the Whangaparaoa Peninsula.

He'd been jolted by one particular sentence: 'Membership has dwindled and the club is struggling to survive.'

He had a special affection for the club on the Manly foreshore. Fifty years previously he had been one of a small volunteer party who had built and paid for the first small clubhouse. He had also helped lay down the first concrete boat ramp alongside the one-room building. Manly was also the beach on which Fred had led about a dozen members of his All Blacks squad on early morning training runs before their 1949 tour of South Africa.

He was staying with his friend Roly McCrystal at the time. Roly knew every local resident and arranged for them to billet the All Blacks. After a few weekends of running and swimming twice a day the players were tanned and fit and well prepared for the long tour that lay ahead.

Fred had always loved the sea. As a young man he had crewed on an A-class keeler and he had been a member of the Royal New Zealand Yacht Squadron for 60 years. No one knew better than he how valuable this historic little club was to the Hibiscus Coast. It had been formed as a Christmas holiday club, but as the area developed it had grown into a fulltime facility providing invaluable sailing and coaching programmes. To Fred, the prospect of losing it was unthinkable.

The root of the problem lay with the Rodney District Council. On at least three occasions the club had applied for resource consents to enlarge and upgrade its building, but the applications had been declined.

This left the club with an obsolete clubhouse, a shortage of equipment, a lack of money and, worst of all, a badly weakened morale.

The council had been repeatedly influenced by the damaging submissions of a small protest group who owned nearby properties. Their submissions at the hearings included masterpieces of spin-doctoring such as:

> *There is the fear of having an unofficial pub on Manly Park.*
> *There is concern that young people learn to associate alcohol and sport.*
> *There will be loud noise from music, singing and partying.*
> *We will be unable to walk in the park in the day or night because of intoxicated persons, especially in the children's playground adjacent to the clubhouse.*

'These were cheap shots below the belt levelled at a youth and family sailing club that had never had a black mark against its name in more than 50 years,' Fred told the council. 'And as for alcohol — it had never been a part of this youth and family club, nor will it be in the future.'

The club's desperate situation had been aggravated by the financial burden of fighting the council. After each failed application it had received an account from council running into thousands of dollars.

'It was the same as losing a court case and having to pay costs,' says Fred, who was then deputy patron of the club. 'The last failed submission in 1996 alone brought us a bill for nearly $4000. That brought the total cost of the three failed attempts close to $10,000. That was a tough hurdle — too tough, in fact, for some of the volunteer workers to handle. Many resigned in despair.'

And, even worse, the club was forced to turn down applications for membership because of sub-standard facilities and lack of manpower.

In a community such as the Hibiscus Coast, where every child lived no more than a few hundred yards from the sea, youngsters wishing to learn sailing and water safety skills were being denied the opportunity.

An additional threat came in May 1998 when the same protestors tried to administer the *coup de grâce*. At a hearing in the council chamber they advocated

The rise and rise of the Manly Sailing Club . . .

that the clubhouse be shifted back from its position on the waterfront to where it would have no view of the sea.

It now seemed certain that the club would die.

Fred naturally expected the club's flag officers to fight back and could not believe his ears when he learned that not a single one intended to appear at the council hearing. They were just going to sit back and let the club go under.

When a small group consisting of the club patron and his wife, together with one staunch club member, vowed to continue the fight on the club's behalf, Fred decided to join them.

It was at this stage that Sir Peter Blake, the figurehead of New Zealand yachting, also agreed to help in spite of his heavy schedule with an approaching defence of the America's Cup. At the council hearing on 20 May 1998, Sir Peter poured scorn on the protestors' submission that the clubhouse be moved further inland with no view of the sailing area. 'For anyone to suggest there is no need for a clubhouse in sight of the racecourse is an absolute nonsense,' he said.

'I certainly would not let my children race at a yacht club which had no surveillance of the sea. That would be foolhardy and unacceptable to me as a parent.

'I hope that the persons writing such submissions will be prepared to front the media if an accident happens that would have been avoidable by the correct siting of such a yacht club facility.'

The appearance in the council chamber of Fred Allen caught the protestors by surprise. His no-nonsense, straight-to-the-point arguments completely refuted the misleading evidence that had been fed to council over the years.

He concluded with the words: 'It's about time these selfish people came to their senses and started to think of the welfare of the youth of the district.'

The lengthy hearing ended in a memorable victory for the Manly Sailing Club. It won consents for the clubhouse to stay on its waterfront site and to be considerably enlarged.

The impact of Fred Allen and Sir Peter Blake was emphasised in a *Rodney Times* article headlined: 'Heavyweights of Sport Support Manly Sailing Club'.

Club members who had expected the worst were delighted. Many who had resigned renewed their memberships and returned to active participation.

'The Hibiscus Coast will now have a fine new clubhouse with everything it needs for youngsters to learn to sail and to race in safety,' said Fred. 'And that's what matters to me.'

A few days later he was thrilled when a letter arrived from a group of members thanking him for the valuable role he had played:

Dear Mr Allen

As members of the Manly Sailing Club we wish to express our sincere thanks for the time and effort you have put in over the past two years to overcome the problems that were threatening to destroy our club.

Thanks to your wealth of experience and considerable knowledge of the club's history you have been of enormous help and the club can now look forward to the future with a great deal of confidence.

We are fortunate indeed to have you as one of our most enthusiastic supporters.

We join in wishing you and your family the best of good health and good fortune for the future.

[Members signatures]

Following the granting of all consents and building permits the Manly Sailing Club raised sufficient money to demolish its obsolete building and construct a fine new clubhouse. Today, in addition to its own all-year-round training and sailing programme, it hosts provincial as well as national championships.

A Remarkable Year

Fred receives a unique tribute from the city of Auckland and a knighthood from the Queen.

The day Fred turned 90, the Mayor of Auckland and his councillors transformed the Town Hall council chamber into City Party Central, and invited Fred's closest friends, along with a galaxy of 100 celebrities, to a civic luncheon in his honour. Among the many dignitaries present were former All Blacks captains, knights of the realm, captains of industry, prominent politicians and sporting icons.

As he presented the living legend with an engraved silver plaque, and helped him cut an enormous cake, Mayor Banks said:

'Today, in the historic Auckland Town Hall on Queen Street, the number of high-quality patriots gathered around you to celebrate your 90th birthday speaks volumes for your extensive contributions to this city and this country.

'Fred, you are a true example of what makes New Zealand great. You are a very special man, much admired, greatly respected and loved by those of us who are privileged to have been touched by your greatness.'

He described Fred as 'one of our greatest living New Zealanders', and thanked him for being 'such a wonderful role model for all of us'.

'On behalf of the citizens of Auckland we thank you for your enormous

Bob Scott (rear) has the microphone during the mayoral luncheon, hosted in honour of Fred on the day he turned 90. Fred, centre, is flanked by Auckland Mayor John Banks and June and Alan Sayers.

contribution to our society and today, Fred Allen, we put you on a pedestal.'

One of the 12 former All Blacks captains at the luncheon, Sir Wilson Whineray, had these words to say: 'Fred Allen is a precious jewel in the crown of New Zealand rugby. His philosophy of the game is based on discipline, precision and respect.'

Bob Scott, legendary All Blacks fullback: 'Fred, your character has left an indelible mark on our national game and on the lives of the many fine young men who have passed through your hands.'

Sir Brian Lochore described himself as one of the country's luckiest players because he was the All Blacks captain right through Fred's unbeaten reign.

'He wasn't nicknamed The Needle because he loved to sew,' said Sir Brian. 'He could strip a player of any pretensions with a word and a withering look. He was ruthless but his heart beat for rugby and for his players.'

The chairman of the New Zealand Rugby Football Union, Jock Hobbs, had this to say: 'Fred's unblemished record as an All Blacks coach will be hard to surpass. He remains an icon of our game and it's great that his 90th birthday is being recognised by so many people.'

The chief executive of the Auckland Rugby Union, Andy Dalton: 'We are extremely proud to have Fred as our patron. His service to rugby is extraordinary and we are thrilled to see this amazing man reach yet another wonderful milestone in his life.'

Sir Fred Allen receives his knighthood from New Zealand's Governor-General Sir Anand Satyanand, June 2010.

In an emotional reply Fred said: 'It is difficult for me to explain how I feel today. To be honoured in this fashion by the mayor of New Zealand's largest city and his councillors is indeed a humbling experience and one that will remain a treasured memory for the rest of my life.'

He praised the loyalty and companionship of the many great men he had enjoyed having in his teams before quoting from a famous rugby poem: 'It matters not whether you play on some rain-soaked winter field in front of 200 spectators — or 10, or even none — or in front of 80,000 at Twickenham — the sensation is the same. There's the exhilaration of the body and soul that will forever linger in the minds of all who have known rugby.'

Another 'exhilaration', the biggest of them all, came in June 2010 when football fans around the world shared the delight of New Zealanders over the announcement that Fred Allen had at long last received a knighthood and henceforth would be called "Sir Fred".

Hundreds of letters arrived, the first from Prime Minister John Key:

Dear Fred

I am writing to congratulate you on your appointment as a Knight Companion of The New Zealand Order of Merit for your services to New Zealand in the Queen's Birthday Honours 2010.

Our success as a nation relies on citizens from all walks of life stepping forward, helping others, seeking new ways of doing things, and reaching for their dreams. You have made an outstanding contribution to that success and enriched the lives of us all.

This honour gives the people you have touched the chance to show their appreciation for your hard work, your dedication, and your achievements. It also gives the New Zealand public the opportunity to recognise your efforts.

On behalf of the government, my parliamentary colleagues, and all New Zealanders, thank you.

John Key

Among the many letters was one that Fred particularly treasured. It came from an 86-year-old Christchurch woman who admitted she knew little about rugby. She was Hope O'Connell who had often ordered Fred Allen garments during the 32 years she worked as a buyer for Ballantynes in Christchurch.

'Wonderful, wonderful and so well deserved,' she wrote. 'With your continued interest in the game there will be many young men out there who will be listening for your advice. Keep well and happy.'

'Fancy writing to me after all those years,' says Fred. 'When I opened that letter I was really touched.'

Sir Fred and his granddaughter 'Nessie' after his investiture at Government House.

The Dream Team

Having been involved in rugby for more than 80 years, no one is better qualified than Fred Allen to assess the greatest players of all time.

I've been watching, playing or coaching rugby now for more than eight decades and in that time I've been fortunate to see many great players and many wonderful teams. Picking my top team from across all those years in New Zealand rugby has not been easy. I have had to leave out so many great players, and that is something I have found very difficult, especially as I played alongside or coached so many of them.

The fact of the matter is that I could easily have picked four or five teams and there would not have been much between them. In the end I decided that this team would be picked on 'best form'. That means that all the players selected in both my Dream Team and my Second XV are playing at the peak of their powers.

Of all the players in my two teams, I have named just one on reputation. He is the incomparable Maurice Brownlie who, like Colin Meads, was the dominant forward of his time in the All Blacks. The remaining 29 players I have had the good fortune to see represent New Zealand in test matches from as far back as 1930.

Fullbacks

As I've said earlier in the book, I was hugely excited to be taken to Lancaster Park to see George Nepia play for New Zealand in the second test against the British and Irish Lions in 1930. By then he had a huge reputation and in Christchurch that day he certainly lived up to it. The All Blacks got home 13–10 and I think it was George's wonderful defence that was the difference between the two teams. I remember him stopping an almost certain try when he completely mesmerised the Lions' backs, Aarvold and Morley. They had broken clear and, with only the fullback to beat, Aarvold chose to go alone. Mistake. George levelled him in a copybook tackle.

I played a lot with Bob Scott and he was also a tremendous defensive player. When Scotty was at the back you didn't have a worry in the world — the Rock of Gibraltar as far as I was concerned. Bob also had great feet and was a terrific attacking player. His punting and place kicking were top notch, although he did have an unlucky run with his goal-kicking on the 1949 tour of South Africa. He wasn't missing by much, often hitting the uprights or the crossbar. It was bad luck for him and for us because the Springboks' kicker, Okey Geffin, kicked everything. To be fair, Scotty did not get that many opportunities in the test series in '49 and many of his attempts were from a long way out.

Of the other fullbacks, Fergie McCormick was very much like Bob Scott in that very few players ever got past him. He was such a gutsy footballer. Don Clarke was solid and possessed that famously prodigious boot. Christian Cullen was a brilliant player in his day, although I always thought they could have used him more as an attacking weapon on the blindside. Still, a brilliant player to watch in full flight. The current All Blacks' fullback, Mils Muliaina, has really come on in the last couple of years and has scored some great tries for New Zealand. He's top drawer as well.

Wings

I can never forget the feats of Bryan Williams in South Africa in 1970. I was leading an All Blacks supporters' tour to the republic and he was just sensational. Of course I was aware of his reputation before he left for that tour, but some of his performances were breathtaking. He was a great sight when he was in full flight — pace, sidestep, fend, he had it all. There's no doubt that he'll always be remembered for that South African tour, but I also saw him play some sensational games for Auckland and the All Blacks in later years. On top of everything else, 'BG' is a class act, a real nice guy and a man who has been a great ambassador for rugby.

I thought I'd seen it all when it came to great wings prior to the 1995 World Cup, but Jonah Lomu was something else altogether. What pace and power. He was virtually impossible to stop when he was at his best. I was on another All Blacks' World Cup supporters tour in 1995 so I was privileged to see him as a youngster — just like Bryan Williams in 1970 — and what a great attacking weapon he was.

I remember coming down to breakfast at our hotel a couple of days before the All Blacks played Scotland in the quarter-final at Pretoria. The Scots were also in our hotel and their captain, Gavin Hastings — a hell of a nice guy — invited me to have breakfast with him and his brother Scott. Midway through our meal, Gavin asked me, 'Fred, how can we stop Lomu?'

'Gavin,' I said, 'you won't stop him with a bloody steamroller.'

We've been blessed with many great wingers, going right back to the 1905 Originals. I saw George Hart play in the 1930s and he was pretty handy and had great pace. Ron Jarden was a pacey, thinking winger and the best player of his generation. Thirty-five tries in 37 matches for the All Blacks is hard to argue with. Then you've got guys like Stu Wilson, Grant Batty and Jeff Wilson, all of whom were exceptional in their time. John Kirwan was a bloody good footballer who, like Jonah, had pace, strength and size and a great ability to beat a player one on one.

So Bryan Williams is my first-choice wing. After that I've really struggled to decide between Jonah and 'JK'. In the end, I've given the nod to Jonah. I know that both he and Bryan were, strictly speaking, left wingers, but it's my Dream Team and I'm allowed a bit of latitude.

Centres

Johnny Smith was the greatest centre I ever saw and I have no hesitation in naming him in my Dream Team. Johnny was a superstar for the Kiwis in 1945–46 and there was no doubt he was the British league scouts' main target after the tour. He played outstandingly for the All Blacks against the Aussies in 1946 and 1947, and what a tragedy it was that he was barred from touring with us in South Africa in 1949 because of his Maori descent. Smithy could beat a man half a dozen ways — half the time the opposition had no idea of where he was, or what he was going to do. He was quick, too, but not perhaps as quick as the real speedsters. It's just that he had such great feet and so many tricks in his bag. Many of the legendary Welsh backs, like Bleddyn Williams, Jackie Matthews and Cliff Morgan, rated 'JB' Smith as one of the greatest backs they'd ever seen.

Bruce Robertson was a wonderful player to watch, with great speed and silky running skills. He must have been a real delight for the wingers he played inside. We've had a crop of really good centres come through in the last

20 years or so. Joe Stanley, Frank Bunce and Tana Umaga were all strong attackers and defenders and each had great careers for the All Blacks. As a testament to their abilities, I believe most international sides of their time would have welcomed all three of them. I rate Conrad Smith highly as well.

Second-fives

I saw Bert Cooke play for New Zealand against the touring Lions in 1930, right at the end of his involvement with the All Blacks. By this time, though, he had carved out a wonderful playing career. He was, of course, one of the greats on the 'Invincibles' tour of 1924–25. Bert shuffled between second-five and centre, but wherever he was in the backline he always posed a threat. He wasn't a big man, but he was elusive and had great speed and acceleration.

I played quite a bit of All Blacks rugby with Ron Elvidge in the 1940s and what a great footballer he was. A quiet, almost shy person off the field, he was a great player to have on your side. He was a big, strong man for his time and always reliable. I held Ron in very high esteem. Ian MacRae was another big, strong second-five who I coached for a fair bit of his career. Ian was a complete player, too. We've been well served at second-five for some time. Bill Osborne, Warwick Taylor and Walter Little and more latterly Ma'a Nonu spring to mind.

First-fives

Dan Carter. No question about it. He hasn't got a single weakness and where he has it over some of the other great players in that position is that he's not afraid to tackle. He's actually bigger than he looks on television and he has a great ability to shrug or fend off defenders. Kicks well, runs well, distributes and tackles well. What more could you want? Other players in my very top drawer would include Ross Brown, who was a very good runner and kicker at different stages of his career, and Grant Fox and Andrew Mehrtens. Both Foxy and Mehrts were exceptional kickers and Mehrts also had a good running game.

Halfbacks

I firmly believe that Des Connor was the greatest halfback I ever saw. A great all-rounder with a kicking, passing and running game. He came over to New Zealand from Australia in 1960 and I had a lot to do with him as coach of the Auckland team. It always amazed me that he wasn't taken away on the

1963–64 tour of the British Isles. Sid Going got better and better as his career went on — his performance at Eden Park against the French in the third test of the 1968 series was unbelievable. It was my final test as All Blacks coach. I really wanted to win that day and I told Sid to run as much as he wanted and that I wanted him to score at least one try. He had a blinder that day, scoring two tries and very nearly a third. Chris Laidlaw was a very accomplished player with a great pass and Dave Loveridge was also a mighty all-rounder.

No.8s

Brian Lochore would be my pick, although I was always a huge admirer of Buck Shelford. I surprised a lot of people when I made Brian my first All Blacks captain back in 1966. To me, though, he was the logical choice after Wilson Whineray's retirement. He was by no means the most senior player in the side, but I had a gut feeling about Brian and it proved correct. He was a born leader of men. As a player he was big and robust, a very good lineout forward and, although not a classical runner, he was faster than he looked and linked well with his backs. He was also a great corner-flagger and he possessed a very, very strong left-footed kick. Buck was also a great leader and a real hard man on the field. He's a close second to 'BJ'. I should also mention Zinzan Brooke, who was a wonderfully skilled player.

Flankers

I've said on many occasions that Colin Meads is the greatest all-round footballer I've ever seen. In saying that, Richie McCaw is right up there. He must be immensely strong both mentally and physically because I cannot believe how much work he gets through. He just doesn't stop. I'm amazed by how he gets up time and again after he's been completely done over. Ian Kirkpatrick was a mighty footballer in his day — a real athlete. Kel Tremain was a big, strong player and very difficult to stop close to the line. You also had Waka Nathan, another fine player. Graham Mourie was a fine captain who read a game well. I rated him very highly. Before Richie arrived on the scene I thought Michael Jones was as good as it got. Michael was a terrific athlete and he played both openside and blindside flanker equally well. He would be a hard player to leave out of any all-time great side.

Locks

Colin Meads would be my first pick. No question about it. He could do absolutely anything on a rugby field and there is no doubt in my mind that he would have footed it with today's players. I get annoyed when people say he was a dirty player. He wasn't. He might have been caught a few times doing a couple of things, but they were always in the interests of the team. If a young halfback or first-five was getting done over, Colin would sort it out. A dirty player? Never.

In the 1920s Maurice Brownlie was the greatest forward of his era. Although he was generally regarded as a loose forward, the scrum formation was vastly different back then — a 2-3-2 formation and the roles of the forwards were different from those of today. Brownlie was, in fact, the main lineout forward on the 1924–25 'Invincibles' tour of Britain and France. He was feared right around the world, firstly with the 'Invincibles' and then as captain of the 1928 All Blacks in South Africa where the series was drawn.

There are a number of players who have served New Zealand well at lock over the years. 'Tiny' Hill and 'Tiny' White were both fine forwards as well as Stan Meads, Peter Whiting, Andy Haden, Robin Brooke, Ian Jones, Ali Williams, Brad Thorn . . . the list goes on.

Props

Kevin Skinner wasn't a big man. He was just out and out tough. Never took a backwards step. Kevin could play on both sides of the scrum — as the Springboks found out in 1956. On the other hand, Ken Gray was a very big man, a tighthead, who was immensely strong. I never saw him bettered in the scrum. Wilson Whineray was a fine prop and a quite wonderful All Blacks captain. I had a lot of time, too, for Johnny Simpson. He was another very strong front-rower — they used to call him the Iron Man. Like Kevin Skinner, he never stood for any nonsense.

Of today's players, I had a lot of time for Carl Hayman. He was such a strong tighthead and the best in the world when he left New Zealand. He was a big loss.

Hookers

Sean Fitzpatrick is the obvious standout. He won a World Cup very early in his career and continued to develop as a forward until his career ended in 2007. He was very strong and pretty single-minded. A very good all-rounder who turned into a great All Blacks captain. Back in the 1960s Bruce McLeod was also a good all-rounder who probably did a bit more tight work then Fitzy. Ron Hemi and Tane Norton were exceptional hookers in their time and I've been impressed with how Keven Mealamu has come on as well.

Fred Allen's dream team

Fullback
Bob Scott
1946–47, 1949–50, 1953–54

Wing
Bryan Williams
1970–78

Wing
Jonah Lomu
1994–2002

Centre
Johnny Smith
1946–47, 1949

Second-five
Bert Cooke
1924–26, 1928, 1930

First-five
Dan Carter
2003–

Halfback
Des Connor
1961–64

No.8
Brian Lochore (c)
1963–71

Flanker
Michael Jones
1987–98

Flanker
Richie McCaw
2001–

Lock
Colin Meads
1957–71

Lock
Maurice Brownlie
1922–26, 1928

Prop
Kevin Skinner
1949–54, 1956

Prop
Ken Gray
1963–69

Hooker
Sean Fitzpatrick
1986–97

Fred Allen's Second XV

Fullback
George Nepia
1924–25, 1929–30

Wing
Ron Jarden
1951–56

Wing
John Kirwan
1984–94

Centre
Bruce Robertson
1972–74, 1976–81

Second-five
Ron Elvidge
1946, 1949–50

First-five
Ross Brown
1946, 1949–50

Halfback
Sid Going
1967–77

No.8
Wayne Shelford
1985–90

Flanker
Ian Kirkpatrick
1967–77

Flanker
Graham Mourie
1976–82

Lock
Richard 'Tiny' White
1949–56

Lock
Stan 'Tiny' Hill
1955–59

Prop
Wilson Whineray (c)
1957–65

Prop
Carl Hayman
2001–02, 2004–07

Hooker
Ron Hemi
1953–57, 1959–60

The Legacy

Every Christmas Fred's two granddaughters fly from the South Island to spend time with their 'Grandy'.

It's a sunny Sunday morning and Fred is enjoying his morning cup of coffee in the conservatory of his cliff-top home overlooking Manly beach. He is so pleased with what he sees in the bay below that he simply has to phone a friend. The sight has given him a flashback to the time when, together, they saved the Manly Sailing Club from extinction.

Wearing that same familiar smile which lights up his face and is so much part of his personality, he lifts up the phone . . .

'You should see what's going on right in front of me,' he says. 'What a beautiful sight. There's at least 50 yachts in full flight — it's great how the club has flourished.'

Now 91, Fred lives alone since Norma passed away. All around him are his memories — memories of happy days, memories of precious friendships, memories of great sporting triumphs around the world. This is where he is happiest. It is the home that he and Norma designed when their world was young.

In the evenings he sits in Norma's chair surrounded by photographs and treasures. On a wall behind him is a painting of his beloved mother, Flossie. Nearby are two framed photographs, one of Norma as a beautiful young nurse and one of himself as a handsome young soldier.

Occasionally, his memories are tinged with sadness. He thinks of his late son Murray when he was a smiling, happy young man — and all the hopes he had for him when he grew to manhood.

And he thinks of his daughter Marianne who lives in Dunedin with his two granddaughters, Inés and Katia, who he loves dearly. Both his grandchildren have made him very proud. Inés is studying law and political science at Otago University while Katia, gifted with a beautiful voice, has recently won a prestigious musical scholarship. He looks forward to them coming to stay with him at Christmas and loves how they call him 'Grandy'.

One of the pleasures Fred misses in his life is the companionship of a dog. He has had dogs all his life and every day neighbours waved to him as he walked past with a four-legged friend on a lead.

His last one was a small grey and white terrier named Polly, but since she has gone he feels that, at his age, it would be unfair to have another.

The years have brought so much memorabilia into the house that space had to be found to store it. Very few people, even some of his closest friends, have ever seen the storeroom in the basement of his home. Much of the collection has been packed into cardboard boxes. Still more is hidden away in an old metal sea-chest. The room is so filled with mementoes of all descriptions that one friend who has been down the 16 steps has likened it to 'Aladdin's Cave'.

Although he lives alone Fred is never lonely. Quite the opposite, as each day he enjoys the company of friends and neighbours who come to see him. Sometimes there are so many it can be a little overpowering — but he makes sure he never misses his afternoon nap.

A cleaning lady comes twice a week. She keeps his home immaculate, does his washing and sometimes cooks him a nourishing meal. And he never misses driving himself at least twice a week to the Silverdale RSA where he meets a regular group of mates for an hour or so.

Backing his car out of his garage and up his steep drive is no problem. 'Of course not,' he smiles, 'I learned to go up hills this way when I was just a boy.'

He is still patron of the Auckland Rugby Union and because of his passion for the game he never misses an important match at Eden Park. He doesn't drive himself into Auckland because he likes to have a few drinks with his old rugby comrades after each game.

A good deal of his time is spent in front of a large TV watching rugby and cricket. He is pleased to see rugby reverting to its former pattern of fast, open play as he taught in his heyday — the old, spectacular format of possession, position and pace.

Fred at his Whangaparaoa home with daughter Marianne and granddaughters Katia (left) and 'Nessie'.

He bought the latest digital set for Norma when she fell ill and partially bed-ridden so she could watch her favourite programmes. She did not want to go into care — she wanted to spend the eventide of her life in the home they built together. For the last three years of her life Fred looked after her 24 hours a day.

He sits in her old chair now because it makes him feel closer to her. On a table beside him are scores of letters, including one from his niece Carla in Hawaii. He reads it often.

Words seem so empty when my heart is so full. I am deeply grateful for the loving, dedicated care you gave my dear Auntie Norma. Being there and seeing what you did for her on a daily basis was so amazing and I was touched beyond words. Mother and I will always be grateful for the loving care you gave her. We are so sorry that we are so far away and not there to comfort you. Please know that we love you and are eternally grateful.

Because of his recent knighthood, his mailbox has been crammed with correspondence from all over the world. So much arrived that he had to call on friends to help him deal with it. He was determined to reply to every one of the hundreds who wrote to him.

All his life he has been inundated with requests wanting him to attend weddings, birthdays, prize-givings, fund-raising events, club anniversaries and funerals. They still arrive, many from people he has never even heard of. It is impossible to attend them all and he hates having to say no. But at his age, he has little choice.

One evening in the first week of spring, 2010, memories of great days filled Fred's home to overflowing. He had recently been knighted and was determined, when all the formalities of the past few weeks were over, to enjoy a few hours of relaxation with his closest friends and his great players of yesteryear who were all so dear to his heart.

He was 90 now, his body was tired but his mind was as sharp as ever and he was certainly not too old to enjoy clinking glasses and swapping reminiscences. The friendships in the Allen home on that special occasion had not been won by kind words or deeds — quite the opposite. They had been forged in the heat of many a gut-wrenching physical and mental confrontation on the rugby fields of the world between men of immense character for the honour and glory of their country.

And he had been, for a while, the person whose responsibility it was to tutor them, to inspire them, to correct them whenever they went wrong and to imbue them with such fighting spirit and will to win that in the end they would become the finest rugby team in the world.

When Fred Allen spoke that night, it was in a manner they had never experienced before. It wasn't The Needle they were listening to, it was a completely different person, a man who spoke softly and with great feeling, as he thanked them from the bottom of his heart for what they had achieved together and for the affection and respect in which he held them.

Directly behind him, smiling gently from her portrait on the wall, was the loving mother who had made it all possible, the mother who had skimped and saved to buy her son an old, second-hand pair of rugby boots when he was only seven.

And when Sir Fred had finished what he wanted to say, the room was quietly silent with heads bowed and many hands brushing away a tear.

They knew, beyond all doubt, that they had just listened to a truly remarkable human being who would leave a glorious legacy for others to follow — a legacy of loyalty, integrity and abounding love for his country.

Fred looked after his wife Norma 24 hours a day after she became ill in 2006. She passed away in 2009.

Record

Playing record

Canterbury 1939–41	13 matches
Marlborough 1944	1 match
Waikato 1944	1 match
Auckland 1946-48	21 matches
Barbarians (UK) 1946	2 matches
Barbarians (NZ) 1950–52	4 matches
Olympians 1951–52	2 matches
Centurions 1952	1 match
South-Burnham Army 1941	1 match
30th Infantry Battalion 1942	1 match
3rd NZ Division 1942	2 matches
North Services (Army) 1944	1 match
2nd NZEF 1945–46 (Kiwis)	28 matches
North Island 1946–48	3 matches
NZ trials 1947–48	4 matches
New Zealand 1946–47,49	21 matches

Coaching record

Auckland coach 1957–63
All Blacks selector 1964–68
All Blacks coach 1966–68

Auckland Ranfurly Shield record

1959

Auckland 13, Southland 9 (won shield)	Invercargill

1960

Auckland 22, Thames Valley 6	Auckland
Auckland 14, Counties 3	Auckland
North Auckland 17, Auckland 11 (lost shield)	Auckland
Auckland 6, North Auckland 3 (regained shield)	Whangarei
Auckland 31, Manawatu 8	Auckland
Auckland 9, Bay of Plenty 6	Auckland
Auckland 22, Wellington 9	Auckland
Auckland 25, Taranaki 6	Auckland
Auckland 19, Canterbury 18	Auckland

1961

Auckland 5, Hawke's Bay 3	Auckland
Auckland 17, King Country 3	Auckland
Auckland 17, Counties 12	Auckland
Auckland 14, Otago 9	Auckland
Auckland 9, Southland 6	Auckland
Auckland 13, Wellington 8	Auckland
Auckland 10, Waikato 0	Auckland
Auckland 26, North Auckland 11	Auckland

1962

Auckland 24, Thames Valley 9	Auckland
Auckland 29, Bay of Plenty 6	Auckland
Auckland 8, North Auckland 3	Auckland
Auckland 52, West Coast 6	Auckland
Auckland 15, Waikato 11	Auckland
Auckland 27, Taranaki 3	Auckland
Auckland 15, Canterbury 6	Auckland
Auckland 46, Bush 6	Auckland
Auckland 20, Wellington 8	Auckland

1963

Auckland 22, Wairarapa 8	Auckland
Auckland 41, Wanganui 18	Auckland
Auckland 3, Hawke's Bay 3	Auckland
Wellington 8, Auckland 3 (lost shield)	Auckland

Record 25 successful defences of Ranfurly Shield

All Blacks coach

1966

New Zealand 20, British Isles 3	Dunedin
New Zealand 16, British Isles 12	Wellington
New Zealand 19, British Isles 6	Christchurch
New Zealand 24, British Isles 11	Auckland

1967

New Zealand 29, Australia 9	Jubilee Test, Wellington
New Zealand 36, British Columbia 3	Vancouver
New Zealand 40, East Canada 3	Montreal
New Zealand 33, North of England 3	Manchester
New Zealand 15, Midlands, London & Home Counties 3	Leicester
New Zealand 16, South of England 3	Bristol
New Zealand 23, England 11	London
New Zealand 21, West Wales 14	Swansea
New Zealand 13, Wales 6	Cardiff
New Zealand 16, South-east France 3	Lyon
New Zealand 32, France B 19	Toulouse
New Zealand 18, South-west France 14	Bayonne
New Zealand 21, France 15	Paris
New Zealand 35, Scottish Districts 14	Melrose
New Zealand 14, Scotland 3	Edinburgh
New Zealand 23, Monmouthshire 12	Newport
New Zealand 3, East Wales 3	Cardiff
New Zealand 11, Barbarians 6	London

1968

New Zealand 14, Sydney 9	Sydney
New Zealand 74, Tasmania 0	Hobart
New Zealand 43, Junior Wallabies 3	Adelaide
New Zealand 68, Victoria 0	Melbourne
New Zealand 44, ACT 0	Canberra
New Zealand 30, New South Wales 5	Sydney
New Zealand 29, NSW Country 3	Newcastle
New Zealand 45, Australian Combined Services 8	Sydney
New Zealand 27, Australia 11	Sydney

New Zealand 34, Queensland 3	Brisbane
New Zealand 19, Australia 18	Brisbane
New Zealand XV 33, Fiji President's XV 6	Suva
New Zealand 12, France 9	Christchurch
New Zealand 9, France 3	Wellington
New Zealand 19, France 12	Auckland

Played 37, won 36, drew 1, lost 0, points for 978 — against 266.
Recognised as the most successful coach in All Blacks history.

Official rugby positions

- Captain Canterbury at age 20
- Captain Auckland
- North Island selection panel
- North Island coach
- New Zealand selection panel
- New Zealand coaching panel
- Patron Auckland Union
- President Auckland Union

Honours and accolades

- Captain of British Barbarians, 1946
- Silver Jug of Appreciation from undefeated All Blacks, 1966,67,68
- NZ Rugby Hall of Fame 1995
- NZ Rugby Hall of Fame 1996 as a member of the Kiwis Army team
- Steinlager Silver Salver for an outstanding contribution to NZ rugby, 2002
- Halberg Trust Service to Sport award, 2003
- 'Night with the Needle', Special Tribute, 550 guests, Eden Park, 2004
- International Rugby Hall of Fame, London, 2005
- Represented 120,000 NZ returned service personnel at Passchendaele Memorial Service, Belgium, 2005
- Represented NZ returned service personnel at Anzac Day Memorial Service, Westminster Abbey, 2007
- New Zealand Rugby Union Special Award for services to coaching

- Auckland Rugby Union Special Award for services as captain, selector, coach, president, patron and life member
- New Zealand Rugby Union life member
- Citizens of Auckland Award at civic function in Town Hall
- Trustee Silverdale cemetery with Fred Allen Walk of Honour
- Royal New Zealand Yacht Squadron 50-year badge
- Member Auckland Club for more than 60 years
- Member Auckland Racing Club for more than 65 years
- Life member Royal New Zealand Returned Services Association
- Life member Silverdale & Districts Returned Services Association
- Patron or life member of many rugby clubs throughout New Zealand, including his childhood club, Linwood
- Honorary member of numerous rugby clubs throughout the world
- Officer of the Order of the British Empire, 1991
- Knight Companion of the New Zealand Order of Merit 2010

About the Authors

On a wet and muddy day in 1946 Alan Sayers was in the press box at Eden Park reporting a rugby game for the *Auckland Star*. Shortly after halftime a Grammar player scored a try alongside the corner flag on the terrace side of the field. Because the players were covered in mud, and the rain was pelting down, it was impossible to see who had grounded the ball in the pile-up over the line.

Anxious to give credit for the try to the right player, Alan went to the team's dressing room after the game and asked to see the captain. He introduced himself and the captain gave him the name of the forward who had forced the ball. As Alan turned to walk away, the captain said, 'Keep up that accurate reporting, son, and you'll do well.'

Little did the young reporter know that the man who had just given him that friendly advice would shortly become a life-long friend who would propose the toast at Alan's ninetieth birthday celebration 62 years later!

That man was Fred Allen. Today they live not far apart on the Hibiscus Coast north of Auckland where they see each other often. They have socialised, fished, played bowls and watched rugby together.

Alan went from Auckland Grammar to the *New Zealand Herald* where he was trained as both reporter and photographer. After the Second World War, during which he served as an officer in naval intelligence, he joined the *Auckland Star* where he became the first by-lined feature writer in a New Zealand daily newspaper, as well as its chief photographer. He was also a key figure in the formation of our first major Sunday newspaper, the *Sunday News*.

He was an official New Zealand photo-journalist on the Royal Tour in 1953 before embarking on a freelance career.

An all-round sportsman, he twice represented New Zealand at Empire and Commonwealth Games. He was also a Waikato rugby representative and holds the record of seven tries in one senior game of rugby league. He retired in 1980 and built a home at Arkles Bay where he and his wife June busy themselves with voluntary work for the local community. In 1998 he was made a Member of the New Zealand Order of Merit for his services to journalism and sport.

 Les Watkins is a Welshman by birth and a New Zealand resident by choice. His journalistic career began in 1947 when he was 17, and seven years later he became the youngest columnist on any national daily newspaper in Britain — after his column in a Bristol evening paper brought him an unexpected invitation to join the *Daily Sketch* in London.

He later switched to the *Sketch*'s sister paper, the *Daily Mail*, and travelled extensively as a roving foreign correspondent before doing a stint as that paper's literary editor.

Another unsolicited invitation resulted in him becoming a senior editor with *Reader's Digest* in London and then in Sydney.

In Britain, in addition to writing drama and documentary scripts for Independent Television, he became familiar as a radio and TV broadcaster.

In 1985 he launched himself as a freelance in New Zealand and was soon writing for a mix of publications including the *National Business Review*'s colour magazine and the *Sunday Star-Times*.

Les has written seven books which, between them, have been published in more than a dozen countries. They include *The Unexploded Man*, *The Real Exorcists* and the science fiction *Alternative 3* which, inadvertently, sparked immense controversy in America and Britain. His first novel, *The Killing of Idi Amin*, was partly set in a filthy cellblock in Kampala. He was imprisoned there and threatened with execution after being arrested at gunpoint as a suspected spy while covering a mini-war between Uganda and Tanzania.

Journalistic assignments provided other valuable background material for his work as an author. They were as diverse as spending Christmas on patrol with troops in Northern Ireland, and interviewing former inmates of Russia's notorious mental hospitals — most of whom had been cynically diagnosed as 'politically insane' — and psychiatrists who had served in these places of terror.

He and his wife, Kathleen, split their time between their home at Arkles Bay and their lifestyle block at Mangawhai where they have their 11 pet sheep.

Bibliography

Chester, Rod, Palenski, Ron & McMillan, Neville. *The Encyclopedia of New Zealand Rugby*, Hodder Moa Beckett, Auckland, 1998.

David, G.R. *Rugby and Be Damned*, Hicks, Smith and Sons Ltd, Wellington, 1970.

Frost, David. *The All Blacks 1967 Tour of the British Isles and France*, Wolfe Publishing Ltd, London, 1968.

Howitt, Bob. *New Zealand Rugby Greats*, Hodder Moa Beckett, Auckland, 1975.

Lewis, Paul & McLean, Jock. *The Life and Times of Sir Terry McLean*, HarperCollins, Auckland, 2010.

McLean, Terry. *All Black Magic*, A.H. & A.W. Reed, Wellington, 1968.

McLean, Terry. *All Black Power*, A.H. & A.W. Reed, Wellington, 1968.

Scott, R.W.H. & McLean T.P. *The Bob Scott Story*, A.H. & A.W. Reed, Wellington, 1956.

Veysey, Alex, *Colin Meads All Black*, Collins, Auckland, 1974.

Veysey, Alex, Caffell, Gary & Palenski, Ron. *Lochore*, Hodder Moa Beckett, Auckland, 1996.

Photo credits

Index

Page numbers in **bold** refer to photographs.